Homeboys

Homeboys

Gangs, Drugs, and Prison in the Barrios of Los Angeles

By Joan W. Moore

with Robert Garcia
Carlos Garcia
Luis Cerda
Frank Valencia

Temple University Press

Philadelphia

Temple University Press, Philadelphia 19122
© 1978 by Temple University. All rights reserved
Published 1978
Printed in the United States of America

Library of Congress Cataloging in Publication Data

Moore, Joan W
    Homeboys: gangs, drugs, and prison in the barrios
of Los Angeles.

    A publication of the Chicano Pinto Research Project.
    Bibliography: p.
    Includes index.
    1. Gangs—California—Los Angeles. 2. Mexican
American youth—California—Los Angeles. 3. Mexican
Americans and drugs—California—Los Angeles.
4. Mexican American prisoners—California—Los Angeles.
I. Garcia, Robert, joint author. II. Chicano Pinto
Research Project. III. Title.
HV6439.U7L75   364.3'09794'94   78-11808
ISBN 0-87722-121-9

The opinions, findings, conclusions, and recommendations expressed in this book are those of the
authors and do not necessarily reflect the
positions or policies of the National Institute
on Drug Abuse, the Department of Health,
Education, and Welfare, or the National
Science Foundation.

Contents

Maps, Figures, and Tables

Acknowledgments

THE CHICANO PINTO RESEARCH PROJECT was funded in 1974–75 by the National Science Foundation (#ERP GI43926) and the National Institute on Drug Abuse (#1–R01 DAO 1053–01). We are especially grateful to the two project officers (Gladys Handy from NSF and the late Eleanor Carroll from NIDA) for encouraging the initial grant application and for nurturing the project through its eventful history. Too seldom do "Washington bureaucrats" receive compliments for arduous and risk-taking work; we hope that this volume will represent some degree of justification for the risks that were undertaken in funding our project. Neither the National Science Foundation nor the National Institute on Drug Abuse bears any responsibility for the statements and opinions expressed in this volume.

The earlier publications of the Pinto Project (*The L.A. Pinto: Background Papers and Advance Report*, 1975a and the *Final Report*, 1975b) acknowledge the fact that the project and the materials derived from it are to a large extent outcomes of the pinto movement. It is doubtful that anything approaching this current volume could have been developed in the absence of that movement. Thus our primary gratitude is to the nameless Chicanos in the California and federal prisons who developed and created a real movement in conditions of near hopelessness. We are, specifically, grateful to seven Chicano prison groups who helped the project immeasurably. They are COPA (at the California Institution for Men, Chino), MACHO (at the California Correctional Institution, Tehachapi), MARA (at the California Institution for Women, Frontera), MASH (at the McNeil Federal Institution), MAYO (at the California Rehabilitation Center for Men and at the California Rehabilitation Center for Women); and PUMA (at the Federal Correctional Institution, Lompoc). Administrative problems kept us from forming working relationships with the culture groups at San Luis Obispo and at Terminal Island, though both groups extended us considerable courtesy and cooperation.

In addition, three funded pinto-serving agencies in Los Angeles were very helpful: these were the Proyecto del Barrio of San Fernando, and its director Roberto Castro; the Narcotics Prevention Project of Boyle Heights, and its director Juan Acevedo, and Community Concern Corporation and its director Manuel Ortiz. We are grateful to all three groups. The voluntary association of ex-convicts, the Chicano Ex-Pinto Association, was particularly helpful to us under the direction of Enrique Guillen.

The Pinto Project staff, by and large, shared collective traumas and most of us went through individual crises in connection with the work. All of the staff put some major efforts into the project, and all deserve recognition for those efforts. In addition to staff members who received authorship credit, we would like to mention pinto research staff members Gene Jimenez, Frank Yudico, Alex Torres, Jerry Cannett, and Robert Yribe, and the non-pinto research staff members Frank Carrillo, Steve Contreras, Mary Daddio, Richard Diaz, Leonel Garcia, Trinidad Macias, Rubén Ruiz and Carol Sigala. Among the administrative staff the pintos were Louis Acosta, Andres Hernandez, Vera Leon, Robert Maher and Mary Resendez—all of whom added to the substantive discussions in the project. Roy Madrid, Gloria Ortiz, Cristine Candelaria, and Rosemary Franco were the effective non-pinto staff members. Kaye Briegel, Douglas Scott and John Irwin helped us as consultants in the project.

At the University of Wisconsin-Milwaukee I have received considerable encouragement from the Urban Research Center, under the direction of Ann Greer. A small grant from the center permitted the analysis of survey data, ably performed by Steven Sansone with the advice of Ronald Edari and Carla Garnham. Mimi Michels, Deborah Ritchie Kolberg and Maryl Kasch cheerfully produced reams of manuscript, usually on short notice, with remarkable accuracy. Among my professional colleagues Alberto Mata has been consistently encouraging and generous with his time and expertise, and Walter Fogel, John Palen, and Harry Pachon offered valuable comments.

A special word of appreciation to the many people of the barrios who helped research, write and criticize this book and its predecessors. Some of them are dead and some are incarcerated and some are lost, perhaps even to themselves, but if this book accomplishes any happy changes for their own neighborhoods and for their own people they can consider it their memorial.

JWM
1978

Homeboys

Introduction

THIS BOOK is a research collaboration between the academic world and Chicano ex-convicts and gang members. No other minority group in America is more alienated and more suspicious than the Chicano homeboys of East Los Angeles.

The research process that produced the book required a complex chain of interactions—and for the Chicano men, a hope that more knowledge about their lives and barrios will, eventually, help the Mexican American communities of Los Angeles to a better life. Without some background on this fruitful and interesting research relationship, neither the purposes nor the findings of the study are fully intelligible.

Most of the research was done in only one year of intensive work during the funding of 1974 and 1975. But the actual collaboration began several years earlier and continued long after funding was cut off. Some important features of both the academic and the ex-convict subcultures made this long interaction possible.

First we will consider the ways in which research has been defined by Chicano convicts and ex-convicts since the early 1960s. Then we will discuss the funded project that produced the systemic data on which this book is largely based. Finally, we will discuss the Chicago field work tradition that is one ultimate source of this kind of approach. More complete details and a complete natural history of the Chicano Pinto Research Project are given in Appendix A.

Research and the Pinto

Chicanos who serve sentences in California prisons tend to come from territorially-based youth gang backgrounds, and to have been imprisoned for offenses that involve narcotics. They are essentially the subject of this book; they are the homeboys. They have developed a subculture with, among other features, a clearly defined slang. (This slang, in turn, is a variety of Spanish that goes back to the early 1940s, to the days of the Los Angeles pachucho; cf. Barker, 1947.) For this book, the three critical slang terms are: pinto, meaning convict or ex-convict (one who has served time in *la pinta*, or the penitentiary); barrio, meaning equally the neighborhood and gang (always a neighborhood with a name); and tecato, meaning addict. Thus, to rephrase the first sentence of this paragraph: most pintos tend to be barrio boys, and many pintos are also tecatos.

Official Research

The pinto-tecato-barrio subculture is suspicious of research, because both Chicano addicts and Chicano convicts have been subjected to many experiences that are defined as "research" and that would horrify any academic social scientist. Medical "research" in particular is often grossly exploitative and is described by Jessica Mitford quite accurately in her book (1974) about certain experiments done with convict "volunteers." (The chapter title is "Cheaper Than Chimpanzees," a quotation from a medical researcher.) In addition, the convicts see legitimate research consistently misused in order to label behavior for purposes of control.

Many such labels are derived from psychological research. The consequences are clearly evident to prisoners from the battery of psychological tests given every California prisoner shortly after sentencing. The results are used to determine an appropriate prison with an appropriate custodial rating (cf. Irwin, 1970). Prisoners classified homosexual or violent are examples of potential problems to the custodial staff. Program diagnosis is much less important.

Every prisoner has experienced these questionnaire-like psychological instruments. Most know how they are utilized, and have acquired a strong distrust for batteries of questionnaires. They equally distrust qualitative approaches because of their similarity to the use of informers by law enforcement people. Many convictions (especially for narcotics offenses) are the result of testimony given either by undercover law enforcement agents or by rats or snitches—that is, criminals who provide evidence in return for some degree of immunity. Unfortunately, police "informers" and scholarly "informants" are not far apart in the perspective of the pinto. He has experienced negative consequences from both.

The adaptations of individual pinto-tecato-barrio men toward official research are reasonably clear. Their overt compliance with researchers conceals a covert noncompliance that goes far beyond simple acquiescence. "Just check any answer." "Tell them something good." "Tell them you don't know." "Look dumb." There is no reason for any convict—and especially for any Chicano convict—to believe assurances of confidentiality. (Chicano communities also have their own strong hostility to conventional research.) But there are many good reasons for them to con the researcher into believing that he/she is getting what he/she wants.[1] This is not to cast doubt on the validity of the existing research findings based on data from institutionalized men and women. It simply indicates how strongly the pinto-tecato-barrio subculture resists official research. The normal array of techniques available to the academic researcher (indigenous interviewers, participant observation, use of informants) are defined as extraneous to the research enterprise. They simply don't address the subculture of distrust, disdain and contempt that has developed over the years.

The Background for Collaboration

The main problem with official research is, of course, the well-founded suspicions about its purpose. Beginning in the mid-1960s, however, convicts in the California prisons began to develop their own research materials. Inmates at San Quentin compiled a *Convict Report* that discussed the indeterminate sentence and the convicts disillusionment with treatment-oriented reforms. Portions of this document were written by John Irwin, then incarcerated at San Quentin. Irwin later completed graduate training in sociology and included portions of the *Convict Report* in his book *The Felon* (1970).

This effort at San Quentin directly inspired an organization of Chicano ex-prisoners active in the prison self-help movement to use research to change narcotics laws. (California narcotics laws are severe and then included penalties for addiction itself.) It was hoped this change could be made through signatures on an initiative submitted to voters on the California ballot. LUCHA (a Chicano pinto self-help group based in Los Angeles) spearheaded the effort. The result was the two-hundred-page *Peoples Resolution* (1970), a substantial and well-developed statement of life in and after prison for Chicano drug offenders. It included two small-scale surveys. The first was taken among inmates at Folsom prison and recorded the preincarceration experiences of Chicano convicts with the justice system. The other was a "snowball" sample of predominantly Chicano ex-addict parolees in Los Angeles. It concerned their perceptions of the conditions of parole, and the extent to which parole was helpful (see Appendix B). It was at this point that the senior author of this book became involved, giving technical assistance on the latter survey and generally assisting the LUCHA group.

The response to the *Resolution* was so good, particularly in Chicano communities, that the notion that laws could be changed by means of Chicano pinto research was firmly implanted. A number of convicts active in the prison self-help movement became interested in a wide range of research. Some, done by convicts working in administrative offices with access to case records, attempted to overcome stereotypes of "dumb" Chicanos (see MASH survey, Appendix B). Most notably, it proved that Chicanos served more time in both federal and state prisons than did Anglo or black convicts. Another noteworthy example studied the basic economics of the prison system, and established a strong case both for possible corruption in the Inmate Welfare Fund and for some degree of inmate control of its expenditure. The charges were so well documented that the Department of Corrections was compelled to answer some probing questions from Ernesto Duran, a Chicano ex-convict, in a 1974 legislative hearing. The primary lesson in the barrios was that research could have positive consequences if it accurately documented and analyzed the operations of the prison system and the potential of the Chicano pintos.

This experience of more than ten years is the background for the research undertaken by the Chicano Pinto Project in 1974 and 1975, and represented in this book. The lesson was long and hard; it is unlikely that these working relationships could have been established any other way. Through the prison self-help groups, the pinto movement had demonstrated that research, normally an instrument to manipulate convicts, could be used to change as well as to sustain a system.

The Chicano Pinto Research Project

From the first days of the funded project, it was clearly understood by all participants that the pinto viewpoint would be a consistent, significant, and often determining influence over the project. Half of the professional staff were ex-convicts. The project focussed on the post-prison adaptations of Chicano addicts and convicts. But within that focus there were many alternative ways of producing data that meant something to the research participants themselves, the barrio men and women. And there were many alternative ways of exploring policy issues—a sincere discussion of what might work and what might help.

The process was not smooth, easy, or simple. Yet a year of funded research demonstrated to the participants in the project that the collaborative pattern worked. The sources of strain, and the strengths of the collaboration, the phases in the project, and the actual effects of the collaboration are detailed more fully in Appendix A.

The principal investigator and senior author was active with pinto affairs since the 1970 publication of the *Peoples Resolution*. She chaired the first board of a Model Cities agency based on the principles of LUCHA and directed the agency during the summer of 1973, after the leadership collapsed and the project lost its funding. She subsequently worked with pintos on several projects to develop the proposals that were funded for the Pinto Project discussed above. The years of involvement with pinto groups and other pariah associations in the Los Angeles area made it possible for her to build an unusual and close working relationship with the research participants.

The three barrios that are the focus of the study were selected because of their immediate relevance to ongoing community projects. However, they form an interesting sample of the hard-core barrios of Mexican East Los Angeles. Men from each of the gangs in these three neighborhoods were part of the project staff. Robert Garcia of White Fence and Carlos Garcia of Hoyo Maravilla contributed substantially to the project and to the book; both men are pintos. Robert Garcia became the president of the Chicano Pinto Research Project, Inc., after the funded project was over and the group decided that the experience was worth extending. Largely through the efforts of Robert Garcia, the project survived without financial support for three years. In 1978, further funding came from the Department of Labor and the National Institute on Drug Abuse. This was the first government support of any organization directed by Chicano ex-convicts.

Materials on the third barrio, San Fernando, were written by a pinto from the Alpine barrio, Luis Cerda. Roberto Castro of San Fernando's Proyecto del Barrio, a pinto and former LUCHA member, was instrumental in assisting the Pinto Project. Frank Valencia, a pinto from the Happy Valley barrio, was responsible for the basic research on the heroin and barbiturates market.

The donation of time and effort by pintos, both inside and outside prison, was one of the most significant features of the project. Organized Chicano groups in the state and federal prisons cooperated both in criticizing working documents and in administering questionnaires.[2] Other pintos organized groups of street acquaintances into formal seminars to criticize drafts of the manuscript as it emerged. Enrique Guillen was particularly helpful in these efforts. Of course, the prisoners and the ex-prisoners got something out of this participation. There were enough diverse views among the pintos that no faction could monopolize either the direction of the study or any interpretations. In fact, there were continuing disagreements and controversies, both within the project staff and among pintos outside the staff. But the participating men, both in and out of the staff, gained a perspective, a sense that personal and subgroup preoccupations can be conceptualized in broader terms, and a confirmation of the notion that subjects can participate in research. Most important for our colleagues, there is some remote hope that this activity might lead to policy changes that would help Chicano convicts.

Academia and the Community Field Study Tradition

Just as the pintos drew on the values of a subculture which could accept research as a neutral activity (rather than as the special privilege of an institution), so also the academic interests drew on a methodological subculture that could accept the subjects as participants in research. In addition, this subculture had been reinforced by the years of protest against the dominant scientific mode of social science research. Research traditions in social science go far beyond the impersonal questionnaire, although it may not seem that way to many pintos.

In fact, the collaborative methodology developed in the Chicano Pinto Research Project represents a substantial degree of continuity with the community field work tradition, especially as that tradition appeared in the Chicago school. This is the tradition on which a remarkable group of Chicano barrio men have built something quite new and useful—but it is only fair that the roots in Chicago be recognized.

The field work tradition of the University of Chicago, which began in the 1920s, virtually mandated that major consideration be given to the point of view of the communities and the people under study. Some of the sociologists in the Chicago school did this with what came to be called (with careful objectivity) "personal documents." Thomas and Znaniecki's five-volume study of the Polish peasant in Europe and America (1918) used letters, life histories, and the like as major elements. Works in this tradition also included detailed life histories of deviants, most notably *The Professional Thief* (Conwell and Sutherland, 1937); Clifford Shaw's *The Jackroller* (1930); and Helen Hughes' edited version of a woman heroin addict's personal story (Clark and Hughes, 1961). Survey tradition was combined with field work in Thrasher's work on 1,313 Chicago gangs (1927). The field work tradition of Robert Ezra Park continued in a direct line of descent with Everett C. Hughes and his students in sociology and Robert Redfield and his students in anthropology. At Chicago, the field work in these two disciplines remained very close through the early 1960s. W. Lloyd Warner joined the faculties of both departments and shared with the sociology undergraduates his experiences and attachments with the Murngin tribe of Australia as well as his work in Yankee City. There were also the real world concerns that motivated the social gospelist Albion Small in his interaction with Jane Addams (of Hull House) early in the century. Everett Hughes, Allison Davis, Robert Havighurst, W. F. Whyte, and Burleigh Gardner had an interdisciplinary program on industrial relations. Men like Horace Cayton and St. Clair Drake were motivated to do their massive study of the Black Belt in Chicago (1962). Both men were black; Cayton spent some years administering a community center on Chicago's South Side. As a result, *Black Metropolis* was a remarkable joining of the traditions of Chicago field work. It was dedicated to Robert E. Park; Warner and Allison Davis were closely associated with the study and Hughes wrote the introduction to the 1962 edition. There was also a tradition of cross-racial collaboration at Chicago: the white anthropologist Burleigh Gardner and his wife developed a cross-racial view of Mississippi life with black anthropologist Allison Davis in the book *Deep South*. Both men became associated with Warner. In more recent years, Whyte (1943) and Gans (1962) continued the Chicago tradition with studies of the Italian community in Boston. Unlike Gans, Whyte did not train at Chicago, although he found strong intellectual support there for his work.

For a number of reasons, the Chicago tradition began to fade after World War II. For one thing, the number of institutions granting doctorates in sociology had proliferated by the late 1950s. The tradition of field work developed at Chicago (with its pragmatic intellectual base) lost ground because it took much time and highly individualized training to produce a researcher. When performed in mediocre fashion, field work easily slips into poor journalism. Discipleship is virtually impossible, and the Chicago tradition had no dogma.

A serious crisis soon appeared in the acceptability of social research, directly traceable to the exclusion of minority subjects from the research process. (The Chicago tradition usually assumed some form of subject participation, even if it wasn't emphasized.) The apparent cause was the movement of the equality revolution of the 1960s into academic research. But the real cause was a great deal of "objective," dogmatic, and not very good research. The most publicized crisis occurred over the *Moynihan Report*, a compendium of what was, by then, the generally accepted social science wisdom about the black family (cf. Rainwater and Yancey, 1967). The *Report* became closely tied to the issue of minority representation in academia, and led to a long controversy in the academic journals about the relative importance of insiders and outsiders in research about minorities (Merton, 1972; Moore, 1973; Bernard, 1973). The response to this criticism of academic research did not immediately revive the Chicago tradition of community research, for there was no longer a base at Chicago. Community research was revived in the old Chicago field sites (e.g., Suttles, 1968; Kornblum, 1974), but with somewhat different interests. In addition, many of the liveliest contemporary social scientists trained in the older Chicago tradition have tended to move either into more theoretical issues (a good example is the work of Erving Goffman), or into more specialized matters (such as the study of medical settings). Community research was still alive and well, but its best exemplars in minorities studies (e.g., Liebow, 1967; Hannerz, 1969; Blackwell, 1975; Lewis, 1955) were seldom associated with an institutional setting that could provide a base for a revival and updating of any community research tradition. Also, the Chicago tradition (despite strong praise from some minority scholars, e.g., Blackwell and Janowitz, 1974) was coming under attack from some of the revisionist sociologists of the left (e.g., Schwendinger and Schwendinger, 1974). Most importantly, unless community participants are actively involved in both the research and its uses, as we have done in this study, both the research and its ultimate uses tend to be highly suspect. While this can be termed politicization, the alternative is not very pleasant either. Unless the community is involved, so-called objective research will almost inevitably be politicized beyond the researcher's control.

The work reported here reflects a merging and amplification of a new thread of field research that stems from the struggle of neglected minorities and the Chicago tradition of field work in minority communities (the principal author was a student of both W. Lloyd Warner and Everett C. Hughes). In this respect, the project represents strong continuity with both the barrio tradition and an academic tradition. It might also be considered an early step in policy and action research that deinstitutionalizes the academic and, with luck, reintegrates the dispossessed. It is our hope that this study will help show the way to yet more collaboration between academics and minorities.

The Problem

BOTH THE CITY of Los Angeles and the Chicano people who are its oldest and poorest citizens are fascinating in themselves. Even the most casual visitor is impressed by a Sunbelt city so large that it may be the prototype of a new kind of urban sprawl. The Mexican Americans who founded the city are still its largest and fastest-growing minority. Together, the Chicanos and Los Angeles are growing and shaping each other.

Whatever the future of this relationship, there are always the realities of conflict and poverty. More precisely, there is a range of realities that, although complex in origin and effect, are quite understandable.

This understanding is our immediate concern. It can never be complete because of the great city's complexities; but if we are careful to follow a narrow range of interconnected phenomena, to weight them against the factors of Chicano life in Los Angeles, to listen to the men who lead these lives, there is much to be learned.

We are directly concerned with the facts of life in the barrios of Los Angeles. First, we will examine specifically the persistence and influence of the neighborhood (or barrio) Chicano youth gangs. Second, we will follow the growth of the use of heroin and barbiturates in Chicano neighborhoods and the growth of the markets for those drugs. Third, we will consider how the norms of these barrios not only survive among the men of the barrios who go to prison in California, but reemerge in the self-help groups created in those prisons. Fourth, we will observe the twists and turns of opinion that make it possible for the average residents of the barrio to live in, and even maintain some optimism about, their neighborhoods.

On the surface, these realities seem simple enough. They can be observed. With the expert help of our collaborators, they can be accurately measured. The critical problem is understanding, because each reality is the outcome of at least three basic factors, each complex within itself. Each factor is controversial, involving some of the most powerful values and habits of thought in the dominant Anglo community and the institutions that execute those values. Most difficult of all, the factors are intermeshed in ways that we can only begin to understand.

The first is the distinctive ethnic-minority context of Chicanos in Los Angeles. The second is the well-developed institutional system of the city and county of Los Angeles and the state and federal governments. The third is the barrio economic system, which shares much with ghetto economic systems in other cities.

Myths and Misconceptions

Mexican Americans and the American West are so distant from the center of national attention that we must first deal with a persistent myth. It appears in the popular conception of a romantic rural past, of César Chávez and his farmworkers, and in terms of the "illegal" aliens pouring into the Southwest. Yet Chicanos live in large cities by the millions; in Los Angeles County alone there are approximately one and one-quarter million Chicanos. It is true that many Chicanos and undocumented persons work on farms, but they are a tiny fraction of the population and are significant mainly as a symbol. Chicano urban problems first appeared in the 1920s, if not earlier, and Southwestern cities built their institutions around those problems—persistent youth street gangs, an active drug problem, and an expensive and growing welfare system.

But somehow these problems were seldom conceptualized as intrinsic to poor urban populations. In the big Western cities, particularly Los Angeles, they were conceptualized as "Mexican" issues, probably because of the special characteristics of Chicanos. Mexicans were foreign in appearance and language, and reflected the presence of a nearby homeland.

We must note that the urban problems of Los Angeles and other Southwestern cities are rapidly becoming critical to American society as a whole. While the shift of the American population from older Eastern and Midwestern cities to the newer, expanding, clean cities of the South and the Southwest is attracting national attention (Sale, 1975; Berry and Dahmann, 1977), Chicanos are also moving north and beginning to replace other low-wage workers in many older industrial areas. Thus the national image of minorities must expand to include Mexican Americans. It is equally necessary that the concept of urban ghetto expand to include the shacktowns, enclaves, and barrios of the Sunbelt cities. These "new" ghettos have a historical origin and ecological linkage quite different from the older, decayed central city slums of the Chicago type. As developed in particular by writers of the Chicago school, the Eastern models have become American paradigms of minority settlement in typical cities. Habits of thought change slowly, even among the students of American cities.

First, we will examine the distinctive context of the Chicanos in the city of Los Angeles.

The Ethnic-Minority Context

Mexicans settled in the American Southwest very early, and founded many of its cities. During the westward push of settlers from the United States, Mexicans were displaced from power. They remain almost powerless politically, except in some very small towns and in the rather special conditions of the state of New Mexico.

Immigration from Mexico continued from the earliest times, most notably through the years 1910–1920, when a series of revolutions sent many people northward across the border. Since then the flow varied in response to labor needs in this country and to difficulties in the homeland. Between 1900 and 1910 only about 24,000 Mexican nationals entered the United States, followed by 225,000 in the following decade. During the 1920s, labor demands in the rapidly developing Southwest attracted nearly half a million immigrants. The flow dwindled during the decade of the Great Depression, and there were selective deportations, but it rose again in World War II, ebbed after the war and then rose sharply again in the decade of the 1970s (Moore, 1975).

Thus the Mexican Americans were not only living in the Southwest long before the first Anglo pioneers, but they continued to enter the Southwest in waves of immigration that match in scale any arrival in American history. This strange mixture of native-born urban Americans, immigrants from rural areas of the United States, new immigrants from Mexico (many of them undocumented and therefore "illegal"), and third-generation urbanites live intermixed in the traditional barrios of Southwestern cities.

Los Angeles experienced these waves of Mexican immigration during the course of its own precipitous growth. Between 1887, when the railroads first reached Los Angeles, and 1900, Los Angeles county grew from 12,000 to 120,000 (Pitt, 1966). The city doubled in population every subsequent decade until 1940; by 1970 it was the second-largest in the nation. This rapid expansion attracted national attention—yet the continuous immigration of Mexican nationals and Mexican Americans from other parts of the Southwest went unnoticed, even though in 1970 the city had more Mexican-born residents than at any time in its past. Asians, Mexicans, European immigrants and, later, blacks came to fill the labor needs of the city. By 1970 there were more people of Mexican descent in Los Angeles than in any other city in the Western hemisphere except Mexico City and Guadalajara. These million and a quarter individuals were approximately a fourth of the entire population of Los Angeles.

Chicano patterns of settlement never quite matched the sociological traditions developed in Eastern and Midwestern cities. In Los Angeles, these patterns were dictated by the land itself—approximately four thousand square miles of relatively cheap land that included mountain ranges, beaches, farmland, and desert. The area is pocketed with narrow ravines that are subject to mud slides and intermittent flooding. The Mexican settlers of the early nineteenth century built homes near the Los Angeles river and in the two outlying mission settlements of San Gabriel and San Fernando (see Map 1). Later, the homes near the river were described as shacks "of hammered-out cans, old boxes, or burlap" (Bartlett, 1907).

In the heart of old Los Angeles, the Plaza area just north of the present Civic Center was labelled Sonoratown when large numbers of Anglos came to Los Angeles in the late nineteenth century. Here adobe homes were crowded together wall-to-wall, and by 1907, when large numbers of Southern European immigrants arrived, one-story shacks were built in the rear of the old Mexican houses (Bartlett, 1907). As the city expanded east across the Los Angeles river, a group of stately homes were built in the Hollenbeck area on high, well-drained, relatively accessible ground. Mexicans, Russians, and Italians began to move into the unsettled ravines and hollows. Land was cheap, if not safe. North of the Plaza area the Mexicans settled in hilly Chavez Ravine (McWilliams, 1968), an area that was renewed immediately after World War II as Dodger Stadium.

A major pattern of Chicano settlement in Los Angeles is a slow thrust running eastward from the downtown area (Map 2). In the decade of the 1970s Chicanos were beginning to form major fractions of small cities ten to fifteen miles east of the center of the city.

The Barrio Pattern

The East Los Angeles area is the largest contiguous settlement of Chicanos in Los Angeles County. Extending through most of the eastern part of Los Angeles, it is so large that its name is a familiar euphemism for the Mexican portion of the city. It will be so used in this book, although what appears to be a familiar concentrated pattern of minority settlement should not obscure the distinctive features of Chicano settlement, both within the city of Los Angeles proper and within other portions of the county. (Although Los Angeles is a very large city, it is important to remember that it covers only a fraction of the county, which contains a complex of some seventy cities of varying size.)

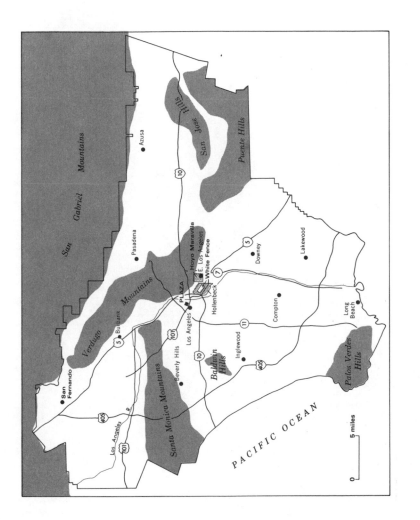

Map 1
Los Angeles County

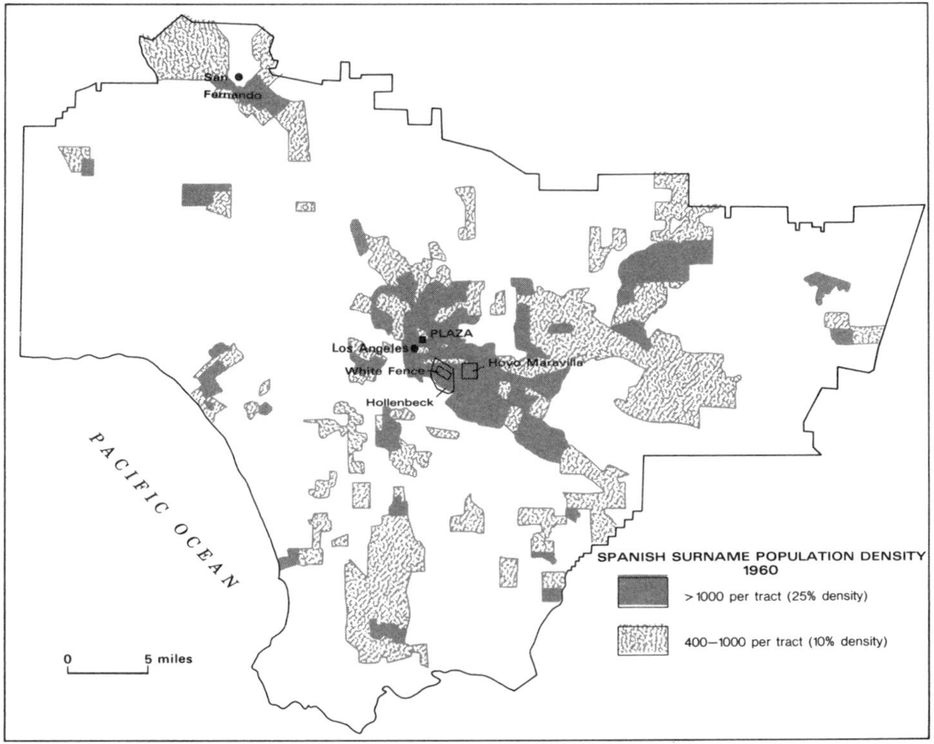

Map 2
Chicano Settlement

SPANISH SURNAME POPULATION DENSITY
1960

>1000 per tract (25% density)

400—1000 per tract (10% density)

PACIFIC OCEAN

0   5 miles

Los Angeles
PLAZA
White Fence
Hoyo-Maravilla
Hollenbeck
San Fernando

The Chicano sections, whether original or expansion settlements, were always tightly contained; in some instances they were almost like small towns. This is the typical barrio pattern. In some Los Angeles County barrios (e.g., San Fernando and Azusa), the original barrio was composed of ranch workers, forty to fifty miles from the downtown Plaza of Los Angeles. Soon these settlements became the typical Mextown of every California city, located somewhere beyond the railroad tracks and near the packing sheds and small factories, remote from Anglo residential areas. In other cities, such as Santa Monica in western Los Angeles County, the original barrio began with workers for the streetcar lines. When the surrounding bean fields gave way to expensive housing tracts (as in West Los Angeles and Westwood), the barrio simply became the lower class part of town. In the eastern portion of the county barrio isolation was preserved by settlement in the ravines. Other city barrios were cut off by important traffic arteries.

Most of the areas of Mexican settlement soon established an individual identity among Mexican Americans and bore their own names. Thus the barrios near downtown Los Angeles (Macy Street and Dogtown, the latter named for the animal shelter) established identities that had to do with local industries and the activities of the residents. "Los de Macy" (literally "those of Macy") were poor, and many worked in the nearby packinghouses (cf. Oxnam, 1920). In the 1920s an outbreak of bubonic plague led city inspectors to demand improvements in their homes that the poorer Mexicans could not meet. Some moved to Dogtown, where Chicanos had been mixing with immigrants from Italy, Syria, and Central Europe. Dogtown Mexicans also included a sprinkling of more respectable refugees from the Mexican Revolution, who fled the influx of the poorer people from Macy by moving east to newly-developed areas.

Only a few of these barrios gained identity from common town origins in Mexico. One such was Simons, a brickyard in eastern Los Angeles County, which was populated almost exclusively by people from Pénjamo, Mexico. Simons had its own school, company store, church, private police, band, and baseball team (cf. Grebler, et al., 1970, p. 311). Most of the Los Angeles barrios got their identities not from Mexican village origins but from a combination of geographical isolation and the work characteristics of their new location.

The Minority Experience

Work was overwhelmingly the dominant reason for Mexican settlement in the 1920s. In railroads, meatpacking, foundries, and clay and brick manufacturing, the need for a convenient work force explained the Mexican presence. Mexicans were essential to the olive, citrus, and

livestock ranches in outlying portions of Los Angeles County. Many of
the urban residents sent family members to work in agriculture elsewhere in California during the harvest season to supplement low wages
(Scott, 1971). Organized labor, always weak in Southern California,
considered Mexicans an unorganizable threat, despite Mexican participation in some important strikes during the 1920s. Just as they had
fought Japanese immigration, the California Federation of Labor opposed Mexican immigration and union membership (Grebler, et al.,
1970). Yet even in the prosperous 1920s, Mexicans were attracting
unfavorable attention because they were overrepresented in the relief
rolls. Then, as now, the fact that Mexicans gave much more to the
economy than they took away was ignored by the press. (The best
available figures show that from 25 to 35 percent of California relief
recipients were Mexican. Los Angeles county had an estimated 167,000
persons of Mexican descent on welfare; Scott, 1971.)

Social workers, school teachers, and public health workers joined
with the Federation in the late 1920s to call for quota restrictions on
Mexican immigration (Scott, 1971). Although this attempt to influence
federal legislation was unsuccessful, mounting unemployment led the
County of Los Angeles into negotiations with officials of the Mexican
consulate in the early 1930s. An ingenious repatriation scheme was developed for Mexican families on relief. By a combination of persuasion, incentive, and coercion, 13,000 Mexicans were repatriated between 1931
and 1934 (Hoffman, 1974; McWilliams, 1968; Grebler, et al., 1966). Not
until the late 1930s were Chicanos accepted into the Los Angeles labor
movement, in trades such as cement finishing, painting, upholstery, and
garments. And by the beginning of World War II, Chicanos were moving into more standard industrial jobs, with somewhat less hostility from
the institutional forces of the city.

But World War II brought many other kinds of people to Los Angeles, and although the institutional restrictions were easing, there were
a series of riots of considerable consequence. In 1943 the first of these
so-called Zoot Suit Riots began in Los Angeles between army and navy
servicemen and young Chicanos, with the tacit approval of at least some
official elements in Los Angeles. The riots were brutal and dangerous,
although to this day few outside the Chicano population think of them
as race riots. Because the consequences of this open warfare between
roving gangs of Anglo servicemen and young Chicanos will last several
generations, they will be an integral part of our discussion of Chicano
youth gangs (Chapter 3).

The first important organization of Los Angeles Mexican Americans
for political purposes began after World War II. The reasons for this

are not well understood, except that during the war many young Chicanos left the isolation of their barrios for the first time, and an unusual flow of cash came into the dilapidated shantytowns of East Los Angeles: wartime allotment checks, steady work for both men and women, and an acute demand for casual labor caused barrio family incomes to increase substantially. Whatever the reasons, this early political consciousness resulted in the election of a Chicano from the East Los Angeles barrios to the Los Angeles City Council. Yet when Edward Roybal was shortly thereafter elected to Congress, the East Los Angeles people were once again represented on the council by an Anglo. Neither the City Council nor the powerful Board of Supervisors seated an elected Mexican American after that first flush of power. Throughout the following three decades the elected officials have been Anglos that typically employ Chicano field men to represent their Chicano constituency.

It is so difficult for non-Californians to accept this reality of California politics that it is worth repeating: about one and one-quarter million Mexican American citizens of Los Angeles County have no elected representative in city or county government. Yet the blacks, much newer to the city, are substantially represented in the Council and elected Tom Bradley mayor. The East Side barrios described in this book are in the 1970s represented by Anglos.

In the late 1960s and early 1970s these barrios were swept into organized Chicano *Movimiento* activities. The movement organizations that appeared ranged from the militant quasi-military Brown Berets to the quasi-professional Educational Issues Coordinating Committee, which organized teachers, parents, ministers, and students for change in the school system after a series of high school blowouts (walkouts). A smaller, but nonetheless significant, group of community-based organizations were created by OEO, Model Cities, and various volunteer efforts to meet the needs of East Los Angeles communities for services in health, mental health, housing, education, aging, youth services, narcotics, alcoholism, and other problems obvious to the most casual visitor. The militant approach resulted in a series of riots which climaxed in a particularly bloody day of street-fighting on August 29, 1970. Although these activities were concentrated in East Los Angeles, their impact extended throughout the county and the state. Other barrios in outlying cities were drawn into the movement, and other Chicano settlements began to express their needs and develop locally-based programs.

It is significant that the history of Chicanos in Los Angeles is quite different from those of either blacks or Puerto Ricans. Chicanos were the founders of the city of Los Angeles, but remain its reservoir of low-paid casual labor. They are both the oldest and, because of the stream of undocumented persons, the newest and most deprived. Chicano claims to a distinctive culture are unquestionable. Because the denser and older concentrations of East Los Angeles tend to attract the newest immigrants from Mexico, some of these areas were more distinctly Mexican in the mid-1970s than a generation ago. The resulting conflict with the larger Anglo society appears to be endless. Usually the friction appears indirectly in law enforcement and in education, but it can also appear directly, as in the deportations and the major riots of 1943 and 1970. Once insiders, Mexicans are now outsiders in the city, the county, and the state.

This painful sense of being strangers in their own land is intense. Most of the old barrios endure in isolation, sometimes sharpened by freeways that at one stroke rip mile-long barriers through old neighborhoods. Middle class and upper-middle class Anglos move west in Los Angeles to the cooler climate nearer the coast, or up into the hills to escape the smog and the congestion, and young Anglo families move out to the traditional first houses in the enormous tracts of the San Fernando Valley. The old Chicano neighborhoods remain. Most Los Angeles people are completely unaware of the Chicano neighborhoods, now several generations old. And when people from East Los Angeles drive one or two miles to downtown Los Angeles, perhaps twelve miles to Beverly Hills, perhaps fifteen or twenty miles to Mar Vista or out over a range of mountains to the San Fernando Valley, they are entering an alien land that is denied them by prejudice, income, or both.

Later we will return to the special traditions and emphases of the Chicano barrios and their cohesiveness as communities. This group of issues is difficult to handle, except in careful detail. These neighborhoods cannot be easily epitomized as gemeinschaft or folk islands in the urban stream (cf. Bernard, 1973); the phenomena that will concern us show that the poor barrios of Los Angeles exhibit more of the qualities of true communities than do most urban neighborhoods (cf. Yancey, et al., 1976, on urban structures related to the salience of ethnicity). But these are matters for later chapters. First, we must consider how the institutional system has shaped the lives of people living in the barrios.

The Institutional Context

On one level, the array of helping and controlling institutions in Los Angeles represents the most progressive face of twentieth-century America. On another, this group of institutions is one of the more intractable aspects of what is variously called internal colonialism, "blaming the victim," and "programming for failure."

Health, Education, and Welfare: A Progressive Place

By the mid-1970s, California and Los Angeles had a national reputation among some sectors of the helping professions as an "advanced"
state and an "advanced" city. To be sure, there was a mass media
stereotype of a westward tilt of insanity, but in one institutional setting
after another California's pioneers and innovators developed models for
other urban areas. The county maintained a large health system with
both neighborhood clinics and large county hospitals. A matching network of mental health agencies provided strong localized services and
innovative programming. Both were paralleled by strong private networks that were innovative in prepaid medical care. The Department
of Public Social Services administered the usual array of federally-sub-
sidized support programs. But the more innovative types of private social
welfare programs were weaker than in many cities in the East and Midwest, and, importantly for a primarily Catholic population, the Catholic
charitable effort was extremely weak; the local Catholic hierarchy earlier
chose to spend much of its money in building a strong parochial school
system (cf. Grebler, et al., 1970).[1]

The elementary and secondary school system was dominated by the
Los Angeles Unified School District, which educated the children of
many smaller satellite cities in addition to Los Angeles proper. By the
late 1960s the quality of the school system had been eroded by a series
of bond-issue failures. Curricular innovations were largely confined to
upper-middle class high schools and their feeder elementary and junior
high schools. Archaic curriculum and instructional methods characterized the schools of the Chicano barrios. Protests at the declining quality
of education in Chicano areas were a consistent theme in the Chicano
movement activities of the period. In response, the district was decentralized, and East Los Angeles became one of some dozen areas, each
with its own superintendent, administrative staff, and a mandate to
develop innovative programming. On the state level, task forces of
minority educators were assembled to evaluate existing textbooks and
recommend changes. (These changes were implemented largely because
California purchases a great many textbooks.) Accountability legislation
was passed to require teachers to show that their pupils met certain educational standards at each grade level. Other legislation required general
bilingual/bicultural educational requirements for prospective teachers in
minority areas. Thus it is not possible to criticize the educational system
of the state of California and Los Angeles for lack of action.

In the most widely publicized aspect of urban education, desegregation, the Los Angeles school system moved slowly, understandably so
in view of the difficulties of designing a pupil transfer program across

the vast area of the district. For our interests, this is a positive sign. On a national level, as well as in Los Angeles, the special minority experience of Chicanos has long been directed toward the improvement of education at the local school level—which means opposition to desegregation (even though some of the Chicano political activities of the 1940s were centered around protesting school segregation; cf. Grebler, et al., 1970). Thus in California there has been emphasis on bilingual programming and, most notably, on attaining equity in school finance within and between districts (see *Serrano* v. *Priest*, the landmark decision on school financing in the action brought by John Serrano of East Los Angeles in protest against the poor quality of education received by his children). The strongest efforts of the relatively powerful Chicano educational groups are implicitly opposed to desegregation as a means of improving education.

Criminal Justice: A Progressive Place

Los Angeles and California offer models in professional law enforcement. The Los Angeles police were radically reformed by Chief William Parker, who in 1949 took command of a "department principally known for its anti-labor goon squad, subject to frequent lapses into racism and corruption," and transformed it into what is "generally regarded as the country's most professional and incorruptible police department" (Farrell, 1977, pp. 30, 31). In the unincorporated areas of Los Angeles County, including much of Mexican Los Angeles, the equally professional Sheriff's Department is the law enforcement agency. It also runs the county jails. The miles of freeways in the county are efficiently and effectively patrolled by the California Highway Patrol.

Although the Los Angeles juvenile, municipal, and superior courts are occasionally studied (Greenwood, et al., 1973), they appear unremarkable. Although a bit larger than other such systems (the Juvenile Hall is reputedly the largest such institution in the world), only the large number of county probation camps is particularly noteworthy. But in the corrections system, both youth and adult, California's national reputation is one of progressivism. The state developed a Youth Authority in 1941, one of the first states to implement the 1938 American Law Institute models. The Adult Authority followed in 1944. California led the movement toward a treatment model, for both youthful and adult offenders (Tappan, 1949). As Irwin (1970) comments, it was this treatment philosophy and its indeterminate sentence that justified the spectacular expansion of the California prison system from three to ten adult male institutions within twenty years. In scale, the California correctional system is impressive, with a 1972–73 budget of 96.5 million dollars (Mitford, 1974). It continues to enjoy high regard throughout the national professional community of correctional personnel.

While professional praise for the Los Angeles and the California criminal justice systems has been a dominant theme since the 1940s, there have been warning notes. Patrick Murphy, President of the Police Foundation and former chief of police in New York, Detroit, and Washington, D.C., was quoted in 1977 as deploring the lack of professionalism of the then-Chief of the Los Angeles Police Department, Edward Davis. Murphy commented, "He exemplifies one of our major problems—we don't know how to control the enormous power that rests with the police. And when that power falls into the hands of someone like Ed, well, watch out!" (Farrell, 1977, p. 34).

In turn, the California correctional system has drawn much recent criticism. Some is in response to black prison writings (e.g., Cleaver, 1968; Jackson, 1970), carefully documented journalism (Mitford, 1974), or local efforts to develop professionally-supported alternatives to incarceration or deinstitutionalization. Some has been sociological, and is concerned with the system's stubborn resistance to change (e.g., Dunbar, 1975, on the structural sources of the system's rejection of a model Department of Labor program). Some criticism comes from the self-styled "new" radical criminologists (e.g., Quinney, 1977), many of whom are based in California (e.g., Wright, 1973; Krisberg, 1975). But all of these criticisms come from persons who are more or less outsiders to the correctional system, rather than from the correctional system professionals themselves. California has not made innovations, and thus has at least lost leadership among, if not the respect of, corrections professionals.

Barrios and Institutions

It is typical of the 1970s that the professional opinions of institutional officials were increasingly challenged as ultimate judgments of effectiveness in minority areas. Some of this challenge is part of a general, and radical, critique of society, but much of it is quite specific.

There are three fundamental themes: internal colonialism; "blaming the victim"; and "programming for failure." Some of these themes are accepted in the professional literature; others are still popular phrases.

Internal colonialism describes a body of literature developing about Chicanos (see Moore, 1970, and citations in Moore, 1976) that argues that the present oppression of Chicanos is a direct continuation of institutional means of suppression that were developed immediately after the conquest of the Southwest by the United States. "Blaming the victim" (the phrase is from Ryan, 1971) is based largely on the black experience; it argues that the failures of institutional structures (like the schools) are generally masked and rationalized by a professional tendency to blame the victim (e.g., failing pupil) rather than the institution (e.g., the school). "Programming for failure" has become a minority cliché describing the structural barriers that are set up in the way of achievement. One of the clearest academic versions of this theme can be found in Rist's *The Urban School: A Factory for Failure* (1973). This is a careful analysis of the values, norms, and social structure of an inner-city elementary school that creates a systematic program for failure, or failing career life, for a large proportion of its students entering at kindergarten.

All three themes emphasize the importance of the institution as it shapes and molds behavior, and as that behavior affects the continued degraded status of minorities. Thus all three points of view state that the professional judgment of the health, education, and welfare systems (and especially the criminal justice system) are completely irrelevant to an understanding of the minority experience. In the more despairing and nihilistic postures, professional judgments are no more and no less relevant to the amelioration of minority problems than were the judgments of Eichmann and his colleagues about the amelioration of the plight of German Jews. In the more pragmatic postures, the three themes unremittingly call attention to the actual experience of clients with the institutions that are supposed to serve them.

In the Los Angeles barrios, the significance of the health, education, welfare, and criminal justice institutions is shown both statistically and experientially. All residents with children have contact with the schools, even if a high proportion continue to drop out before completing high school. In a 1964–65 survey of Los Angeles Chicanos, we found that 22 percent of the poor barrio residents derived income from welfare agencies. An additional 28 percent derived income from Social Security payments and other federal pensions. Only 54 percent were dependent on salaries and wages for their income (Grebler, et al., 1970, p. 330). Thus a relatively large proportion of the barrio residents were dependent on what we term the "welfare economy."

But poverty means not only dependency from income, but also dependence upon a full range of other institutional services. Especially in the past, state and local agencies were designed to meet only a very narrow legislative intent. Eligibility is checked carefully in the funds for Aid to Families with Dependent Children, unemployment benefits, food stamps, and medical care. Furthermore, the service agencies are highly fractionated. A notable example is the distinct separation of the network of agencies serving mental health needs from the cluster of agencies meeting problems of alcoholism and drug abuse. In turn, both groups are distinct from the "County Hospital"—which, in turn, is distinct from the County Health Clinics working at the neighborhood level. The network of agencies serving the aged is yet again separated from the network serving children.

For the poor Chicano family, the practical effect is that even if there is no special problem, an inordinate amount of time is spent locating the appropriate service resources, obtaining bureaucratic clearance for service, making funding arrangements that allow the agency to be reimbursed, and then, ultimately, waiting for the actual service. Often the service rendered may be of a quality that inspires distrust. Among other agencies, the Los Angeles County U.S.C. Medical Center has a persistent decades-old problem with Spanish-speaking patients and non-Spanish-speaking medical personnel. Malpractice is often a consequence. It is a normal practice in the barrio for a group of family members to serve as "paramedical" personnel; they gather at a health agency and stand watch around the clock so that the patient doesn't die of neglect.

Justice is also rendered to the barrio poor by bureaucracy. We estimate that close to 20 percent of the barrio men experience prison (Tables 1 and 2); undoubtedly many more have contact with the justice system at its lower levels. It is difficult to explain the importance to barrio families of the process of rendering justice by bureaucracy. We might make this point by beginning with the family car—essential to livelihood in far-flung Los Angeles.[2] Most cars fit the family income. They are second-hand, they often break down completely, and they often cannot be repaired immediately because there is no money. They are rarely insured because there is no money for insurance and rates have been especially high in Chicano Los Angeles; any street accident is a matter of negotiation between the participants.

The police get involved through the family car because of traffic warrants. Because barrio people frequently fail to pay parking tickets, they get warrants which require an appearance in court. Drunk driving is a common offense; it is a misdemeanor that requires a court appearance.[3] Traffic court and municipal court are a curious mob scene, a bureaucratized, time-consuming, Hogarthian madhouse with crowds of people milling around or standing in lines for hours. Actual court appearances are a ritualized mumble of incomprehensible routines and often, to the participants, silly questions. Traffic court, municipal court, juvenile court. The impression that justice is bureaucratized is important because the routines of justice are similar to those necessary for getting clothing, getting an education, or getting an eye examination, for example.

It is important also to notice the intermingling of welfare and punitive functions of the operation of institutional agencies in Los Angeles. It was "the welfare" that was responsible for the deportations of the 1930s;

in 1977 it was the County Health Services that led the bureaucratic fight against costs arising from services to "illegal aliens." The federal Immigration and Naturalization Service has always been a real presence in Chicano Los Angeles, penetrating the helping as well as the law-enforcement agencies, and affecting the functioning of all institutional agencies about all Chicanos, not only Mexican nationals. It might be argued that this special experience of Chicanos, extending over fifty years of ever-present law enforcement activity, has given barrio residents a suspicion that the constitutional rights of Americans don't apply to them, no matter how remote they may be from Mexican nationality.

The Absence of Brokers

California cities were never permitted to develop the kind of political machine that characterizes so many of the Eastern and Middle Western cities (cf. Sale, 1975). Such machines have undoubtedly helped some minority poor as brokers with institutional agencies. Without this mechanism, the Chicanos of Los Angeles were comparatively less equipped to cope with civic institutions than were, for example, the black people on the South Side of Chicago. In this context, it is interesting that so many of the agencies developed by community initiative under poverty programs in East Los Angeles were designed either to supplement agencies or to correct agency malfunctions. Thus services were created to supplement the County Hospital (a Spanish-language ward) and the County Mental Health Services. There were many youth services supplementing the school system. Notably, there was a comprehensive one-stop counselling service for undocumented foreign nationals. Services for addicts and ex-convicts filled gaps left in the criminal justice system. Such inventions only hint at the gaps in service left by the traditional agencies, and, ironically, the new service needs created by their malfunctions. Significantly, the riots that led to the Moratorium disturbances of 1970 were directed toward the school system, a longstanding source of resentment in East Los Angeles:

> When I was a kid and first started going to school, thinking of getting out of the barrio, you know, get myself a good home, and stuff like that, and find out that, you start going to school and when you go to the boundaries of the barrio, somehow you're stopped and knocked back and you fall back into the barrio, and again you try and take a step again farther and there you go again, down again.

Although the Chicano experience with institutions is very much like that of other minorities, two special factors—the omnipresent Immigration Service and the absence of an urban political machine—make the Chicanos' case unique.

The Barrio Economy

In the large cities of the Southwest (most notably, Los Angeles, San Diego, Phoenix, San Antonio, and El Paso), the Mexican ghettos appeared for the same reason as the ethnic and racial ghettos of the Eastern and Midwestern industrial cities—to meet the needs and opportunities of the local labor markets. But in the early decades of the twentieth century, when Mexicans first entered the U.S. in large numbers, Southwestern labor markets were different from those of New York and Chicago. Railroads, mines, and large-scale agriculture offered the major workplaces. In the East, new immigrants worked in such labor-intensive manufactures as the garment sweatshops of New York.

There was a much smaller range of labor-intensive industry in the Southwest; this difference dictated the pattern of settlement for Chicanos and for other racial minorities. Yet slowly, through the past few years, the market for workers at the bottom of the urban job structure has grown to resemble that of Eastern cities as the Western economy has diversified.

The Segmented Labor Market of the Barrios

It is now common wisdom that the opportunity structure has changed substantially for the "new" urban minorities. In turn, this changing structure is greatly affecting community social structure—and therefore the ways in which people solve their problems of survival (cf. Handlin, 1962). In general, this new structure is the segmented labor market. An understanding of its structure and function is essential for understanding any of the social or cultural features of modern urban ethnic neighborhoods and communities.

We will begin with a sociological version of a rather controversial theory in labor economics of labor market processes. In its assumption of a segmented labor market, this theory departs from both conventional economics and popular conceptions by arguing at the outset that the type of job always described in the American dream of normalcy (with security, good pay, and a career ladder) is relatively scarce (Gordon, 1972; Doeringer and Piore, 1971; Freedman, 1976). The fact is that only a minority of American workers hold jobs with these features.[4]

Yet it is more significant to our study that very few people on the bottom of the labor market will ever have access to good jobs. This is because of the segmentation that is caused not only by differences between types of workers (varying levels of education, motivation, and skills, and more or less attractiveness because of age, race, and sex), but also by differences among the employing organizations. Urban minority workers are found disproportionately in the lowest-paying segments of the labor market. These are unstable jobs, often only part-time, with below-average wages and virtually no possibility of advancement. The only protections for such employees are those required by the government, such as compensation in case of injury and social security deductions in lieu of private pensions. These are *types* that we are talking about; peripheral firms (marginal employers) are as likely to demand workers with the job habits of the casual laborer as a large, well-established employer is to demand workers with the job habits of the middle-class Protestant ethic.[5] These firms and employers constitute the "secondary labor market" to which many people in today's urban ghettos are largely confined.[6] The employees are simply making do with the inadequate best that is available in the barrio or ghetto.

This view has important implications. Not the least of them is the well-founded suspicion that, just as the inner-city schools produce workers for the secondary labor market, so do other schools in other areas produce workers for managerial positions. Rist (1973) has called the inner-city minority schools "factories for failure" after a careful study of interaction processes at the lower grade levels. This term accurately describes the chances of the individual failure to attain a good job. But, in another sense, the young school dropout is *well* prepared for jobs in the peripheral firms. He has been thoroughly socialized in the schools to expect very little: he learns to cope with, and finally abandons all hope of, pleasing the teacher, and he establishes patterns of "truancy, tardiness and evasion of school rules." Finally, the young dropout acquires habits and attitudes ("tastes for work"; cf. Cain, 1976, pp. 18, 19) that can qualify him (or her) only for jobs in the secondary labor market (cf. also Bowles, 1972; Gintis, 1971). It is essential for peripheral employers that their workers not expect much, as they must be hired and fired as finances permit and as the market demands.

Yet another aspect of labor market segmentation has to do with the geographic distribution of jobs, and of access to those jobs. Peripheral or secondary labor market hiring is generally concentrated in specific areas of the city. More commonly in the past (although even today in modern ghettos), employers took advantage of labor pools by contract hiring. Liebow (1967) studied the operations of labor recruiters in a black ghetto in Washington, D.C., and noted that contractors dominated casual employment at the time of his study; they still do in some black areas of the Deep South. In the Southwest, jobs in the construction and agricultural industries and on the railroads were historically dominated by labor contractors who simply rounded up truckloads of day workers.

While this practice is not as dominant today as in the past, it underlines the general point, which is that job search patterns of workers in primary labor markets are quite different from the experiences of workers in the secondary labor markets. The state unemployment office and union hiring hall serve similar functions to those of the old-time labor contractors, but the more common pattern of non-union membership shows even more particularistic and less "rational" job search patterns (cf. Bullock, 1973). In recent years, when new job opportunities appeared in industrial belts on the edge of the city (as is happening in older industrial cities), a certain amount of commuter labor from central city to suburbs appeared. This parallels the old and familiar migration of domestic workers from the ghettos to the suburbs (Berry and Kasarda, 1977). But such commuting is costly, especially in Los Angeles and other Southwestern cities, where workers must rely on the private automobile. Increasing costs of gasoline mean that several dollars a day may be spent in commuting to a job that may pay no more than thirty or forty dollars per day, at best. Minority residences tend to concentrate in areas of the city deserted by industry. Making a rational job search and commuting are very expensive. These geographic patterns add to the segmentation of the labor market—that is, the market becomes differentiated spatially, which especially affects minority ghetto concentrations.

From the point of view of the employer, segmentation of the labor market means that the ghetto worker rarely competes with the workers in the primary labor market for the scarce good jobs.

Supplemental Economic Structures

What, then, keeps workers in the secondary labor market working? As we suggest in an earlier book (Grebler, et al., 1970), middle-class communities are filled with role models for the new entry into the labor market. In general, the young, college-educated Anglo can expect his income to increase regularly with age. Younger workers can see the shape of their future in the jobs of the older men around them. But poorer communities lack such exemplars. Black high school dropouts see little relationship between age and income in their community. Many young white males who participate in the secondary labor market can consider such a work experience a normal, and temporary, part of gaining maturity. But this is not true for women and for minorities. And even during youthful experience in the secondary labor market, minorities are treated differently. As Freedman (1976) comments, during the "critical period of work establishment, they experience higher unemployment rates, lower earnings, and more involuntary mobility than their white counterparts" (p. 23). Much the same appears to be true for young Chicanos (Bullock, 1973). The norm in poor communities does not provide much incentive to send young people to work. Nor do older workers offer much of a desirable model of the future. It is not possible for them to term this a pattern of failure, because it is normal in poor communities. Therefore the question, Why do people work? is serious enough to have led theorists of the segmented labor market to suggest that alternative sources of income deserve the most serious attention in designing policy for the working poor (cf. Cain, 1976).

Besides the normal wage-labor market, there are two important economic structures in the poverty areas of American cities: the welfare structure and the illegal structure. The welfare economy is the familiar combination of income from food stamps, Aid to Families with Dependent Children, programs for the aged and veterans, unemployment compensation, and other benefits. There are also occasional special programs, such as the Cuban Refugee program. In the mid-1960s a careful survey found that about a quarter of the residents of the barrios of Los Angeles received income from welfare and related services (Grebler, et al., 1970). One may also add the numerous and elaborate manpower programs (such as the Neighborhood Youth Corps), which were intended to provide socialization experiences for youth in the secondary labor market but have become straightforward programs to keep kids off the streets (cf. U.S. Department of Labor, 1976). These employment and training programs tend to offer minimum wages for specified periods of time for a limited number of jobs.

The second important economic structure in the barrios of Los Angeles is the illegal economy. It is elaborate and well-funded. It includes casual labor (part-time drug dealers and, in some cities, numbers runers), middle management, and top management. Of course, illegal structures differ somewhat from legal businesses. Some economists consider them the essence of the truly competitive enterprise in their response to market conditions. Middle-management heroin dealers, for example, enter and leave their business rapidly in response to supply factors and consumer demand. In addition, they respond to warnings about law enforcement activity. Bullock (1973) discusses the role of police corruption in the illegal economy (what he calls the "sub-economy") of the black and Chicano slums of Los Angeles. Providing information about impending "heat" that leads to shutdowns of illegal businesses is a major aspect of police corruption and an additional element of barrio business operations in the illegal economy; yet this critical point appears nowhere in the literature on narcotics in poverty neighborhoods. Perhaps this is because the literature on narcotics is gained almost entirely from law enforcement sources.

Correct and prompt information is as essential to large narcotics dealers as it is to grain or sugar dealers. It is obvious that such information can be obtained in Los Angeles without too much difficulty. Many people can name the larger drug enterprises in Los Angeles and not fear the consequences because, after all, this is general knowledge. It must also be said that the essential information need not come from law enforcement officers; often there are other persons with reliable market information. The important fact is that this information is indeed available and reliable. Even the slightest reflection on the dedication to duty of Los Angeles area law enforcement agencies is a dangerous area of speculation; Bullock's fragmentary scraps of information from poverty-level blacks and Chicanos caused wide public controversy in Los Angeles. Yet it is a fact that large dealers can be well known and still continue to operate for years, even decades. Several dealers who began shortly after World War II are reputed to be still active.

It is also important to note that illegal activities (particularly those less spectacular and bizarre than narcotics) may shade so gradually into ordinary business enterprise and marginal interpretations of welfare that it is hard to determine illegality. A slightly illegal (unlicensed and uninsured, to cut costs) trucking operation may employ drivers on a part-time cash basis who also collect unemployment compensation. One of them may share some of his pay with a woman who receives aid for her dependent children. Ianni (1974) describes a jitney-cab operation in New York City that survives through just such a combination. And yet this is all part of the illegal economy.

Tripartite Economic Structure

This interpretation of three economic structures makes it difficult to estimate the importance of the illegal economy in the total economic structure of poor urban minority areas. One of the few attempts was based on the Urban Employment Survey of Harlem in 1966. The author states:

> A conservative estimate places 10 percent of the population engaged in illegal activities, at the average income earned of $6,000 per year. The total illegal income thus amounts to . . . 22.5 percent of the earned income during the year. The estimate is considered conservative, because 38 percent of the population in the survey had unaccountable sources of income. (Friedlander, 1972, p. 180.)

It should be added that the sources of illegal income should not be thought of entirely in terms of a business analogy. The casual worker may earn just a few dollars a week, exactly in the manner of the Puerto Rican welfare mother described by Susan Sheehan (1976). For example, small-scale soft drug dealing seldom provides a full-time income, but it may supplement other earnings. Even the larger narcotics dealers may earn some portion of their total income from legitimate front jobs.

The three-part economy that makes up the core income career opportunity structure of America's inner city poverty areas is illustrated in the accompanying diagram. The structures within the peripheral sector are interconnected at both individual and family levels. That is, it is common for a worker to migrate back and forth from positions in one or another economic structure in the peripheral sector of the economy. He may change, for example, from a minimum-wage job to unemployment compensation to the illegal labor market. Many sources of income in the welfare economy are conditional upon losing a position in the work economy, as Cain (1976) and others point out. Multiple roles may also exist within one family, with one member working part time, another receiving welfare or unemployment compensation, and yet another working some type of hustle. In general, the welfare and illegal economies subsidize the marginal industries of the peripheral sector of the secondary labor market. Without "fall-back" and supplementary sources of income, the minimum wage is not enough to support a family. Even if an individual primarily identifies himself with work—legitimate jobs, in the secondary labor market—this person (or other members of his family) must often resort to alternative sources of income.

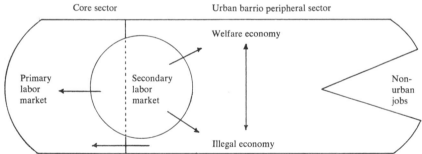

Figure 1
Tripartite Economy of the Urban Barrio
Source: Adapted from Bennett Harrison, "Education, Training and the Urban Ghetto," in Manpower Research Monograph No. 27; U.S. Department of Labor, Manpower Administration.

The structure is also connected to the core sector and to the good jobs in the primary labor market. Some people manage to move from youthful jobs in the secondary market to permanent jobs in the primary market. Historically, residents of the barrios were in demand for good jobs during World War II, and *braceros*, or contract laborers, were imported from Mexico to work in the agribusinesses of the Southwest. Yet many of these workers returned to the peripheral sector when the manpower emergency ended, and the *braceros* returned to Mexico. Then, too, the illegal economy provides capital for legitimate ventures in the core sector, such as real estate and restaurants (cf. Kaplan and Kessler, 1976). The extent of lifetime mobility from the peripheral to the primary or core sector of the economy is difficult to estimate, and even more difficult to project into the future, with unknown changes in the industrial structure.

Implications of the Tripartite Model

The tripartite model offers a view of the American opportunity structure that differs from both common sense and many sociological writings. The model's primary assumption is rooted in the structure of the American economy; there are not enough jobs in the core or primary structure for all—or even most—Americans to attain the vision of normalcy. The model effectively illustrates the economic situation of the urban barrio resident. This is a world of limited opportunities, with legitimate jobs generally offering little prospect for lifetime satisfaction. In this respect, the segmented labor market becomes an essential concept for understanding the structure and context of the Chicano gang, the use and marketing of illegal drugs and stolen merchandise, and the prison involvements of the residents of the Los Angeles barrios.[7]

It is important to remember that the continuous shuttle from one economic structure to another consumes a great amount of time and energy. Each structure is differently organized. Hiring in the secondary labor market entails different and often informal job search patterns (cf. Bullock, 1973), which take a great deal of time. Obtaining income from the welfare economy means establishing a status in at least one—and usually several—bureaucracies. Getting income from the illegal economy means establishing—and sustaining—yet another status with a very different set of income-givers. Economic survival, especially in times of inflation, is a more than full-time occupation for the barrio resident. While it is true that there are sometimes high levels of income, for most of the casual participants in the illegal economy the income generated is small. Ultimately, total income only maintains survival, even when an individual participates in several economic structures simultaneously.

The segmented, or dual, labor market is a controversial idea among labor economists (cf. Cain, 1976). Yet it helps substantially to an understanding of the otherwise incomprehensible patterns of behavior in urban ghettos and barrios. We suggest that segmentation within this peripheral economic structure is the economic base for most of the families in the poorer areas of American cities.

In this respect, the Chicanos differ only in degree from other poor minorities. In Los Angeles the welfare structure is more extensive than, say, in the cities of Texas, a state with a strong anti-welfare orientation. In New York the gambling subsector is much more extensive (poor Chicanos show very little involvement in gambling); New York may offer yet other opportunities for illegal income that are not available or are not common in Los Angeles.

These are the realities of conflict and poverty for Chicanos in Los Angeles. The most critical of these realities are their ethnic distinctiveness, the institutional system, and the nature of the barrio economy. In this context, the persistence and influence of the youth gangs is much easier to understand.

2

The Chicano Gang in Context

WHAT, THEN, is so distinctive about the Chicano youth gangs in Los Angeles? What characteristics do they share with other urban gangs— and how can the study of such groups help us understand other gang phenomena? In this chapter we will describe Chicano gangs in general.

Distinctive Structures and Activity Patterns

The Chicano youth gang is a significant structure in a large proportion of poor urban Chicano barrios, not only in Los Angeles but in El Paso, San Antonio, and perhaps in other large cities as well. The gangs in these cities share some common features.

First, the gang is territorially based. This is a truism in most gang studies, because young male peer groups all tend to be based in some local network. But for Chicanos the territoriality is very deep. For gang members the word for gang and for neighborhood is identical. *"Mi barrio"* refers equally to "my gang" and "my neighborhood." This complete intermingling of peer group and neighborhood identity is a core characteristic of the Chicano gang, and extends even to the gang member who resides in a different barrio.

Second, Chicano gangs are age graded, with a new klika, or cohort, forming every two years or so. Regardless of the degree of discipline and cohesiveness of any given klika, their origin lies in interbarrio conflicts between teenage boys in school or in sports.

The gang and the klika remain salient lifelong membership and reference groups for some, but not all, members of the gang. During the peak years of barrio-based participation, a meaningful source of cohesiveness appears to lie in fighting. During adulthood, the primary loyalty may be reinforced by experiences in Juvenile Hall, prison, and other institutional structures outside the barrio, confrontations with active racism, and experiences in the illegal economy. In adulthood, the territoriality of the gang diminishes sharply. It becomes less of a locally-based social network. The network is strengthened, not only because other family members join the street gang, but also because members will marry into the families of fellow gang members, sponsor children in baptism (*compadrazgo*), and so on. Age grading remains a consistent feature of this structure and its lifetime significance for Chicano gangs is very unusual.

→ Finally, all Chicano gangs are fighting gangs—and most, if not all, use drugs. In fact, the gang is the principal context for both use and marketing of heroin. This combination of fighting and drugs is unique to Chicano gangs.

The gang is a quasi-institution in many Chicano communities, and it is best understood as such, rather than as a specialized juvenile phenomenon whose main feature is the production of delinquent acts. It is intertwined into the adult world, and thus cannot be understood outside the whole barrio and the ethnic context. At the same time the youth gang is a specialized structure of the barrio, and like any other specialized structure (such as the neighborhood church), it develops a specialized subculture, a set of values, norms, and specialized traditions, and sources of status honor. These gain special significance when it is remembered that the adolescent gang is a semisecret organization of adolescents and that gang cliques are organizations that in later life may be involved in illegal economic activities.

The Chicano Gang Subculture

Three general points must be made about the specialized subculture developed within the Chicano gangs. The first is that much of the behavior and activity of the gangs can be seen as a symbolic challenge to the world. The second point is that the gang subculture is innovative like any other live phenomenon and develops within its own logic. These first two points are not novel; they appear in studies of other types of gangs, as they stem from the quasi-isolation of the semisecret juvenile group. We will develop them here descriptively, with special reference to the distinctive history of Chicanos as a minority group. The third point is that Chicano gang subcultures are consistently responsive to certain types of programs.

Symbolic Challenge

In the 1940s the symbolic challenge offered by the pachucos attracted national attention. They developed a complete dress style and a full-blown, enduring argot (Barker, 1947). Octavio Paz, a Mexican philosopher writing in the 1950s about identity issues in Mexico, started his work by attempting to relate the rise of pachuquismo to a "spiritual condition" of Los Angeles Mexicans, in which "sensibilities are like a

pendulum . . . that has lost its reason and swings violently and errati-
cally back and forth" (1961, p .13). Paz saw the pachucos as characterized by a "fanatical will-to-be, but this will affirms nothing specific
except their determination . . . not to be like those around them" (p.
14). Paz believes that the pachuchos illuminated the "labyrinth of solitude" within which the Mexican roams, but he points to the fact that the
time of the *pachuchos* was one in which establishing vitality was an end
in itself—vitality denied by the grinding poverty, huge families, and
alcoholism of so many of the older Mexican men—vitality denied by
the opportunity structures. The zoot suits worn by the Chicano gang
boys of 1942 and 1943 had huge oversized trousers and accessories that
gave the new wartime austerity regulations (narrowly cut trousers and
no cuffs) a finger, a gesture of symbolic challenge. Such a challenge,
of course, immediately attracted attention at dance halls. It is interesting that in the White Fence barrio (see Chapter 3), where the opportunity structures were seen as somewhat more open, the pachucho style
never caught on. The message was that if the young Chicano was going
no place in the Anglo system, at least he would not be caught in the
dreary grind of the past.

In the 1970s, the challenge's mildest and most peaceable form is a
can of spray paint. Every clean wall in the county offers a challenge to
the boys from White Fence, El Hoyo, and other barrios. Park buildings,
bridges, public buildings, barrio stores, and residential fences and walls
all carry graffiti. After a gang worker flew a group of teenagers to Sacramento, he found that felt-tipped pens had marked the *placas* (gang
insignia) throughout the airliner. Gang graffiti are everywhere—on inaccessible high rocks in mountain areas, on the walls of toilets far from the
barrio. Recently East Los Angeles residents were distracted from a
movie set in San Francisco when they recognized a gang *placa* (VNE,
for Varrio-Nuevo-Estrada Courts, a rival of White Fence) spray painted
on a church wall. In the early 1970s an imaginative program of mural
painting attempted to build on this. By 1975 350 murals had been
painted, largely by gang boys. One artist designs his murals to permit
the gang graffiti to be incorporated. The murals also present the boys
with an opportunity to look at the evil side of gang activity. Scrolls with
dead members' names were painted in El Hoyo's mural. Needles com-
memorating the death-in-life of heroin addiction are a common theme.
The most important recurrent themes of these murals are always Mexican: Zapata, Villa, Aztec heroes, suffering, and pain.

At its most severe, the challenge means violence. By the mid-1970s,
death in gang fights had become fairly common in East Los Angeles.
The first clique of White Fence lost one young man in a gang fight when
he went to help a younger clique. The second clique lost a boy to a

police bullet. In 1972 the Los Angeles County Department of Community Services surveyed police records on gang activity in the county; their report noted thirty-three deaths among youngsters in East Los Angeles in a single year, and commented that "at least half of these are directly attributable to inter-gang violence" ("The Gangs of the Barrio," *L.A.*, December 16, 1972, p. 5). The violence appears largely in early adolescence, and is an extension of the general challenge that gang boys offer to their environment as a whole.[1]

The challenge expressed ties in with ethnic identity; it is made not only to the neighboring barrio, but to the Anglo world. To the larger system, the challenge in adolescence remains largely symbolic (graffitti, talk, and occasional symbolic vandalism). In adulthood, the challenge shifts. Gang members are extraordinarily proud of those clique members who have made it in the Anglo system. These members are more numerous than might be expected. The bottom lines in Table 2 include a man who became a C.P.A., and another who now owns his own business, although he dropped out of high school. Beating the system is always a source of pride, and even an occasion for group celebration. Older members of the powerful Clanton gang (a territory near downtown Los Angeles) formed an association that now holds reunions, accompanied by good dance bands, good liquor, and the other signs of "making it." But the truth is that for the older gang member, often an ex-convict or an ex-addict, making it is very hard indeed (see Chapter 5).

Innovation

We use the word innovation in both its ordinary meaning and as a sociological term from Robert Merton. To sociologists, innovation occurs when normal means to normal ends are inaccessible, and specialized means to those ends are developed. In Los Angeles County the desirable ends are always visible. Poor Chicanos exist both within their own stratified world and within the stratified world of the Anglo system. In the agricultural world of Chicano San Fernando (about an hour's drive from East Los Angeles), the barrios of the 1930s were stratified by occupation (Chapter 3). Workers in the packing houses were better off than workers in the fields. In their turn, the boys of the San Fernando barrios could visit and envy Chicano life in glittering East Los Angeles. Thus gang boys felt themselves at the bottom of two systems of stratification—that of Chicano neighborhoods and a rural-urban differentiation, and that of Anglo society. In our time the attractiveness and inaccessibility of the larger Anglo system is becoming even more obvious through television.

The gangs are innovative stylistically and symbolically. The pachuco fad is an extraordinary example of a stylistic innovation that expressed the core symbolic pattern of challenge. In a sense, the escalating violence since the 1950s is innovation that means that substance has taken the place of symbol.

Innovation, both symbolic and stylistic, also affected the patterns of drug use. The wide use of marijuana in the gangs of the late 1930s and early 1940s represented a symbolic stylistic break with the past. The gang kids were dandies and spent incredible sums of money on looking sharp, thus distinguishing themselves from the sloppily dressed males around them. Partying with liquor—the ubiquitous beer of the barrio taverns or the wine that began to be popular at this time—can also be a fairly sloppy business. Marijuana and yellowjackets (secobarbital) give a high that is not only different (interesting to an experimental risk taker), but is also "clean." Much the same is true of heroin. Some of the earlier users of heroin comment explicitly on the fact that heroin was used by the sharp-looking men in the barrio, unlike the messy Saturday night drunks from the bars. The risk element in heroin, of course, is even greater than in marijuana and pill use. We are suggesting here that the early and deepening involvement of gang youth in drugs and narcotics was—in the tightly bounded Chicano world of the 1940s—akin to the symbolic innovations of the pachuco dress and argot. Some support for this view can be found in addicts' reminiscences on the role of men from out of town, and several men who commented about the role of returning servicemen who had been "turned on" in military service, especially in Asia.

There is no doubt whatever that heroin and pills (both "uppers" and downers") came into the barrio through the gangs. There is also no doubt (see Chapter 4) that drug and opiate marketing came to be based on barrio gangs.

Historically, heroin changed the nature of interbarrio conflicts. When heroin first appeared (as shown in San Fernando, Chapter 3) barrio members began to deal across "turf" lines. Gang warfare declined. As heroin became more "normal" in the barrios, addicts continued to enter each others' territories, but the newer gang cohorts revived the interbarrio fighting. It is our conclusion that drugs did not destroy the gangs; they simply altered relationships between older clique members.

Crime is seen by many criminologists as innovatory: it provides a deviant means to the normal American end of making it. Some youth crime performed in the context of the gangs certainly appears to be innovative in this respect. In the poverty environment, small scale extortion was (and is) fairly common among teenagers to obtain specific consumption ends.

I mostly identified with our dress, our zoot suit. Sometimes when we didn't have any money to go to the show, we would go to the show lines about one o'clock. You know how they line up, all the school kids. We would tell them, "Hey give us a dime, or a quarter." By the time we reached the end we had about five or six dollars, enough for candy, popcorn, even dinner. That was about the most delinquent thing we did. We never did any major stealing. Maybe sometimes we would steal a couple of pairs of socks and stuff like that but no real stealing.

It was out of this pattern of extorting lunches and lunch money that the neighborhood "squares" began to develop fear of the gang members.[2] Small-scale dealing, in drugs or marijuana, also tends to be gang based. But other delinquent acts, apart from some incidents of vandalism, appear not to be conducted by the gang nor by one of its cliques, but by crime partners, usually from one clique in the gang but later, as people age, often involving men from other barrios. In a study of the Clover gang of Lincoln Heights in East Los Angeles, Klein (1971) concluded that delinquency is a minor part of gang life and is performed cafeteria-style, trying a little of everything. The most common offenses are theft and such juvenile status offenses as truancy and incorrigibility. In addition, sporadic individual crimes of violence occur when a boy has partied too long on a mixture of alcohol and barbiturates. Ironically, given the early motivation to "stay cool" on drugs other than alcohol, it is not uncommon in the barrios to see a boy stumbling down the street, obviously stoned on pills. Pills and heroin are no longer a clean high for the dandified gang member.

Yet innovation in the gang clearly occurs in the sense that every behavior pattern is accelerated by successive klikas. White Fence violated a gang code when they first used guns; by the mid-1970s guns were normal, and a fair fight (one person on one person without weapons) was fairly unusual, although it was the norm of an earlier period. In the mid-1970s, violations of gang codes (accelerating the "badness") included firing into a household where there was "a mother" present, that is, gang fighting involving non-combatants. Twenty-five years earlier, heroin accelerated the innovatory pattern of yellowjackets and bennies (barbiturates and amphetamines; see Chapter 4). In recent years, inhalants have become a widespread youthful "high," as has experimentation with hallucinogens and, rarely, cocaine. But Chicanos have retained an unusual commitment to heroin as "the drug that drives other drugs out."

One of the most depressing aspects of gang life and its acceleratory aspect is the strong anticipatory socialization to life in prison. Many youngsters believe that they will wind up in San Quentin, and the special schools (Jackson and Ramona High Schools) confirm their belief. The coping mechanisms they develop in juvenile detention facilities and camps are often explicitly related to their adult mechanisms for coping with prison.

Response to Programs

Chicano gang subculture is responsive to programs. Because the purpose of all gang-oriented programs in Los Angeles since World War II has been either to destroy the gang or to drastically modify its course, this may be hard to believe. But the Los Angeles gangs generally, and specifically the three gangs of the next chapter, were neither destroyed nor persuaded to deviate in any important way from the logic of their own innovative subcultural development. These "hard to reach" gangs have in fact eagerly responded to three types of official attention.

Some of these were conventional street programs, such as those of the Federation of the Barrios of a generation ago. This group tried off and on over the years to turn the barrio gangs into competitive sports clubs, emphasizing baseball or boxing, to or convert them into party-planning groups. Poor gang boys tend to respond eagerly to any kind of expansion of their resources through this kind of activity. Yet in some cases, as in the mid-1940s, the true intent of the program was to eliminate the gangs. We talked to one older social worker who claimed that he had "destroyed White Fence" in about 1950. This rumor of White Fence's death was wildly exaggerated. Similarly, Klein (1971) documents the "success" of a two-year program in reducing gang recruitment in Clover to the zero point. Again, the rumor of Clover's death was greatly exaggerated.

We have mentioned the mural projects of East Los Angeles. Gang boys have eagerly participated in this type of project, viewing them as both constructive, by relating them to the larger community life (leaving a beautifying contribution in the neighborhood), and cathartic or therapeutic, in that guilt and concern about barrio violence can be symbolically expiated or transmuted into an identification with the Mexican Revolution.

One of the most interesting of the "programs" that attracted a number of gang members was the Brown Berets, a short-lived militant *Movimiento* group that involved older as well as younger gang members in a paramilitary organization. The Berets were especially active in Santa Barbara, working to deter narcotics use in the barrios. Their more widely publicized activities included the takeover of Catalina Island in 1974, a symbolic invasion that drew a great deal of public attention.

It may seem ironic to discuss gang responsiveness in a section on gang subculture, but the question of responsiveness is important. Many funded and unfunded groups in Los Angeles have seen the enduring and quasi-institutionalized gangs as a worthwhile target for their activities.

Almost without pause since the early 1950s, one or another kind of program has been a regular part of the environment of the barrio gangs. In fact, these omnipresent programs are part of the normal institutional environment of the barrios themselves. Several years ago an ex-convict serving agency in East Los Angeles employed twenty White Fence boys at the minimum wage "simply to keep them off the streets during the summer." Even without the nominal pretense of social usefulness or fun, the boys cheerfully accepted these summer Neighborhood Youth Corps jobs, because of the money involved. There are many other examples. We can observe the ambivalent but nonetheless consistent utilization of the resources of city, county, and private agencies throughout the years. It is a reasonable conclusion that opportunistic utilization of the resources available for gang purposes is simply another aspect of the welfare economy of East Los Angeles.

Other Portrayals of Chicano Gang Behavior

Early Studies

There is some hint about the precursors of Chicano urban gangs in the portrayals of young male sociability groups in the small rural towns of South Texas (Madsen, 1964; Rubel, 1966). The *palomilla* (literally, "flock of doves") are a group of young men who cheerfully go from one village to another, drinking, dating, and raiding. Fights are a considerable part of the fun when, for example, they crash the weekend dance of another Mexican community. We are by no means suggesting that the urban gangs of Los Angeles are a simple importation of such cultural items, either from the rural United States or from Mexico. But very little attention has been given in the literature on rural or urban barrio life to gang phenomena. In his reminiscences of life in Sacramento, California, during World War I, Ernesto Galarza provides one of the very rare evocations of what urban life in America meant to the incoming Mexican. He includes a tantalizing (because it is personal, rather than barrio) vignette of his own "club" that "might have become a gang." As early as 1926, Emory Bogardus noted the presence of gangs among the Mexican Americans in Los Angeles. Then, after World War II, a series of scholarly studies of city and small town barrios (Goldschmidt, 1947; Tuck, 1946) begin to fill in the picture of the origins. Yet the studies of the 1940s rarely indicate that the youthful fighting gangs were likely to become quasi-institutionalized in the urban Chicano barrios.

There may have been a special reason for the scholarly neglect of Chicano gangs in the 1940s. The memory of the racism expressed in the Zoot Suit Riots and the argument that the violence of the Chicano youngsters was directly traceable to Aztec blood lust was still fresh (as in the "Ayres Report" of the Los Angeles Sheriff's Department, described in McWilliams, 1949).

When Carey McWilliams wrote his now-classic *North from Mexico* (1949) he virtually dismissed the media campaign against pachuco gangs as pure unfounded stereotype. In his book the word "gangs" is always used in quotation marks, as if the gangs were yet one more creation of a racist Anglo press. By contrast, in the late 1940s a sympathetic community worker, Beatrice Griffith, attempted to put the media portraits of, and the statistical material about, young Chicanos into a context of vignettes of life settings. Her book, *American Me* (1948) offers an interesting evocation of life during the pachucho era, emphasizing the role of traditionalism and transition. The social distance sociologist Emory Bogardus, then teaching at the University of Southern California, called attention to situational factors related to the persistence of the "45 to 70" Los Angeles Chicano gangs in a brief 1943 article. In 1946, Lemert and Rosberg emphasized the institutional factors, most importantly the police practices with the gangs.

Studies of the 1960s

These forerunners were followed by the work of Celia Heller (1966) and Malcolm Klein (1971).[3] Heller did no original work on gangs, but she focussed her analysis of Mexican American youth on what she called "two polar types—the 'ambitious' boys and the 'delinquent' boys . . . to gain insight into the problems of Mexican American youth as a whole" (p. 5). In what was later to be seen as an absurd point, she argued that "the excess of juvenile delinquents among Mexican Americans . . . is not composed of deviants from the cultural pattern but rather of boys who overconform to this pattern. In this view, the most striking 'deviants' among Mexican American youth are not these delinquents but the youngsters . . . who aspire to or who do attend college" (pp. 76–77). In both his early and later work, Bogardus implicitly used a model of "disorganization and deprivation" to account for the Chicano gangs as well as the other youth gangs. Lemert and Rosberg focussed on police practices. Heller, however, unequivocally opted for a *particular* cultural pattern to explain gang behavior.

Klein sharply rejected the notion that there are cultural ("racial and ethnic") connotations to the traditional Chicano gang (pp. 66–69). He argues that this kind of structure appears in "stable slum" areas, where a gang may exist for decades, in contrast to the "spontaneous gang" of interstitial, or transitional, areas in the city. Klein's generalized account of the structure of gangs (traditional and other) differs from ours in several major respects. These differences are so critical to our argument that they deserve close attention.

First, rather than seeing age as the primary basis for the formation of substructures within the gangs, Klein sees age as only one of several bases for the formation of cliques. Second, Klein's primary distinction is made between core and fringe members. The core members are characterized (after analyzing questionnaires from gang social workers) by a cluster of personal characteristics (labelled the "Deficient Aggressive" factor) and by a higher group involvement and commitment. Third, Klein (with most other students of traditional gangs) sees gang members as "withdrawing" from gang identity "as the member approaches the age of majority," that is, the early twenties (p. 77). By contrast, we see the continued salience of klika and gang membership well into adulthood. Fourth, Klein ignores the relationship between gang structure and institutional experiences.

The major differences between our study and Klein's work probably lie in the context of the two studies. Klein's experiences with the Clover gang (which he calls Ladino Hills) lasted only eighteen months.[4] His contacts were primarily through student assistants and a reluctant "detached worker." He records difficulties with staff morale and, notably, with application of his core-fringe dichotomy to the Clover gang. In fact, they were forced to drop this typology (derived from an earlier study of four black gangs) and develop a more complex basis for his intervention strategy in the Chicano community. It is odd that he does not acknowledge this fact in his generalized account of gang structure.

One of the major points we emphasize is that each klika and each barrio is somewhat different, reflecting its immediate historical circumstances. Klein's work in Clover was conducted during 1966, 1967, and 1968, a very interesting period and place in Chicano history, and the klika he studied had a unique set of experiences. Father Luce, to whom Klein refers merely as a "social activist" (p. 275), was administering a program affiliated with the Lincoln Heights Teen Post. In fact, Father Luce was an Episcopalian priest whose social activism went far beyond bland church work with teen posts. He was actively allied with a group of Chicano militants who were headquartered in the Clover area, publishing the radical newspaper *La Raza*. Luce made a direct effort to radicalize the young people of the Clover barrio into the Chicano *Movimiento* activities of the time. It was an innovative and reasonably successful attempt at gang work that is reminiscent of the Blackstone Nation in Chicago and the Young Lords in New York City. There is no doubt whatsoever that the Chicano youth of this district, gang members and squares alike, were deeply involved in Chicano militancy in the late 1960s. César Chávez held his famous marches in 1966. Reies Tijerina was organizing the land grant claimants in Texas and New Mexico. The Brown Berets and the militant college youth group (UMAS, later

MECHA) was organized in 1967. The East Los Angeles high school protest blowouts occurred in 1968. Street demonstrations, protest meetings, and militant propaganda against the overkill of Chicanos in the Vietnam war began in 1969.[5] Clover was a center of this *Movimiento* activity, yet this powerful resurgence of ideology is never mentioned as a condition for the project's experimentally-induced changes in group cohesiveness.

Yet another minor note on the importance of the barrio context. Klein and his workers were puzzled that gang cohesiveness and the related delinquent activities increased not during the summer, but rather, "in direct relationship to school activity," before Easter, Christmas, Thanksgiving, *Cinco de Mayo* (the traditional Mexican holiday), and semester breaks (p. 120). This happened even though almost no gang members were attending school. Because they were concentrating on the supposedly closed world of adolescence, the researchers failed to see that these are general community holidays with many parties, festive preparations, celebrations, and fighting. In addition, gang members also have large families, with many brothers and sisters in school. An observation of the context of barrio life would take the mystery out of the observed relationship.

But the most important contextual fact is the unresearched reiteration of the truism that gangs dissolve when the members reach their 20s. Members of older klikas appear to vanish from the barrio, it is true. A very high proportion of them (see Tables 1 and 2) go underground —into drug addiction and/or prison. Yet in prison the barrio becomes even more important, and gang cohesiveness increases. Younger klika members do not lose contact with these veteranos.

In one important respect, Klein's work has contributed to knowledge of both Chicano gangs and gangs in general. He appears to be the first researcher to abandon the fiction that intervention programs are not part of the slum opportunity structure. Other theorists focus on factors such as "lower class culture" (Miller, 1958), "delinquent subcultures" (Cohen, 1955), and "delinquent opportunity structures" (Cloward and Ohlin, 1960), as if there were no institutional forces impinging on the gangs other than the police. Gang social workers not only label and possibly stigmatize the gang members, but they also provide resources. In our earlier discussion of this point we place these resources on a par with those to be acquired by work (like the White Fence klika in the early days) or by other means. It is something desirable for teenaged boys living in poverty. Klein argues on a more psychological level that it is the attention of the gang worker, and his own seduction into gang activities, that provides reinforcement for the gang's cohesiveness and ultimately of its delinquencies. The Ladino Hills phase of Klein's Los

Angeles study was designed to change the role of the worker and test whether or not this would tend to dissolve the gang.

Klein does not argue for the abolition of gang social work, but rather for its redirection. He concludes that his own form of gang work in Clover served to reduce cohesiveness, membership, and delinquencies, and that it altogether stopped recruitment into the gang. As we said earlier, these findings were valid only in the short run, if at all. There is good reason to suspect that the conclusions are contaminated by Klein's failure to examine the contextual factors that we stressed in Chapter 1.

It is ironic that the Los Angeles law enforcement agencies that directly face the street gangs ignored the Clover findings and concentrated on results from black gangs. They have, in fact, used Klein's research in a continuing campaign against community projects, on occasion directly misrepresenting it. As recently as April, 1977, the *El Sereno Bulletin* in East Los Angeles stated that Klein's study reported an increase of violence among gangs when programs were instituted to help them. Thus the Sheriff's Department's juvenile gang expert applied the findings from the black gangs directly to the Chicano gangs.[6] Although this is a direct misrepresentation of Klein's research, suppression rather than redirection is the ultimate purpose in most action.[7] Klein's remarks about the inaccurate information and insights of the police gang detail were prophetic (pp. 18–19).

Thus the studies done by Heller and Klein emphasized, respectively, the ethnic subculture and at least one institutional factor, that of the gang intervention programs. At about the time Klein was writing about the Clover gang, Paul Bullock began his extensive study of the youth labor market in East Los Angeles and Watts (1973). Based on some three hundred interviews in each area, the study is generally congruent with our outline of the barrio economic opportunity structures,[8] and is part of the evidence for that description. About a third of the East Los Angeles youngsters aspired to professional careers and to relatively high incomes. Yet their information and job search patterns were limited to informal and personal networks that were incongruent with their aspirations. Schools, employment offices, and fathers provided neither models nor guidance, and progress within the first three jobs was slight. About a quarter of the young Chicanos (in their early twenties) were still working in jobs that paid less than two dollars per hour.

The contrast with Celia Heller is sharp. For Bullock, it is not deviant to aspire to a good job; it is just unrealistic, given the resources available to barrio youth. The "subeconomy"—the illegal economy—supplements their income. Bullock makes no estimate of the relative proportion of income to his respondents from their tax-free dealing in pills and marijuana, but he makes clear that a position in this structure is an important (but not highly valued) part of their array of economic opportunities. They do not, generally, aspire to careers in crime. Bullock argues (as we do) that the subeconomy has been a persistent feature of urban life for many decades and was not invented by the minorities of today. He also makes the point that youth in these areas are fully aware of the obstacle that arrest and detention records present to job attainment. (In many cases, arrests are not related to offenses, but are either unfounded or for acts which would not be crimes for adults.) Bullock details the "ovewhelming" impact of police records on the employability of minority youth in both the private and the public sectors; this is amply confirmed by our researchers.[9]

One of the few studies of Chicano gangs that has succeeded in attracting the attention of social scientists who do not specialize in delinquency is that of Suttles (1968) in the old Chicago Halstead-Hull House area (called Addams by the author). Though his work involves some degree of participant observation, most of his information appears to be derived from gang social workers and law enforcement agencies. Suttles emphasizes gang subculture, as does Cohen, for example, rather than some of the more general issues that are addressed here.

Chicanas and Gangs

There is virtually no research on the gang membership of Chicanas (women), except for some passing remarks on girls' affiliates (cf. Klein, 1971, p. 265, and a marvelously stereotypical master's thesis done in the mid-1950s about girls who were involved with boys of the White Fence gang: Ranker, 1957). In 1974 John Quicker argued in "The Chicana Gang" that there has been a real change in role structure for Chicanas, with a decline in traditionalism in the barrios. It is based on interviews of thirteen girls from East Los Angeles and of institutional officials. He sees the girls' gangs as "ambivalent" about their relationship to the boys' gangs of the same neighborhoods—and ambivalent about the extent to which the girls' groups are "bounded gangs" or simply a cluster of girls who go with gang boys. Quicker also comments on some of the same features we note in the boys' gangs, most notably, fighting, and loyalty to ones' homies. In 1978, *Ms.* magazine published a short set of interviews with girls associated with East Los Angeles gangs, but failed to distinguish between girl's gangs and girls who were associated with boys' gangs (Murphy, 1978).

Chicano Gangs and the Literature on Gangs

The "Alien" Theme

The urban gang had become a well-established phenomenon by 1927, when Frederick Thrasher published his monumental study of 1,313 Chicago gangs and Bogardus tried to do the same in Los Angeles (1926).

A generation earlier, Jacob Riis wrote of the "wild children" of New York as part of the "shame of our cities." Obviously, gangs were not merely epiphenomena of the turn-of-the-century urban chaos and the gradual withdrawal of children from the labor market.[10] In the public mind and in the mass media they were consistently associated with foreign and unassimilable influences. Youth gangs of the new immigrants prompted groups like the American Social Science Association to demand in 1875 that the state act *in loco parentis* for "wild" youth because it was apparent that the immigrants were not good parents (Bakan, 1972, p. 75). Later, Thrasher concluded that ganging was "largely a phenomenon of the immigrant community."[11] It is estimated that half of all cases of juvenile delinquency before 1930 involved the children of immigrants (Haskell and Yablonsky, 1974).

The foreignness theme in gangs is still current in the mass media, although in recent years the alienness of the urban minority has replaced the largely outdated alienness of the European immigrant. Chicanos are perceived as alien both in culture and as a minority. This is forcibly demonstrated in Carey McWilliams' 1949 account of the role of the Los Angeles newspapers in the wartime Zoot Suit Riots. Although the fiercest week of rioting was unmistakably initiated by sailors, the newspapers maintained that the riots were provoked by "Mexicans." Not until the Watts Riots a generation later did the media promote so diligently the hypothesis that street gangs begin street riots. In both the Zoot Suit Riots and the Watts troubles, there were charges of "subversion" by, respectively, German and/or Japanese agents and Communists. The alien theme is revived sporadically regarding Chicanos (as in a 1972 issue of the tabloid *L.A.*, titled "The Gangs of the Barrio: The Violence Turns Inward").

The Alien as Adult

Whether blaming the parents or trying to classify the immigrants as "disorganized," the earlier studies of gangs as related to "alien" subcultures at least had the virtue of calling attention to the adult context of gang activity. Thrasher's study of the Chicago gangs reached into all aspects of the adult life of the city that affected the emergence and importance of the youth gang. These included the well-developed adult crime structures of the Chinese and the Italians, as well as the demoralization and bewilderment of some of the other ethnic groups. It included a survey of the city's physical resources for boys' play: vacant lots, railroad embankments, and even teeming Maxwell Street, with its pushcart market and hustlers. In more recent years, however, the adult context has almost vanished as a matter of scholarly interest.

William Foot Whyte, one of the last to focus on ethnicity and to view the gang in a full adult and urban context, studied the Italian corner boy gang in 1942. Even the urban anthropology of the late 1960s viewed Chicago's Vice Lords without any consideration of its adult context (Keiser, 1969), as, oddly enough considering the purpose of his work, did Suttles (1968). Klein's study of the Chicano gang illustrates this trend very well; he was content to label the context "stable slum," the gang "traditional," and continue his analysis with no attention to either the adult or the ethnic context for either the gang activity or his own intervention program. How did this shift in emphasis occur? A review of the literature seems to indicate not only a shift in the conceptualization of young people, but also a shift in interest in adolescent deviance.

We note this shift most clearly in Coleman's *Adolescent Society* (1961), when he argues that adolescents are "structurally isolated" in American society, with comparatively little linkage with adults of either parental age or younger (like older brothers and sisters). Along with the notion of structural isolation went the notion of youth culture. It became academically fashionable to view adolescents as separate from adults. Then students of youth problems lost interest in boys' activities and began to concentrate on explanations of delinquent acts. Gangs became only one of many possible contexts for delinquency, and not a very interesting context at that. Thus the shift in emphasis meant that gangs became associated almost exclusively with delinquency (because that was almost the only interest in the gang). Although such students as Klein say repeatedly that most gang activities are not delinquent, and that when delinquency does occur it is generally the activity of a small group rather than an entire gang, the equation of gangs and delinquency continues, especially in the mass media.

Theories of Gangs: The Adult Context

We will briefly survey some of the gang theory that was widely current during the mid-1970s, specifically on the question of the adult context.

It is obvious that Yablonsky has the most adult-free approach. In his attempt to account for violent gangs, he sees that they share many features with the "pseudo-community" of paranoids. These "near groups" fall between totally unstructured collectivities, like mobs, and organized groups like "the delinquent gang" (cf. Haskell and Yablonsky, 1974). Yablonsky's conceptualization has been widely criticized; all we need do here is point to it as a case of extreme focus on youth and pathology in gang research. Most sociological theories, by contrast, emphasize the gang as a lower-class adaptation to, or rebellion against, the limitations present in the immediate surroundings.

Miller sees the gang as a normal exaggeration of the "focal concerns of the lower class," that is, a subcultural emphasis on excitement, trouble, toughness, autonomy, and fate (1958, pp. 261–2, 269). Cohen (1955), by contrast, views the delinquency of gang boys as a "nonutilitarian" expression of malicious rebellion against middle class norms encountered in school and elsewhere.

Cloward and Ohlin (1960) see the lower class boys as "located in two opportunity structures—one legitimate, the other illegitimate" (p. 152). The variations in illegitimate means available for obtaining normal success goals in the immediate milieu will affect the form of delinquency. Thus stable slums with bonds between older and younger offenders and between the criminal and the conventional give rise to "instrumental, if criminalistic, ways of life" (p. 171). Cloward and Ohlin see such "criminal gang subcultures" as ruling out either a pattern of violence (which arises in "disorganized slums") or drugs. Narcotics use is seen as "retreatism" for the adolescents who are "double failures," that is, who can succeed neither in the conventional nor in the illegitimate opportunity structure. (Chein, 1964, contrasts narcotics users with "reality oriented" gang boys.) This basic framework was later developed empirically in a study of three delinquent subcultures in an Eastern city (Spergel, 1964).

Chicano and Other Gang Literature Compared

These are scarcely sociological theories about gangs. It would be more accurate to say they are interpretative frameworks, and that our description of the structure and subculture of the Chicano street gangs are in close agreement with some aspects of them. In other ways they are complementary and, of course, at some points sharply divergent. At yet other points there is virtually no overlap at all.

We share Miller's view that gang behavior is not as pathological as Yablonsky would have us believe. Yet we believe that Miller's focal concerns must be close to the ethnic themes of adulthood. In turn, these are going to be more complex and more demanding than the lower-class concerns that Miller identifies as "excitement, trouble, toughness, autonomy and fate." We also share Cohen's view that there are nonutilitarian and rebellious elements, as described in Chapter 3. Many of the men we interviewed once vandalized schools and other Anglo institutions, but these actions carried a strong element of protest against the bureaucratic cruelties of minority status.

> It starts off where you start going to school as a kid, right away you get the impression that going to school is a punishment. I didn't learn that from my parents. How many times did I hear a teacher say they'll put you in jail if you don't come to school. . . .
> I remember one summer it was hot, maybe a hundred degrees, I don't know. Somebody said, let's go to the plunge, but there wasn't any plunge around the area, the closest one around I guess was Evergreen, which was a few miles away from where we lived, the other one

was in Montebello, that we had heard of, but it was in Anglo territory. One day me and a buddy of mine said, "Let's go to Montebello, it's closer," so off we went, walked and walked, finally we got to Montebello plunge. We were gonna go inside, some girl said it's filled up, so we got to wait. So we waited and waited and people would be going in, all Anglos, and they weren't coming out. So finally, we figured it out they weren't letting Mexicans in that day. We were hot and thirsty and mad and everything. We broke two windows of that building and ran. We ran all the way home. We got there laughing and laughing.

They say they vandalize schools because they hated the *gabacho* (Anglo), and there is no reason not to believe them. We also argue strongly against Cohen's suggestion that the gang subculture is structurally separated from the adult world. If there were no other evidence in East Los Angeles, there would be the persistence of gang friendships and associations into adult life, and even into groups organized for field research.

We very much share Cloward, Ohlin, and Spergel's view of the dual opportunity structure. Yet we disagree that one can conclude that the gangs continue in a separate criminalistic structure. It would stretch the evidence too far to say that Chicano gangs are based in stable slums and that the older klikas are criminal. This is simply not true, even given the considerable difference between Chicano street gangs from different areas. And what constitutes a stable slum? Many of the Los Angeles barrios have an invisible turnover, still poor and still Mexican, because families leave and newcomers arrive. This could be stable only in the sense that the families look the same and are still poor. Or perhaps the barrios are "disorganized" because Chicano gangs have always fought and are often violent. Although Cloward and Ohlin see narcotics usage as a sign of individual failure, such usage is usual and normal among Chicano gangs. *Most* of the younger men in *most* barrio gangs become narcotics users.

It may be too easy for conventional sociologists to dismiss these findings about Chicano gangs as peculiar. Certainly they diverge sharply from previous findings about gangs. In fact, they overturn the previous associations made between specialized gangs and neighborhood types. Our findings are not anomalous and they cannot be ignored, even though Klein is able to overlook his own discovery that his typology of internal structure had to be abandoned for Chicano gangs. If Chicano gangs are going to be taken seriously, the current theories of gang behavior must be drastically modified. At this late date it is disturbing that so many people can read about, live near, and do research on these longstanding phenomena without noticing that they do not fit the theories.

Theoretical Contributions in Context

The barrios are Chicano by repeated external definition, both in the past and continuously in the present. It is no accident that the 350 street murals of East Los Angeles are always built around Mexican and Indian themes. Or that the high schools of the area sponsor and train folklorico dance troupes who perform at many community functions with pride and with applause. "Cultural nationalism" did not have to be invented; it is normal and expressive in the life-patterns of the community itself. The daily, weekly, and yearly rhythms of life in the barrios differ from those elsewhere in the city of Los Angeles. They are geared to a social system that emphasizes a large and extended family and to relationships among families that (in small town fashion) go back for decades.

The age-graded gang is one among many barrio structures in which boys play a role; it may be the only structure in which they play a reasonably autonomous role. Chicanismo is expressed in all matters of style and substance, and a highly traditional adult social system is maintained. Gang boys show what Anglo adolescents would consider extraordinary deference to adults. They can be observed apologizing for the use of bad language, or even slang. They may ask permission to smoke. They do not interrupt or contradict an elder or a more prestigeful person. Even the most personally confused boys know how to behave, with respect, in the Chicano system. The barrio system is strongly male-focussed, with deep segregation and complementarity between the male and the female activities and between the activities of older and younger people. Men are expected to do things for women and older—and younger—people.

According to the ideal, the adult man carries a demanding burden of responsibility and a certain corresponding license is expected and accepted. Conservatism and idealization both run very deep in barrio life. However, the realities of the survival economy of the barrios mean that responsibilities often cannot be met. Encounters with institutional callousness and prejudice further diminish self-esteem.

> I remember my mother or father sometimes used to have to go too [to school or court] and every time they come up against the Anglos they were meek. They would bow their heads. And I didn't want to be meek.

Often male license is abused. Daily life can become a succession of small dramas centered on meeting interpersonal and economic crises. (This "daily drama" is well portrayed in Sheehan's 1975 portrait of a New York Puerto Rican *mater familias*.) Gossip, heavily judgmental, is at the heart of much sociability at the frequent parties. Gossip is fun. It also means that everybody—adult and adolescent—has a "reputation" that is continuously shifting and renewed.

What we have been describing has become the hackneyed idea of "machismo," "the code," "the culture," and the like. It is also a description of a fairly intense, if not always effective, system of social controls. One of the core values that has been less talked about than machismo is the belongingness that goes with a system based on familism. Gossip, no matter how judgmental, only rarely closes the doors on a barrio relationship—in barrio terms, "to cut one loose." It shifts relationships and sometimes shifts reference groups. The isolated individual is a rarity in the barrios. In the pervasive barrio atmosphere of attachment, a home with conflict or shame (one does not complain or gossip about one's parents' shortcomings) can be a far more severe source of deprivation than such a home in a middle class Anglo area. It is no accident that gang members refer to each other as homeboys. Even in adulthood, when two strangers discover that they are homies they open up to each other as if they were, in fact, members of the same family.

Examination of the adult and ethnic context of Chicano gangs leads us inevitably to several major themes. The first is the disparity between actual behavior and traditional ideals (which is the ultimate source of most barrio gossip). These ideals become even more idealized in contrast to the remote and stereotyped Anglo world. The second theme is that these ideals center around male behavior. The third theme is the belongingness that pervades life in the barrio. The fourth theme is the insults, large and small, of minority life.

Yet this adult and Chicano context for street gang behavior allows us to move beyond the existing literature in one important respect. If we accept the Cloward and Ohlin's thesis that gang delinquency is a deviant means to a normal success goal, then we must look carefully at what normal success means. The success that Chicanos are oriented to is an idealized version of male strength and male responsibility that the people around them can rarely approach. This success requires belonging to the group. Thus the gang represents a means to what is an expressive, rather than an instrumental, goal: the acting out of a male role of competence and of "being in command" of things. With the police quickly defining a separate and identifiable group of Chicano adolescents as a group and as dangerous, the gang will tend to at least partly redefine its competence in terms of increasing violence. Then, also, drug use becomes understandable because it enhances the sense of belongingness that grows naturally from the use of such party drugs as alcohol, marijuana, and barbiturates. The younger boys help the older shoot heroin and then, finally, the use of drugs leads into the intense psuedo-companionship of the secret and illegal market.

There is one final point about the barrio gang that we hope will demolish the notion of a separate and structurally isolated adolescent gang subculture. For each individual in the gang, the basic belongingness to the neighborhood is, in fact, an accident of parental choice. Where the boy happens to live is rarely a matter of his choice. (Of course, in the case of the White Fence gang, the boys can, and do, join gangs based in barrios outside their own neighborhood of residence, although this is rare among Los Angeles gangs.) The nature of family life is also an accident and, no matter how unsatisfying and deprived this family life, it is shameful to complain publicly about family problems. From the boy's point of view, hopelessness is implicit and overwhelming; he has no power to change things at home. He has no power to change his family's choice of barrio. But he does have the power to enter an intense relationship with boys his own age.[12]

We have demonstrated that the Chicano gangs of the Southwest have some distinctive characteristics, and that a serious consideration of these characteristics could produce more effective theories of urban youth gangs in general. Given the peculiar economic background of the community we have emphasized, it is not surprising that a major opportunity structure should emerge from the Chicano gangs. This structure, the drug and narcotics market, will be described in Chapter 4. First we will detail the history and composition of three barrio gangs that are well-known to our researchers, as some of them are former active members and are now respected veteranos.

3

Three Barrio Gangs

EACH OF THE GANGS considered here is different, reflecting the varying factors of the ethnic context of life in Mexican Los Angeles, the institutional structure, and the economic structure. We will demonstrate that the different conditions of the three barrios produced somewhat different gang subcultures.

El Hoyo Maravilla is one gang from a tiny barrio in the center of a larger group of barrios known roughly as Maravilla. This neighborhood is separated from the other barrios of Maravilla only by its distinctive physical location at the bottom of El Hoyo. In the same general area live its neighbors and gang enemies—Marianna Maravilla, Kern Maravilla, and so on. Although they are enemies on the street, the Maravilla gangs join together to dominate the Chicano factions in California correctional institutions.

The White Fence gang lives not far from El Hoyo and is a traditional enemy. (For all of these locations, see Maps 1, 2 and 3.) White Fence is the clearest case of a gang that emerged as a consequence of major changes in a barrio. It was the first rationalized fighting gang in East Los Angeles, thereby attracting a considerable reputation among law enforcement authorities and in the press. It not only departed from the strict tradition of barrio residence as a condition for membership, but it abandoned the looser tradition prohibiting serious weapons.

The third gang appeared in San Fernando, a rural-suburban area some twenty miles north of downtown Los Angeles. Created during the zoot suit, or pachucho era, it was much more loosely organized than the two East Los Angeles gangs and reflects its quasi-rural origins.

These historical reconstructions of the barrios are derived largely from oral histories taken by the Pinto Project, supplemented by the few contemporary studies.

Hoyo Maravilla: The Gang That Just Grew

Just outside the boundary of Los Angeles proper (east of Rowan Avenue and south of Brooklyn Avenue), the barrios of Maravilla began to open to Mexican settlement well before the 1920s. McWilliams (1949) terms this the "principal area of 'first settlement' for most of the immigrant families," and estimates that by the mid-1920s the Mexican population had reached 50,000 in this unincorporated tract of county land (p. 224). Many, if not most, of the new arrivals owned a bit of this land and built tiny wooden houses of two or three rooms, often doing most of the work themselves. Lots in the tract were very cheap; its most conspicuous feature was its unsuitability for houses. An *arroyo*, or dry river bed, cut a series of low bluffs, and the depressed area became known as El Hoyo—literally, the hole. El Hoyo became a barrio inside an area of barrios. There was no water service, no sewer, no pavement, and no gas main. Water was brought to the top of the hill near El Hoyo every day on a horse-drawn wagon, and residents carried it down to the houses in buckets. Today El Hoyo is still a conspicuously isolated area, cut off from neighboring barrios by steep streets. Many of the original homes are still there, packed close together on tiny lots.

Settlement of El Hoyo began very early. One elderly Mexican remembers hearing of the Maravilla area in Texas as early as 1923—and being told that it contained a large community of Mexicans. This man's arrival is typical: his family crossed the border at El Paso, spent a year working for the railroads, and finally settled in Los Angeles in 1927 when he was sixteen. They moved directly to El Hoyo de Mara Villa (then known as lower Mara Villa).

Even to the people living in the eroded gullies and ravines of nearby White Fence, Maravilla appeared to house the desperately poor. In the late 1920s the dry river bed drained a flash flood which swept houses from their foundations and drowned a number of residents. Shortly thereafter the arroyo was filled by the county. Basic utilities were put in by the end of the 1930s.

In a great sweep of higher ground around Maravilla, extending south as far as the Exposition Park area, farms, mostly owned by Japanese, grew sugar beets, lettuce, cabbage, and potatoes. The Mexicans of El Hoyo worked on these farms, and during the harvest seasons they migrated to work in walnuts and citrus in all the nearby counties. The neighborhood was generally so poor that the Depression is remembered as a time of real hunger. Free food was occasionally distributed by the city from trucks visiting the area. The girls and women worked as domestics. Most of the residents spoke only Spanish.

The farms on the surrounding high country not only provided work but are remembered as recreational areas. The youngsters swam in the irrigation ditches, caught and rode the horses, and explored.

Maravilla was an area of cheap land and cheap housing. It was known and accepted in the surrounding Mexican communities that the people of Maravilla were very poor and only marginally adjusted to life in the city. The children did not do well in school. They were overrepresented in what was known as *escuelas de burro* (dumb schools), where the work was easy, and the children could enjoy themselves without being bothered too much by academic requirements. There was little awareness of the implications of being placed in such schools. By the end of the 1930s some children were learning how to "qualify" for these schools—how to flunk tests and act dumb to the Anglo teachers. By the 1940s the gangs of the Maravilla barrios dominated Jackson, the "special" high school, and their numbers gave them great control. Here barrio solidarities were emphasized; rival groups from Clanton, Hazard, and other barrios outside Maravilla were clearly identified.

Occasionally the Hoyo youngsters would encounter boys from another of the Maravilla barrios. These included Kern, La Marianna, and other small areas that were part of the original Maravilla development. At first a distinction was made between upper and lower Maravilla, with the boys from El Hoyo known as Los Vatos de Abajo. Boys from the various Maravilla barrios fought occasionally and competed with one another in sports, but they shared an odd kind of solidarity that stemmed at least in part from their domination of the special schools. El Hoyo's boundaries were clearly defined by natural features and included a much larger territory than that of the original White Fence. Some of the other Maravilla barrios were much smaller, perhaps only a few blocks in size (see Map 3). The boundaries of El Hoyo have not changed substantially over the years.

Maravilla youngsters were deeply caught up in the pachuco fad and *la vida loca* (the wild life) that went with the drapes, the double-soled shoes, and the entire expensive uniform of the early 1940s. The "chucos" spoke their own argot, a Spanish with words and phrases unintelligible to the outsider, especially those referring to marijuana (cf. Barker, 1947; Griffith, 1948). To speak *gabacho* (English) was to invite ridicule. The barrio identities in Maravilla were emblazoned in tattoos across the wrist, the forearm, the back, or the chest—intertwined with eagles, girls, revolutionary *bandilleras* (flags), and an extraordinary range of what came to be an indigenous prison art. The *cruz del barrio* (cross of the barrio) or pachuco cross was the most common design, especially on the back of the hand between thumb and forefinger.

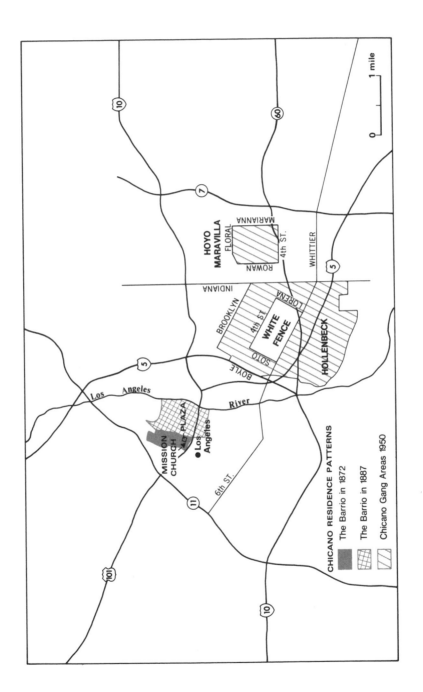

Map 3
Hoyo Maravilla and White Fence Barrios

CHICANO RESIDENCE PATTERNS

The Barrio in 1872

The Barrio in 1887

Chicano Gang Areas 1950

This *vato loco* (crazy guy) *del Hoyo Mara* may be used as a prototype for the well-known *vato loco* image found in Maravilla and elsewhere. His pride in his special culture and his feeling of being against the system and especially against *gabachos* (Anglos) was confirmed by the ferocity of the Zoot Suit Riots. Police and servicemen cruised Brooklyn Avenue (see Map 3), beat the boys from Maravilla unmercifully, cut their long ducktail hair, and stripped off their clothing when possible. The pachucos, in fact, were contemptuous of all squares, including the Chicano squares from their own barrio. In school this contempt was expressed by stealing their lunches and constantly challenging their masculinity. But the enmity for the Anglos and their system was paramount. Respectable Mexicans of the 1940s openly deplored the pachucos. On the Anglo side, the newspapers conducted a sensationalist campaign exploiting the "viciousness" of the gangs.

Yet in spite of the mutual stereotyping, the gang boys of the 1940s were interested in most of the same activities that interested other adolescents—sports, dances, and parties. To the *vatos* of El Hoyo it seemed there were no squares living in the barrio at all. Any Chicanos that were "making it" speedily left the area. As early as 1945 there was some talk about hard drugs in El Hoyo, but very few men (and no women) in this very traditional barrio were using drugs. Furthermore, those who were familiar with hard drugs kept their knowledge from the youngsters.

Until the 1940s, police policy for Hoyo Mara was to let a peculiar community go its peculiar way. Older members recall that police harassment generally occurred only when gang members left their area. This is partially confirmed by the attitude of a deputy sheriff who in 1932 told a researcher, "There is not much we can do to break up these gangs. . . . We talk to the boys and take them home and talk to their parents. . . . After all, the kids themselves know that we are not likely to really do anything to them and so they figure they might as well call our bluff." He saw the problem as one of "keeping order," and believed that order could only come from "some decent older Mexican boys who will set the example themselves" (Lanigan, 1932, p. 23). All this was to change during the pachuco incidents, and there was soon a climate of suspicion and hostility between the barrio and the police. A man from El Hoyo remembers the feeling:

> Let's talk a little bit about a block in a barrio Chicano, you know, on summer nights, all the mothers and fathers would come out with the neighbors and sit on somebody's porch, someone you knew, you'd just sit half the night, just gossip, and as kids will we would go out on the street, there was no sidewalks, just dirt and tar and what have you, we'd play kick the can, ring on the view, or hide-and-go-seek,

and all games we'd use to play and having a hell of a lot of fun. All of a sudden a police car would appear, everybody would freeze, all the kids, mothers start yelling "get off the street, come in the yard."

They used to remind me of big sharks the way they used to cruise through the neighborhood, just looking mean, never saying a word. Soon as they passed, everything became the same way, everybody would start laughing and talking and playing around.

How far back this fear and dread or how far back this fear goes or whatever it is, I don't know, but ever since I can remember, the cops meant something evil to Mexican kids.

Like the gangs in other barrios, a steady succession of cliques followed each other about every two years in Hoyo Mara.[1] The group following the pachucos was Los Cherries del Hoyo Mara, followed in succession by the Jivehounds, the Cutdowns, and the Midgets. In 1975 the youngest clique called itself the Cyclones, with twenty to twenty-five boys aged ten to thirteen. In Table 1 we present data for two cliques of Hoyo Maravilla that were active in the late 1940s and early 1950s.[2] It is a traditionalist picture: twenty-five of the forty-two Midgets lived in the barrio itself and the other seventeen lived on the outer fringes. About seven boys were descendants of the original settlers of the barrio, and a number had brothers in the older cliques. Generally, fathers worked and mothers stayed in the home; there are far fewer boys in these two cliques from broken homes than in White Fence. In itself this is an index of the traditionalism of the gang.

The Midgets had specific hangouts inside the barrio: the corners of Michigan and Carmelita and of Michigan and Gifford. Homes of two members were congregating places, as was the junior high school (Belvedere) and near the Hammel Street School. High up on Brannick Street was a secret gathering place known as Windy Hill.

The succession of cliques in El Hoyo has been continuous, interrupted only by concentrated police action on narcotics. This began in 1947, when a large number of men were arrested for marks (needle punctures) and other minor drug offenses. Harassment was almost continuous thereafter; men were stopped and shaken down for marks, especially when it could embarass them. Maravilla became widely publicized as a drug center following a major federal raid in 1950 and secret federal indictments of the same type that later hit San Fernando and other barrios. While it was true that El Hoyo (along with some other Maravilla barrios) was a significant place for connections, everybody in the neighborhood knew that the main dealers came from other neighborhoods. The neighborhood people were particularly incensed when one such person was named in the newspapers as a leader of El Hoyo Maravilla.

The Maravilla addicts considered him just the *"vato* holding the bag," and worthy of no attention except as a businessman.

The decade of the 1950s saw substantial narcotics usage among the gangs of Maravilla. In the early 1950s yellowjackets (secobarbital), marijuana, and whites (amphetamines) were as popular as heroin but, by the mid-1950s, *carga* (heroin) prevailed. Many that had been using heroin had gone to prison.

Table 1   **Characteristics and Adult Behavior of Members of Successive Cliques of El Hoyo Maravilla Gang, Los Angeles, 1947–1960**

	Clique	
	Cutdowns (1947–57)	Midgets (1949–60)
Characteristics	(%)	(%)
Composition		
Living in barrio	69	60
Living on barrio fringe	25	40
Living far away	6	0
Chicano	100	100
Background		
Born in:		
California	n.a.	100
other Southwest	n.a.	0
Mexico	n.a.	0
From broken families	0	2
by widowhood	0	2
Older or younger relative in gang activity	56	56
Finished high school	9	35
finished later	n.a.	0
In armed forces	37	21
Narcotics and incarceration		
Addicted to heroin	53	45
Served time in youth institution	22	7
Served time in prison	53	35
Current status (1975)		
Deceased	19	0
in armed forces	6	0
of drug overdose	6	0
Has family	37	28
Owns home	12	17
Employed and drug free	44	n.a.
owns business	0	7
civil servant	0	2
Total N (= 100%)	(32)	(42)

NOTE: n.a. = information not available.

The 1950s were the peak period of drug use and gang activity. The disappearance of many men into prison reduced gang activity in the 1960s; cliques became smaller. Out of ten men who were arrested from Hoyo Maravilla in the federal raid of 1950, only one was still having trouble with drugs in 1975. Eight were working in community-based agencies—six in Los Angeles for agencies dealing with the prevention of drug use.

The Hoyo Maravilla gang, like most other Maravilla gangs, evolved from the circumstances of life for very poor Mexicans in the 1930s. Many of the parents were using the barrio as a base for agricultural labor or domestic service; by contrast, the parents of nearby White Fence were highly urbanized and relatively prosperous. Children in the large families did poorly in school and were caught up in a teenage fad that was purely Chicano—the pachuco style of dress and argot.

It is difficult to imagine what might have happened to these gangs if the zoot suit persecution had not occurred. The boys that fought the marauding sailors in East Los Angeles were seen by their younger brothers as heroes of a race war.

> We named ourselves after the veterans that were older than us, the pachucos, the first men to openly meet the enemies and defy the law. They were our heroes. "Cherries" meant younger, but still as bad, we thought. I named myself after my big brother, they called him Teto, his name was mentioned a bit around the barrio. So I called myself Little Teto. I was proud of my brother for fighting the sailors, for wearing a zoot suit, he was one of the soldiers.

Yet few contemporary commentators noticed the nationalist symbolism of the pachucos that clearly echoed their parents' fierce attachment to Mexico. Even fewer noticed that speaking *gabacho* was viewed as disloyalty. The pachuco argot may have been viewed with disdain by respectable Mexican Americans (it still is, among the middle classes), but speaking English was giving in to the system that sent uniformed sailors into the barrios.

For the Hoyo Maravilla gang boys of 1975, it was still disloyal to speak anything but Spanish; intervening events had reinforced the sense that Maravilla was in conflict with the system. In the late 1960s the school blowouts focussed on Garfield High School, which served the Maravilla neighborhoods. These were major events in Chicano urban history, and had major positive consequences for the school system. The most severe Chicano riot of 1970 was concentrated close to Maravilla. Salazar Park, the focus of the riot, was renamed in honor of the Chicano columnist for the *Los Angeles Times* who was killed by a tear gas gun fired by a deputy into a crowded bar nearby. Maravilla is recurrently the scene of conflicts with the Anglo system. Thus it is no real surprise that El Hoyo and the other Maravilla gangs are nationalistic. The gangs accurately reflect Maravilla's roots and its history. Its younger members are following a tradition and an image of substantial proportions.

White Fence: From Traditional Structure to Fighting Gang

The history of the White Fence gang gives us a clear picture of social change. The White Fence barrio originated in the late 1920s and early 1930s. Before World War I the area of Boyle Heights was developed as an exclusive suburb with mansions looking west across the river toward downtown Los Angeles. Shortly after the war, developers began to fill in the area's back streets with cheaper housing that attracted a "Jewish invasion" from the East, as well as Armenians, Italians, Japanese, and Russian Molokans, a pietistic sect (Gustafson, 1940). In the 1920s, Mexicans began to build small houses in the ravines in three particular areas. They were Fickett Hollow, the Hole, and Bernal Gully (known for a time as Tortilla Flats). The homes were shacks, erected on unpaved streets. Unlike Chicano settlements in some other barrios (such as Hoyo Maravilla) these homes had gas service and running water. But the Mexican areas were eyesores to the more prosperous residents of Boyle Heights, and for a time an assessment plan that would tear down their homes and build a park was debated.

The social life of these three Chicano communities in White Fence in the 1920s and 1930s reflects the origins of its settlers from Mexico and from other areas of the American Southwest.[3] The White Fence residents were a little better off than the citizens of Maravilla. They included skilled workers, store owners, brickyard, packinghouse, graveyard, and railroad workers, and, perhaps most important, a refugee Mexican priest who officiated at La Purissima Church. The Whittier Boulevard streetcars offered quick access to most of the county.

For the people of White Fence, life centered around the church. La Purissima offered organizations for old people, children, and young people. By the late 1930s, a group of some sixty to a hundred young men and boys were organized into a church sports group. By any standard the boys of Purissima were extremely conventional. As far as we can trace, they all finished high school and all of them worked, some in Civilian Conservation Corps camps. The "Purissima crowd" was fully integrated into community activities through the church; after Sunday services it was not uncommon for the young men to transport truckloads of families to the San Gabriel River for afternoon picnics. They were active in church bazaars—*jamaicas*—and other events.

This period, which some in the barrio now call the golden age of sports, brought contact with youth from other barrios that emphasized

White Fence's feelings of uniqueness. The compact, church-centered barrio found itself different. The sports sponsor was a bar in the neighborhood. The Purissima crowd was mixed in age, and the young men exerted strong influence over the boys. The few marijuana users were ostracized. In the early 1940s, when the zoot suit fad swept over the Chicano youth of Los Angeles, the young men of La Purissima jeered it as a kid's fad. Families in the neighborhood knew—and were related to—each other. The family, the neighborhood, and the church were well integrated. The barrio was cohesive across age groups, with the young Purissima men integrated with both younger and older cohorts.

There was no tradition of anti-police attitudes; four Purissima boys later became police officers. Three others became priests. There were fights among the young, of course, but weapons were never used and police rarely made arrests. There was the tradition of what later came to be known as the fair fight, one-on-one, using fists only. To the police, White Fence had its own ways and could manage most of its problems. Only three of the Purissima crowd of fifty to one hundred boys used heroin, and those same three were the only ones to go to prison.

In the 1930s, the community felt that the schools were doing a good job. Chicanos were a minority, and teachers were interested in individual students. In 1936, the Lorena Street school was only 22 percent Mexican; the Euclid Street school was 70 percent Mexican (Gustafson, 1940). Although older residents remember that Mexican children often wore embarrassingly identifiable "welfare" clothing, people were pleased with the schools.

Great changes came with World War II. First, the barrio lost all the draft-age men who made up the stabilizing upper level of the youth group. Parents began to work much longer hours as job opportunities opened. The Japanese vanished into relocation camps and were replaced by Mexicans. The younger brothers of the Purissima crowd began to call themselves the Commandos and the Pansy Gang. Essentially, they were seen by the neighborhood as kids playing street games. Obviously, these were war games. But as older brothers left and more Chicanos came into the area, the boys at the junior high school began to be seriously beaten in fights with long-established gangs from nearby neighborhoods.

It was at this time (the middle and late 1940s) that the White Fence gang clique appeared.[3] The White Fence boys were always vastly outnumbered in the schools by boys from larger barrios. The area considered White Fence turf was then quite small, extending four blocks north from the major thoroughfare of Whittier Boulevard to Fourth Street, and west from Lorena a few blocks to Euclid (see Map 3).[4] In self-defense, a few of the neighborhood boys decided to recruit fighters from other neighborhoods who were not yet linked with gangs. They would be the best and most reliable. Individual reputation was enough; there was no need for the kind of initiation that was a feature of other gangs, in which a prospective member would be jumped by gang boys and would fight until exhausted. Boys were recruited from such nearby barrios as Maravilla, El Hoyo Soto, and even more distant barrios such as Mateo, Clanton, Flats, Lil Town, State, First and Indiana, and First and St. Louis. Members included Mexican nationals, Texas Mexicans, and boys from comparatively comfortable families as well as the very poor. A few of the members were even prosperous enough to drive cars.

Gang boys would be picked up after school in cars (very rare at this time) that made a circuit of the public schools. Then they would be dropped near their homes in rival gang areas and watched until they were safely inside the house. Sometimes the walk home from conflict-ridden schools to a safe or neutral area would be patrolled by White Fence members. To the unknowing observer, it was just a bunch of Mexican kids on the street. To members, it was protection and prestige. The White Fence gang would also expel boys (even if they lived in the barrio) who could not stand up in the fighting. There was a serious gang fight on the average of once every two weeks, so the boys were continually tested.

Two street corners and Chuy's, a neighborhood store in the hollow, were favorite hangouts. The YMCA on Whittier Boulevard displayed banners of league games won by White Fence and La Purissima, and Dutch's Malt Shop displayed basketball trophies won by White Fence. The Crystal Theater was also White Fence territory; sometimes the manager let the boys in free.

Because of its diverse membership, the White Fence clique showed a tolerance for individualism that was unusual among Mexican gangs. Only three of the fifty-five members finished high school, but one of them did very well. He was not pressured to sit in the back rows with the hoodlum members of the gang, nor was he ridiculed or called *lambion*, a gang term for kiss-ass. Several "pretty boys" liked clothes and girls, but they were fully accepted because they would fight. White Fence was diverse and tolerant of all except those who would not fight and *ratas* (rats) who informed. English, not Spanish, was the dominant language of the gang.

White Fence was the first Chicano gang in East Los Angeles to use serious weapons—chains and, occasionally, guns. They felt they were different from other gangs, and as their confidence grew they began to challenge and defeat old and well-established gangs. This caused them to be resented as upstarts who broke the norms. As their reputation grew, isolated members (in Juvenile Hall, for example) would be jumped and badly beaten. Police paid particular attention to them and would loudly announce the arrival of a White Fence boy in the Hall. This kind of discrimination went far beyond the intergang brutality that characterizes places of incarceration in Los Angeles. It greatly increased the solidarity of the gang, since it continued, and gave a special intensity to, the barrio ties of the men who later went to jail and prison.

But the city of Los Angeles was changing. As the men from La Purissima came back from the war, some of them turned attention to the condition of the barrio; they pressured the city for paving, better lighting, and other city facilities. A neighborhood boy named Edward Roybal ran for city council. Although his first campaign, in 1947, ended in defeat, it was now obvious that the Chicanos were determined to obtain full citizenship. (Roybal later served in the city council and became one of the first—and most enduring—of the Chicano representatives in Congress. His council seat, however, remained filled by an Anglo.)

Thus the pressures both from within the barrio and from the Los Angeles institutional environment began to change. A wave of newspaper publicity labeled the White Fence gang especially vicious, and police treatment became more severe. Instead of warnings, they were deliberately harassed. The Los Angeles County Probation Department sent in social workers, hoping to transform the gang into a club. (This was partly in response to the Zoot Suit Riots.) A Federation of Youth Clubs was invented to overcome the territoriality, and consequent fighting, of the barrio gangs. A series of dances and sports events were arranged in various neighborhoods. To preclude fighting, gang representatives were elected to handle the affairs. The Group Guidance workers also tried to find jobs for the gang members, which complemented the constant search for work for party money. Before narcotics, White Fence members were not involved in theft; rather, they would travel long distances for work opportunities. An example is the celery farm of the uncle of a member, thirty miles west in Culver City. They would also travel to Oxnard and Moorpark in Ventura County to pick fruit during the summer.

The social workers of the Los Angeles Probation Department take credit for destroying the White Fence gang. This claim more accurately measures their capacity for self-deception than for insight. By the early 1950s, the original White Fence clique had begun to drift apart. Twenty-five members quit school to enter the armed forces; fourteen of the original fifty-five ultimately went into military service. Several married early and began to have children. The first member to use heroin began in 1947. By the early 1950s, he had been joined by some fifteen others. These men formed a separate clique and hustled for drugs. Later this group was joined by nonaddicted dealers. Unlike the La Purissima crowd, the original White Fence clique had used marijuana and occasionally barbiturates (as well as alcohol) at their parties, but heroin had been rare.

As the White Fence clique matured, however, a younger crowd continued the battles. They called themselves the Monsters from White Fence. Like the older group, they were interested in cars, girls, clothes, and fighting—as a necessity. They had the White Fence image to live up to, and although they lacked many of the characteristics that had made the White Fence such an effective fighting gang, they worked hard to match or to surpass the image of their older "brothers" and cousins.

As each clique matured, it was succeeded by others. Each had a distinct name; the Monsters were followed by the Cherries, the Tinies, and some dozen others, until by 1973 there was again a Monsters clique living up to a twenty-three-year-old image. While some of the Monsters of the 1970s had relatives who had been active in the original gang, there were many new kinds of members, reflecting changes in the barrio since 1950. The gang's reputation for aggressiveness continued. In Roosevelt High School, White Fence was still known as the "trouble-making gang" as late as 1975. And by 1975, its boundaries had grown to cover an area almost twice the size of the original barrio.[5]

The characteristics and careers of members of the first four cliques of the White Fence gang are presented in Table 2. As noted, the first clique called itself simply White Fence; the second, Monsters of White Fence, and the third Lil White Fence or the Cherries. (Cherries, Tinies, Midgets, and Cutdowns are common clique names in Chicano gangs throughout the Southwest). Each clique tends to form in junior high school on the model of the older gang cliques in the barrio. Self-depreciating names like Tinies and Cherries (referring to their virginal status) are tolerable because everyone knows the fearsome reputation of the gang that they belong to—in this case, White Fence. (As far as we know, however, Monsters is unique to White Fence.) In some cases, veteranos (older clique members) are asked by the younger cliques to help in gang fights. This occurred with the Monsters, and advisors from the original White Fence commented disgustedly to each other about the Monsters' lack of fighting discipline.

The careers of successive cliques of White Fence show the gang's processes of institutionalization. Members were increasingly recruited from residents of the barrio; increasingly they came from broken families. Paradoxically, there were declining proportions with relatives involved in gang activity. There were declining proportions who spent time in the Armed Forces. As time passed, increasingly larger proportions of the gang were addicted to heroin and served time in prison. It is apparent that heroin rapidly ceased to be a subclique activity. Yet by 1975, when these data were collected, a high proportion of each clique had outgrown their youthful deviance and were employed and drug free.

In White Fence we can see the rapid evolution of a neighborhood and the development of a rationalized fighting gang. The barrio changed from a village-like enclave to a virtually indistinguishable portion of an

Table 2 **Characteristics and Adult Behavior of Members of Successive Cliques of the White Fence Gang, Los Angeles, 1945–1953**

Characteristics	White Fence 1945–51 (%)	Monsters 1947–56 (%)	Cherries (Lil White Fence) 1949 (peak) (%)	Tinies 1953 (peak) (%)
Composition				
Living in barrio	46	64	55	100
Living on barrio fringe	24	21	27	0
Living far away	30	14	18	0
Chicano	100	100	100	100
Background				
Born in:				
California	90	100	97	100
other Southwest	4	0	3	0
Mexico	6	0	0	0
From broken families	20	36	49	95
by widowhood	11	18	39	0
Older or younger relative in gang activity	56	50	49	32
Finished high school	7	11	3	0
finished later	27	36	18	26
In armed forces	46	21	3	10
Narcotics and incarceration				
Addicted to heroin	35	64	42	58
Served time in youth institution	35	39	91	100
Served time in prison	38	64	76	68
Current Status (1975)				
Deceased	9	7	6	10
in armed forces	4	0	3	0
of drug overdose	4	7	6	10
Has family	60	36	6	42
Owns home	46	18	n.a.	56
Employed and drug free	78	82	94	63
owns business	18	7	9	0
civil servant	7	0	3	0
Total N (= 100%)	(55)	(28)	(33)	(19)

NOTE: n.a. = information not available.

almost all-Mexican neighborhood of increasingly poor immigrants. The successive cliques were involved in increasingly more serious activities at earlier ages as the social controls of the community declined. Nevertheless, Table 2 suggests that gang involvement was never total. The importance of this observation will be developed later. For the moment we will simply note that normal social roles remain available in the barrio, even though they appear to be ever more remote from the experience of the younger cliques.

San Fernando: from Mission to Gang

The Mission San Fernando Rey de España was founded by the Franciscans in 1797. By 1835 it was one of the most prosperous in California. The San Fernando Valley extends nearly thirty miles in length and is clearly separated from the Los Angeles basin by a range of mountains. The present town of San Fernando, in a remote corner of the valley, still maintains its independence from suburban Los Angeles, which now completely surrounds it.

Until World War II, San Fernando was economically independent as a service and marketing center for the citrus and olive industries of the Valley. Like other cities in the Southwest, the Mexican community was literally "across the tracks" (cf. Rubel, 1966). Work was available in the fields, and some Mexicans used San Fernando as a base not only for work in the nearby orchards but also for migratory work in nearby counties and further north. More prestigious jobs were available in the packing houses, where work was cleaner, better paid, and steady.

Housing for some Mexicans was provided by the packing houses, notably Sunkist and Pomroy (Lemon Heights, Blue Goose, and the American Company also provided work). But most of the Pomroy worker's houses were built from material discarded by the railroad companies, and many homes in the barrio were one-room adobe buildings. It was not uncommon to find more than one family crowded into these single units. The communities were called *vecindades*. Once a worker had arrived and gotten a job, he built a house on the inexpensive land from lumber scavenged by dismantling freight cars. As soon as a cluster of homes was built, the area would be given a name—and the barrios began. La Rana (frog) and El Bajillo (lowlands) were two of the first. La Rana was constantly flooded and muddy, because of poor drainage and continual truck traffic that kept the dirt roads muddy. At night the frogs sang—thus the barrio's name. Later, the San Fernando gang boys stereotyped the *Raneros* as those who did the worst of the field jobs—shovelling fertilizer for the orchards.

Mextown in San Fernando was a self-contained community. It was rigidly segregated between San Fernando and Laurel Canyon Boulevards and between Fox and Workman Streets. Until the Santa Rosa church was built in the barrio, Mexicans were sectioned off to one side of the Catholic church; until the construction in the early 1940s of a Spanish-language theater, Mexicans were required to sit in a separate section of the town's only movie theater. Mexicans caught on the Anglo side of the tracks were stopped and questioned. If they could prove no valid reason for being there, they were either jailed for trespassing or told to go back where they belonged. The barrio had its own grammar school, but the dropout rate from high school was high.

Social life centered on house parties marking feast days or other special occasions, and on church bazaars that were held at least twice a month. Dances were promoted at the local hall, baseball was important, and the Circo Escalante visited twice a year. Mextown was small, with a few stores owned, the residents believed, by Spaniards. Wooden sidewalks bordered the businesses. Marijuana was smoked by some men, but it was done with great discretion.

As time passed, similar barrios sprang up in the San Fernando Valley. Some people occasionally drove the length of the Valley and over the mountains to shop in Los Angeles, but only for major items, such as an automobile, because most of life's necessities were available in Mexican stores in the barrios of the Valley. Whenever people went to Los Angeles, they identified themselves as being from San Fer regardless of which barrio in the Valley they actually lived in.

Handball and baseball teams from the Valley barrios played against each other, with fierce rivalry, betting, and occasional fights. From these fights emerged the first recognized gang in San Fernando. They called themselves the Chain Gang, and had about fifteen members. These were boys who supported themselves by promoting and gambling on handball games. Some had a reputation for running bootleg whisky, smuggling marijuana, and pimping. The Chain Gang had a reputation for being tough and united; they were feared. Once a few members went to San Quentin for murdering a youth from a rival barrio.

Of more substantial interest was the Polviados (the Powder Puffs), a San Fer gang of about forty or fifty boys. There seems to have some continuity between the Chain Gang and the Polviados. But the real model for the Polviados were the pachucos of Los Angeles. The gang started in the early 1940s, and made a point of keeping up with the latest clothing fads, going to Murray's and Young's in downtown Los Angeles for their drapes and fingertip coats, and to Price's for their double-soled shoes. The Polviados consciously set themselves apart from the rural Chicanos of Pacoima, Canoga Park, Van Nuys and other Valley barrios, whom they considered backward, square, "farmers."

The conflict between the Polviados and boys from other Valley barrios was clearly a conflict between urban and rural orientations. The

Polviados considered work in the orchards and canneries beneath their dignity. Not many urban jobs were then available in the Valley, so the Polviados hustled for a living. Many committed burglaries and small time thefts, like bike stealing. Later this would become stealing and stripping cars. Many went into Los Angeles and scored pounds of marijuana, which they rolled into joints that were sold for as much as a dollar each. Most were school dropouts or attended continuation schools; they hung around street corners and pool halls, occasionally going up into the nearby mountains to smoke and drink. The square youth of the barrio considered them the biggest "mess-ups," but also sneered at the Polviados' "anti-macho" effort to smell pretty and look dandy.

The Polviados' fights were quite different from the occasional inter-barrio fights of the era of dating and raiding in the 1930s. The Polviados began to use yellowjackets combined with alcohol. Their fighting reputation led them to exclude some San Fernando boys, and to accept "guys with guts" from such other barrios as Pacoima. There was even one boy from the Polviados' main enemy, Los Raneros. Occasionally, a Polviado roaming outside of San Fernando would be attacked and beaten up. Thus carloads of his fellow gang members would cruise "enemy" territories, fighting with knives, tire irons, chains, bottles, and baseball bats. The Polviados began to go to juvenile detention centers and camps, where they made many friends and acquired connections with the Los Angeles gangs.

The gang fights almost ceased when most Polviados became heroin addicts in the late 1940s. Heroin was introduced about 1945 by a newcomer, a *vato loco* who had been addicted in El Paso. Periodically he would get small stashes, which he would sell or give away to his new friends. By 1948 the members we interviewed could not remember anybody who had not become addicted.

Many of the Polviados began to deal heroin, at first relying on connections established in the Los Angeles County jails. Later they established their own connections directly with Mexico. They supplied heroin to addicts throughout the Valley, including North Hollywood, Van Nuys, and even as far away as Glendale and Pasadena. Addicts from formerly rival barrios were allowed to enter "enemy" territory to buy and sell drugs.

But hustling increased as men stole to support their habits, and with the hustling came greater police attention. When the Polviados were still interested in sports, girls, and dancing, and using only marijuana and alcohol, there was very little harrassment. By the early 1950s, however, almost all of the Polviados had served some time in jail.

In 1952 almost two-thirds of the Polviados went to state prison as the result of a single group of secret indictments. An undercover agent managed to infiltrate the network and made numerous buys. Every three or four months, members reminisce, some of the Polviados would be rounded up and sent to San Quentin. By late 1952 there were thirty to forty gang members meeting each other in the big yard.

By 1975, many of the original Polviados were back in San Fernando. Many had respectable jobs, some of them in community agencies. The cliques that followed the Polviados (and revived their tradition of fighting with other barrios) appear to be more loosely organized than the cliques of the two East Los Angeles gangs. The Delinquents (clearly compensating for the sissy Polviado name), and La Mott (referring to a particular street) were followed by a set of car clubs, such as the Gear Grinders. (Car clubs are not considered nearly as negatively by barrio people as are gangs; as gang theorist Walter Miller suggests, they tend more to be groups of adolescents that reflect focal concerns of the working class community.)

Since the Polviados and the Chain Gang appeared when stress between rural and big city life styles was at its height, they seem to be a transitional phenomenon. Gang membership provided a way to elevate one's status above the local hicks. A few years later, the members were in prison, the town of San Fernando was surrounded by tract homes of the lower middle classes expanding out from Los Angeles, and new kinds of opportunities were beginning to open up for Chicanos.

The Three Gangs Contrasted

It should be clear by now that even within one city the Chicano gangs are different in composition, in motivation, and even in the degree to which they are institutionalized into the barrio social structure. The gangs also vary internally, even from one clique to the next.

The Hoyo Maravilla gangs of the mid-1940s were consciously emulating both the pachucho heroes of the early 1940s and their soldier brothers. The gang was strongly barrio-based. Older cohorts maintained cohesiveness and were still visible to the younger cohorts. In other words, the full aged-graded structure was already present. When the Cherries, Midgets and Cutdowns organized themselves, they were following a tradition which evolved out of both the conditions of settlement of the very poor Mexicans in the Maravilla area and out of exposure to active discrimination. Loyalty and Chicanismo (cultural nationalism) were the bywords and sources of honor.

White Fence appears to be a rationalized fighting gang that is only partially based in a single barrio. Yet it was organized by a core of residents who actively recruited good street fighters in order to protect barrio members from the larger and more cohesive barrios in the schools of the area. The older cohorts were not gang boys, but rather sports- and church-oriented young men who had gone to war and were therefore effectively absent. The first clique of the White Fence gang was a group of innovators. Discipline and individualism were the bywords and the source of honor.

The gangs of San Fernando grew out of the loose across-the-tracks affiliations of boys from isolated Mexican agricultural work communities. Clearly transitional, the Polviados emulated the city slickers in another part of the county rather than either the older boys in their home barrio or some abstract model of fighting competence. The subsequent cliques were more loosely organized than in East Los Angeles. Their initiation into drug use probably occurred within more tightly bounded subcliques.

There are several reasons why the 1940s provided a meaningful point of reference for Chicano fighting gangs. World War II and the immediate postwar years were a turning point for the barrios and, in consequence, for the gangs. Among other changes, these years mark the time when the first Los Angeles children from the great immigration of the 1920s were passing into adolescence and maturity. Thus the symbolic rebellion of the pachucos was a significant gesture for them and for the Mexican American minority.

It was the time of the first widespread urban riots involving Chicanos—the first manifestation of conscious racism against Mexicans that would reach national attention. These two factors (the new generation and overt racism) tended to give the barrio gangs a degree of self-consciousness quite different from that of earlier years.

Finally, it was during this period that increasingly hostile law enforcement attitudes toward the gangs appeared, along with the first programs for youth gangs. These are local institutional changes that, with variations, were to dominate the institutional milieu for youth gangs for the next thirty years. In addition, the years of the 1940s saw the beginning of large-scale heroin use and distribution in the barrios of Los Angeles. The barrio histories offered in this chapter make it possible to pinpoint the first beginnings of heroin use inside the gangs. We will show in Chapter 4 that the Chicano gangs' involvement with drugs, both as users and as dealers, is completely unlike that of other groups in other cities.

Three Chicano Gangs as a Sample

These three gangs (El Hoyo Maravilla, White Fence, and Los Polviados of San Fernando) are a tiny number among the more than sixty barrio gangs in Los Angeles in the 1970s. Yet they are among the most enduring gangs and are distinctive in that respect. There are, for example, some gangs that survive only for the lifetime of their originators, such as the Saxons, a small and now defunct East Los Angeles gang. Other gangs exist a longer time, but wane eventually, either because of physical changes in their neighborhoods or because of the defections of members to nearby or rival gangs. A complete natural history of all the gangs would be fascinating, but the task remains to be undertaken.

In other respects, what kind of sample do these three gangs represent? First, they provide a good example of the rural-urban range represented in Los Angeles County. This range includes proximity (and ease of transportation) to central city functions, including commercial and recreational facilities that serve the citywide population. It includes the historical background of the labor force in the barrio itself. (It is important to remember the enormous size of Los Angeles county. Los Angeles, while one of the nation's largest cities, is contained by a county whose agricultural production was first in dollar value in the entire nation in 1977.) Some barrios, like San Fernando, were almost entirely agricultural in their origins. Others, like Hoyo Maravilla, were mixed; still others, like White Fence, were almost entirely urban. This last variable is independent of the location of the barrio with respect to downtown Los Angeles. (One missing dimension that is important for Chicano gangs in recent years is the housing project—that purely urban anomaly in barrio development. Every Chicano housing project in Los Angeles has its own gang.)

Second, the gangs vary in their proportions of Mexican nationals, native-born Chicanos raised in Los Angeles or elsewhere, and non-Chicanos. They also vary in the extent to which linguistic preference reflects their self-conscious identification as Chicano. The three gangs analyzed here differ in this respect, but they do not include any examples of the racially mixed gang, of which there are a number in Los Angeles.

Third, because of their long lives and strong reputation in the Chicano neighborhoods, the two East Los Angeles gangs in our sample have relatively clear images. The image of the San Fernando gang is less extensive than the others because its domination is limited to the San Fernando Valley. White Fence and Hoyo Maravilla are known among Chicano gang-oriented youth and also among Chicano prisoners throughout California. An image is a complex mixture of an aura of power (this phrase might summarize the long-standing reputation of successful gangs), and certain specialized roles. Specialized roles mean, for example, that the *vato loco* image is more likely to be associated with Maravilla than with White Fence. A cool dude image is more likely to be associated with White Fence than with Maravilla. Beyond these subtleties, the point remains that the three gangs sampled include dominant, rather than marginal or "loser" gangs.

In the last two chapters drugs appear only incidentally. Yet drugs and Chicano gangs are very much involved, one with the other, as we shall see.

4

Drugs
and the
Barrios

THERE ARE FOUR POINTS at which drugs and barrio gangs significantly intersect. First, the Chicano youth gangs have been consistently innovative in drugs—with marijuana, then with heroin, and most recently with inhalants and PCP. Second, most heroin use in Chicano barrios begins with gangs. Third, a high proportion of all Chicano gang youth consistently becomes addicted. Fourth, the prison experience of Chicanos is predominantly within a context of narcotics offenses.

It is odd that these points were not noticed in the earlier studies of either Chicano gangs or heroin addicts (Casavantes, 1976; Bullington, 1977). But the omission is understandable, since gang researchers tend not to observe adult behavior, and researchers on addicts do not notice juvenile behavior. Because of the gang influence, this oversight emphasizes the importance of involving participants in research. Men and women who were gang members, and later addicts or dealers, could not possibly overlook the connections, and would find it inconceivable that either topic could be discussed separately. Except for explicit references to written sources, the entire discussion of drug use and marketing in this chapter is based on information from former users and dealers.

Recalling our earlier discussion of the barrio economy, drug dealing and narcotics represents an opportunity in the illegal marketplace. There are two major differences between our findings and most other analyses of the economics of drugs. First, we find the marketing of barbiturates to be a serious and complex illegal activity. It extends far beyond the theft of drugs from pharmaceutical sources, into contracting the manufacture of bootleg barbiturates in Mexico, smuggling them, and marketing them in East Los Angeles. This marketing is done by barrio homeboys from specific neighborhoods.

Second, we find that heroin marketing in East Los Angeles is unlike that of any system previously described. The basic source of heroin is Mexico, rather than Turkey via the so-called French connection. Because Mexican sources are multiple and cannot easily be monopolized (like the Mafia-controlled Near Eastern sources), the marketing of heroin is a significant entrepreneurial opportunity for a number of barrio-based dealers in East Los Angeles.

Chicanos as Distinctive Addicts

There are some demonstrable differences between subgroups of addicts; these differences affect both theory building and treatment and control strategies. They are a favorite topic for many drug researchers, who hope that some simple factor might be found and isolated; but the results to date of this work are not very important. Therefore, although the special characteristics of Chicano addicts are not our principal interest, we will briefly summarize the available information.

The most consistent source of information about addict populations in the United States comes from the patients at the two federal narcotics hospitals, Lexington and Fort Worth. The most important long term change in addict characteristics is the decline in the proportion of white addicts and the increase in the proportion of minority addicts. Between 1936 and 1966, the proportion of minority members among the clients at these two hospitals increased from 12 percent to 44 percent of the case load (Chambers, et al., 1970). In a much shorter time span (between 1961 and 1967), the proportion of Chicanos increased dramatically—from 6 to 12 percent of the case load. Extrapolating from these data and the Treasury Department estimate that there are some 700,000 heroin users in the United States (Mushkin, et al., 1973), we might estimate some 70,000 Chicano addicts in the late 1970s, largely concentrated in the Southwest.

Of course, this estimate is just as tentative as any other effort to estimate the numbers or characteristics of unknowns from a sample of knowns, usually the case load of an agency with some very special intake procedures.[1] Nonetheless, there is substantial consistency between some of the findings about characteristics of Chicano addicts from these two federal hospitals and from other agencies, all collected in the late 1960s or early 1970s. All of these show interesting differences between Chicanos and other addicts.

Compared with the other inmates of Lexington and Fort Worth in 1967, Chicano addicts appear to be more heroin-dominant, to have a higher arrest rate, to start use and to be arrested earlier, to be less likely to finish high school, and to be twice as likely to have been employed legally at the time of admission (Chambers, et al., 1970). A 1969 study of 372 patients in non-hospital drug treatment programs corroborates some, but not all, of these findings (Maddux, 1973; Sells, 1974). The study also found that, while older Chicanos were more heroin-dominant, younger Chicanos were polydrug users. Overall, Chicanos had the highest conviction rates and tended to start heroin at an earlier age. Like the federal data, the study noted a tendency for more Chicanos to come from intact families than do addicts of other ethnic groups. The intake figures from the California Rehabilitation Center, a "hospital" of the California Department of Corrections for civilly committed addicts, also show that Chicanos are heroin-dominant at an earlier age, are arrested earlier, and are from poorer families than addicts of other ethnic groups. Chavez (1973) found that 40 percent of the Chicanos were from welfare families; he estimated twelve thousand Chicano addicts in California in 1971.

Such findings call for some explanation. The response, in general, has been a series of hypotheses that these distinctive user characteristics are rooted in Chicano or Mexican culture. In particular, three culture traits have been repeatedly singled out. These are machismo, personalismo, and carnalismo. Casavantes (1976) has done perhaps the most extensive analysis of these three traits with regard to addiction. Machismo is probably the most familiar. To the general American public, it is a familiar word meaning vulgar male chauvinism. But it has a much wider range of meanings among Chicanos, from the aggressive, risk-taking, phallic masculinity of the macho stereotype to complex notions of responsible adult manliness. Personalismo, less well known outside of Mexican culture, refers to a tendency for relationships to be highly particularized and to command long-lasting loyalties. These relationships may be among peers or among individuals of different status. Carnalismo is a specifically Chicano phrase—that is, it has become a culture trait among lower-status Mexican Americans. It refers to the "blood brother" bond that ties affinity groups together. Thus carnal refers not only to one's barrio homies but also, by extension, to all Chicanos.

Some people feel that these three traits make sense out of the especially tight relationships among Chicano addicts, although Casavantes ultimately abandons the search for specifically cultural explanations and concludes that the specific ethnic subculture is too confounded with the poverty subculture (1976, and see also his annotated bibliography). We would suggest also that some of these special traits have something to do with the special history of drugs in the barrios. In particular, we feel that the circumstances of heroin marketing have encouraged bonding of the kind described by the three culture traits. Yet we are less concerned with the Chicano drug user as a culturally distinctive person than with his gang and the structure of the illegal barbiturates and heroin markets.

Pills

Barbiturates Use in the Barrios

Nonmedical barbiturates use is probably one of the most misunderstood dimensions of drug abuse in the United States. It is widely perceived only in its middle-class manifestation—as a problem of frustrated housewives. Thus the National Commission on Marihuana and Drug Abuse concluded that "barbiturate dependence may be the modern equivalent of the hidden opiate dependence of the late 19th Century" (1973, p. 145). In other words, a way for the unhappy middle-class woman to dull the ache of oppression. In this account, the prime sources of pills are either acquiescent physicians, forged prescriptions, or small-scale suppliers who steal their goods from pharmaceutical houses (Soref, 1975).

We argue that this is a class-biased viewpoint, because for decades barbiturates have been used as a party drug in East Los Angeles. Barrio youngsters used them as early as the 1940s, especially in poorer areas where liquor was too expensive (the effect of alcohol is enhanced when combined with pills). Because the pills were associated with poverty, their reputation was depreciated. As Bullington later found, gang kids in the 1940s "preferred marijuana and alcohol as the primary means of obtaining a 'high' " (1977, p. 96). One of the White Fence members in our study recalls that in this period the primary impetus for working was to get liquor money. "Going over to Dogtown" (then the home of the gang specializing in pills) was a last resort. Gang boys depreciated pills by calling them "fender benders," which describes the cars driven by the pillheads who stumble and slur their speech and are constantly smashing their cars.

Barbiturate Types and Connections

The early barbiturates users called the pills yellowjackets. If they connected through Dogtown, they were buying pills that came from pharmaceutical sources, either by prescriptions or from crooked drugstores in central Los Angeles. The largest quantities available in the 1940s and early 1950s were jars holding a thousand pills. These would sell for fifty or sixty dollars. On the street, a roll of six pills would sell for a dollar.

In the early 1950s, reds (seconal-secobarbital) appeared on the barrio streets. The red capsules were smaller than the yellows, and, although both the color and the chemical composition of the "downers" were to change in future years, the name stuck. Like yellowjackets, reds came from unethical medical and pharmaceutical connections, or from occasional thefts from hospitals and warehouses. Cliques within other barrio gangs outside of Dogtown began to specialize in the pill traffic and to develop mechanisms of distribution.

By the late 1950s, the demand for reds had outgrown the supply from pharmaceutical sources as barbiturates use rapidly spread beyond the gangs to other Chicano young people. (This contrasts sharply with heroin, which is still largely confined to gang boys. This contrast is based partly on the very different legal penalties for use and dealing, and partly on the differing social contexts of use. Barbiturates are used for parties; heroin pulls the user away from the normal adolescent and young adult patterns of sociability. Gang cliques that used heroin were not interested in parties. As one man eloquently put it, "The clock stopped for me when I was seventeen. I didn't go anywhere.")

While heroin is unequivocally illegal, barbiturates are legally and medically ambiguous. Thus the supply of reds in East Los Angeles meant constant complexities. Small-scale supplies continued to be available. There were always doctors in the barrio to write prescriptions, and pharmacists who would fill those prescriptions without question. Workers in hospitals, rest homes, and other such institutions continue to deal in small quantities of stolen pills. Because the profit margins from small pill transactions are low, comparatively few groups entered seriously into barbiturates. One group that did work out an ambitious entrepreneurship—contracting with bootleg manufacturers in Mexico, smuggling, and marketing the pills in East Los Angeles—was a barrio gang.

Bootlegging and Marketing in the 1960s

In the 1960s, a substantial quantity of the barbiturates manufactured for overseas export never went beyond the borders of the United States. Thanks to a system of payoffs, and laxity in the control of drugs, traffickers could pick up their illegal merchandise in the warehouses of such American border towns as San Ysidro, across from Tijuana. The reds were packed in cylindrical cardboard drums in quantities of 50,000. In this form they were called barrels, or kegs, and sold for $1,200 at the time. The large-scale dealers developed middleman dealers, who broke the barrels down to jars of 1,000; these were distributed to the street pushers by a runner, who also collected the money.

In a very short time, the demand for barbiturates increased the price of a barrel to $2,200 (with a street price of four pills per one dollar roll). Increased government regulation of production and distribution for export was the catalyst for smuggling and bootlegging operations; bootleg pill manufacturers appeared in both Los Angeles and Mexico. By the late 1960s, a mule system had been developed to smuggle drugs across the border. Stash cars (*el clavo*) permitted the dealers to minimize the cost of arrests: at the time less than 2 percent of the automobiles coming to the United States from Mexico were inspected, and one barrio clique operated for periods of eight to nine months without any "busts."

Manufacturers in Mexico began to meet the smugglers' need for smaller and more compact pills, but the increased drug traffic across the border and the use of computers led to increased numbers of arrests. Not only were the arrests costly in themselves, but the mules were able to demand more money for their risks. The M&M red was the first tablet exclusively manufactured in Mexico. It was approximately the same size and shape as its candy namesake, and had a red coating. Although more of these pills could be stashed in an automobile, they did not sell. It was discovered that many pill users had been injecting the seconal powder in the red caps. This was not possible with the compacted M&M red, which was purchased only by the pill dropper. The price of the M&Ms went down; middleman dealers were required to buy a barrel of M&Ms for every five barrels of the always-popular amphetamines.

Expensive red caps returned briefly in the early 1970s, but Mexican bootleg manufacturers acquired new pressing machines to produce what came to be known as the marshmallow red, pure secobarbital, held together by high-pressure pressing. The marshmallows were introduced at a price between M&Ms and the caps—$2,000 per barrel of 50,000. The dealers hoped the marshmallows would be more successful than the M&Ms, because they were smaller and the profit margin was higher. But marshmallows were a commercial disaster; users complained that they had no effect. Pushers began to return the merchandise at just about the time it was realized that the pills would not decompose in the stomach. One dealer said he threw a bag of marshmallows against the wall and none of the pills broke. Another pusher claimed that his customers were passing the pills without absorbing them. "Tell them to chew the damn things" was the dealer's advice, but the users failed to comply.

Red caps remained the reliable drug to pill users, but increased surveillance drove prices up. By 1975 a barrel of reds cost $7,000. Technical innovations in the bootleg manufacture continued. In late 1973 a new red, manga, hit the streets in Los Angeles. This pill was round, powdery, somewhat smaller than the M&M, uncoated, and had swirls of red. At first the pill droppers bought them happily, but an epidemic of barbiturate overdoses—six deaths in one month—brought the astonishing discovery that the bootleg pharmacists had introduced a delaying agent into the mangas to prolong the high. At the end of a half hour, pill droppers experienced little effect, so they would drop another. For the inexperienced youth who was just following the actions of his friends, this could be fatal.

Thus the bootleg manufacturers in Mexico and their barrio distributors followed a path of product innovation, product testing, and response to consumer reaction. Pill prices (for the new varieties) were the only indication of success taken seriously by the dealer. Otherwise, consumer satisfaction was ignored. The overdose deaths from the mangas created so much anger that in one barrio the mothers formed a coalition with an activist group (*Casa Carnalismo* and *Los Tres*) to threaten exposure of the pill pushers. But for the dealers in volume, the profits were high and the risk of comparatively mild legal penalties was minimal.

It is important to note the amount of time needed for a complete transaction. From the time a barrel is delivered in Los Angeles to complete collections is usually only about three days. Fast turnaround helps avoid law enforcement. It is a pattern of marketing that we will see again in heroin.

Like other entrepreneurs, the barrio pill peddlers observe market trends and attempt to fit in. One barrio of pill dealers noticed a periodicity in demand for uppers (whites, or amphetamines) and downers, and attributed this to a young adult pattern of alternating the two drugs for weekend partying and preparation for the work week. An adjustment in marketing patterns was made. In the early part of the week the dealers would import whites, turn the money over, and then invest their capital in the purchase of reds for the weekend.

Organizational Consequences of Pills

Contempt for barbiturates and their users continues to linger in the barrios. This is partly because (in spite of use throughout the age spectrum and their increasing price) pills are still seen as a drug of youth and poverty. Even amphetemines appear to generate more respect because of both the well-publicized "Speed Kills" campaign and the danger of paranoid amphetemine users.

There are several consequences of this disrespect. One of them is that few of the large-scale pill dealers use their own drug. Unlike the heroin business, the hierarchy of pill dealing does not employ addicts in the lower ranks. Seller and customer are very clearly opposed. This permits the large-scale operators to be highly rationalized and commercial. Age differentials exacerbate the social distance between user and dealer. In the larger Chicano community, pill use is rarely stigmatized as much as heroin. This may be because pill use carries comparatively little legal consequence. And it may be because of widespread pill use by squares in the Chicano community.

Besides its effect on the organization of barbiturates dealing, this tendency to take barbiturates casually has had other organizational consequences for barrio users. For one thing, withdrawal sickness for barbiturate addicts has been relatively overlooked, even though it may be considerably more traumatic than for those using the highly diluted heroin of the 1970s. Convulsions are common, but it was only in the early 1970s that any official detoxification facility became available for pill users in Los Angeles. (Treatment was available in such other places as the Fort Worth federal facility as early as the mid-1950s.)

It is also well known that pills and liquor often produce violence. But because of comparative indifference, youthful offenders who are violent after a reds party (using a mixture of beer or wine and barbiturates) are rarely handled by the police or the courts as substance abusers. In the rare cases where there are adversary proceedings, both the prosecution and the defense tend to ignore the question of substance abuse. Instead, they concentrate on the individual's previous history of gang activity or other brushes with the law.

The increased costs and lower availability of barbiturates have sent the youngsters of the 1970s to even more dangerous substances, including solvents, for cheap highs. The extreme hazards of such chemicals as model glue and angel dust (PCP) have generated a degree of public concern in East Los Angeles that never appeared over the barbiturates. Barbiturates continue to be stereotyped as a cheap teenager drug, and not a matter for serious concern.

Research and the Barbiturates

In both the scientific literature and the public mind, barbiturates have been wrongly stereotyped and neglected. For example, it is universally assumed that the ultimate pill source is American pharmaceutical houses (cf. Soref, 1975). Few scholars have noticed the illegal and foreign manufacture of barbiturates described here. But law enforcement people obviously know about illegal Mexican manufacturers; the person who compiled our basic description served a federal prison term.

It is likely that the general depreciation of Chicanos—especially the uneducated—as businessmen has something to do with this oversight. That a gang of Chicanos could develop a high degree of entrepreneurial competence in, and rationalization of, the barbiturate marketing system fits neither the racial stereotypes nor the stereotype of barbiturates. Scientific neglect is thus an interesting phenomenon in itself.

Heroin Use in the Barrios

Barrio gangs received their greatest publicity during the pachucho era of the early 1940s, when heroin was almost unknown in the barrios. But by the middle of the 1950s, heroin-using cliques could be found in all Chicano gangs. It is evident that neither narcotics nor gangs can be understood separately. The heroin market was barrio-based, certainly, but it transcended local neighborhoods and generated its own special subculture.

The sudden spread of opiate addiction among the Chicanos of Los Angeles appears to be related to both technical and market innovations (see Bullington, 1977, for early reminiscences). Black opium, a sticky, tar-like substance, was sold to Chicanos in fan quantities long before World War II and through the early 1950s. It was awkward to use. A lid (from a Prince Albert Tobacco can, only) cost $75 to $125 in Nogales and was sold in Los Angeles for $500 to $600. This would be broken down to fill small jars of the kind women use as purse containers for creams. These were the "fans," in both $25 and $50 sizes. In turn, the fans were split into halves or quarters, and finally into "papers" which sold for $2, $3, $5, $6, $10, and $15. The black opium was smoked, chewed, and injected. Injection required that the opium be diluted, strained, and cooked three or four times. (The drug had to be refined enough to pass through a standard Number 26 needle, unless the addict owned an unusual Number 23 or Number 24 needle.) Injecting "black" was risky; if the addict missed a vein, impurities lodged in the tissues. But the addicts liked the black opium. It is recalled as good stuff, so strong that the users' feet and crotch would itch and a man's face would wrinkle up like the face of an old man for about an hour after injection. Morphine was available only rarely, by theft or from a few cooperative doctors. The opiates present in cough syrup were only strong enough to forestall withdrawal pains.

White opium was comparatively scarce. With very few exceptions, the Chinese refused to deal with outsiders. The westward migration of addicts and dealers (Jews from New York, Italians, Armenians, Syrians, and professional thieves) established only the most fragile connections with the Mexican Americans of Los Angeles.

Texans from the apparently well-established drug port of El Paso seem to have established themselves as dealers in a few barrios, but only as users in the three neighborhoods in this study. Because of these factors, Chicanos were not deeply involved in heroin use. When they were, they seem to have been dealing with an ethnically mixed group. This changed in the 1950s.

Heroin Connections

World War II curtailed heroin supplies from the European refineries. The major New York-based heroin importers turned to Mexico for a new source of supply. Until then, only Chinese immigrant farmers had cultivated the opium poppy in Mexico, but this reputed foreign investment led to thriving industries in the Mexican states of Sinaloa, Durango, Sonora, and Guerrero. By the end of the war, Mexico had become a major supplier, and the border towns were centers of narcotics traffic. For the Chicanos in Los Angeles, the establishment of nearby Tijuana as a drug center was a major turning point. Tecato (addict) lore is uniform in viewing this new drug center as a displacement of El Paso. Some stories relate the deaths of hundreds of El Paso addicts because of lethal heroin, which some attribute to a plot to discredit Mexican dealers. Others believe U.S. law enforcement authorities conspired to eliminate the addicts. But the appearance of *chiva* (light heroin) in Tijuana greatly increased its availability in Los Angeles, as well as the availability of marijuana.

Some Chicano veterans returning from Asian service in World War II had been astonished by the availability and high quality of opiates elsewhere in the world. Some were exposed to amphetamines in combat duty. To the respectable people of the barrios, any obvious drug user was a *marijuano* and an outcast, but the excitement of the wider world of drug use appears to have been contagious.

This allure, the social discontinuities caused by the war, and the availability of high-grade heroin from Tijuana helped establish a basic structure of Chicano drug dealers in Southern California.

Marketing Patterns in the 1940s and 1950s

In the late 1940s, heroin was plentiful. To contemporary eyes, the Chicano street dealers were astonishingly casual. One ex-dealer remembers how he would awake and fix with his coffee can of papers. He would take the trolley to 7th and San Pedro streets near downtown to make the day's sales. If business was slow, he would flag down cars in an open attempt to sell his merchandise. The bindle of papers, which sold for about six dollars, was sufficient for three or four fixes. For chippies (occasional, unaddicted, users), it could be extended to six fixes if one counted the use of *algodones*. (*Algodones* are the cotton balls used as filters when the cooked heroin is drained from the spoon into the dropper or syringe. They were saved to be used another time, or they could be given to a friend in need.)

Use was as informal as sales, for there was no accumulated experience to make gang boys wary of the drug. Because they knew that the dangers of marijuana were greatly exaggerated by non-users, they did not believe the stories about heroin. There were stories in the newspapers that street pushers victimized others into becoming addicts, and that dealers gave parties at which they opened shooting galleries. Actually, addicts simply did not conceal their behavior from younger people, and were apparently willing to share their drug supplies with others. Usually a couple of *vatos locos* went to buy a paper, and if they met a

friend they might invite him along. At times a *chavalo* (a naive young-
ster) would accept the invitation. He might even beg to try some stuff,
in order to relate to the heavier dudes, and to gain status over members
of his own clique. Addicts who had become aware of the problems of
drug dependency actively drove such youngsters away from drug use.
But others saw no harm in sharing with the kids who helped them cook
and fix when they were weak from withdrawal pains.

The spread of narcotics increased some of the existing differentiation
between gangs. The bigger dealers tended to employ the members of
their own barrios in a hierarchy that included nonaddicted dealers, addicted dealers (who, in turn, would supply addict-pushers who sold
heroin for use rather than profit), and finally, the consumer addict. At
the bottom levels the roles could change easily. The addict-dealer was
able to function as a middleman and to control the flow of heroin into
the barrio. Some barrios became major centers for distribution; others
were seen as user gangs.

The acknowledged and overriding importance of the connection meant
that for the first time addicts could legitimately go into a rival gang's
turf to buy drugs. Safety was assured, provided that the visit was to
score. Some tecatos now claim that heroin stopped the endemic violence
of gang warfare between the barrios. Indeed it may have done so for a
time, for the heroin market required both communication among individual users and market-related visits from one barrio to another.[2] However, the younger gang cliques rapidly revived the fighting tradition.

Increased Law Enforcement in the 1950s

The prices of an ordinary fix levelled off during the 1950s at about
$2.00 to $2.50, as the supply of heroin was stabilized. The federal
Jones-Miller Act of 1951 was not a deterrent to heroin use and was
repealed by Congress fifteen years later. At the same time, similarly
punitive state legislation (from five years to life sentences for the first,
and ten and fifteen years to life sentences for successive narcotics offenses) was passed in California.

This increase in law enforcement activity had a dramatic effect on
Chicanos. In 1950, the first mass federal arrests took place in Maravilla,
based on secret federal grand jury indictments secured by undercover
agents. The heroin market was driven underground. Inside the barrios,
the natural reaction was a greater emphasis on security. Sales were made
only to those who were well known to the dealers on an individual basis.

For its part, faced with an almost impenetrable group of individuals
and with growing public demand for control, the law enforcement agencies began to extend the snitch, or informer, system. Addicts are reasonably visible and are often known on sight. Thus it became common

practice to arrest addicts, then draw them from the jail's holding tank after withdrawal pains set in. They are offered a fix in return for information, an offer that many are unable to refuse. Addicts are easily blackmailed by the police, who use them in many ways. But the barrio loyalties, intensified by gang traditions and youthful battles, are strong, and the snitch betrays not only his supply sources but also his barrio. He is ostracized, and, according to the mythology, he is marked for death. Neither the police nor his gang will protect him.[3]

Social Types in the Barrio Heroin Market

In the drug business, the addicted and the nonaddicted tend to have little regard for each other. The non-user looks upon the addict as a man whose weak character let him become addicted, and whose habit will lead him to betray and exploit his most important personal relations. In turn, the addicts despise and envy the non-user dealer, because business norms intrude into a primary group social context (the barrio world), and because of the profit he makes from the miseries and needs of others. But the non-user dealer is seen as a more reliable source of supply than the addicted dealer. The non-user dealers are well known because their life style sometimes borders on the luxurious.

To the people of the barrio, the drug business demonstrates forcibly that money is the great equalizer in American society. Enormous social distances can be spanned with enough cash. The boys from the barrio learn that they can enter the best restaurants in Los Angeles wearing Levi trousers and thong sandals—if they can pay. Some dealers buy legitimate businesses as fronts. The most popular are restaurants and bars; techniques they learn from legitimate business are reapplied to the drug business.

Loyalty to the gang or clique is still stressed, because the members are considered to be a family. But to protect the family, networks of distribution have been established so that the street pusher never knows the ultimate source of the drugs. At each level of distribution, a cut (or step) is made to realize greater profits. By the time the barrio consumers receive the merchandise, it may have been stepped on as many as five times. This merchandising system means that more gang members have become involved in the distribution network, and that addicts pay for increasingly diluted products. Some dealers experiment with heroin, sometimes involuntarily, when the powder is inhaled while cutting. Some use it as a tranquilizer after the daily stresses of evading the law and engaging in high-risk deals.

Marketing in the 1960s

By the mid-1960s, the price of heroin in the Chicano barrios had doubled in ten years. Many of the men who had been incarcerated in the mid-1950s were leaving federal prisons. With them they brought new connections made in prison and greater sophistication in evading the law.

The growing market brought a new cost problem—payoffs. Money, the equalizer, was offered to policemen, sometimes to eliminate competition. It is no secret in the world of drugs that some narcotics agents employ the same tactics as the organization: if they feel cheated they will eliminate those who wronged them. A story from this period involves a pill dealer who began to deal in heroin. When he refused to increase his payment to the local narc, an undercover agent approached him and demanded that he stop dealing in heroin. When the dealer refused to talk to the agent and walked away, the agent shot him in the back. The next day's newspaper carried a story stating that the victim had attempted to knife the narcotics agent.

Prison sentences in California were long and were based on previous records. (The inequity of these sentences can be seen in such cases as that of the addict inmate at the California Men's Colony who in 1975 was doing his seventeenth year of confinement for a sale amounting to less than twenty dollars.) The spread of heroin use and the harsh sentences under previous legislation prompted the state legislature to pass the Civil Commitment Act of 1963.

This legislation established the California Rehabilitation Center (CRC), administered by the Department of Corrections (cf. Bullington, 1977, and Duster, 1970). Here confinement is based on success in the treatment programs. If the released addict has problems with the law, he is returned for further treatment. In practice this often becomes a cycle, so that civil commitment is often equivalent to a sentence of ten years. Inside the barrios, which supply a great many of the inmates, CRC is seen as simply another joint. The psychological treatment programs are not only alien to the Chicano barrio background (because they involve the open disclosure of private and subgroup information), but they are contaminated by an atmosphere of coercion. The inability of Chicano inmates to respond to the treatment model means longer commitments and increased bitterness toward the system. (Street drug programs based on a self-help principle began to appear somewhat later in the 1960s and have had enough success to appear to be one of the more promising alternatives. We will deal with this self-help subject, particularly in the prisons, in Chapter 6.)

For a time in the early 1970s, it appeared to many persons in the Mexican American communities that the market for heroin was leveling off. But in the mid-1970s it appeared to increase again, and the price rose sharply, to $6.25 for the street user. Vietnam veterans appear to have added to the consumption. (Here was a case where Chicanos sought an escape from the barrio, and found themselves among the oppressors.)

But unlike the veterans of World War II, these men returned at a time when anti-heroin sentiment was strong at all levels of the barrio, not just among squares and outsiders. Their return brought them in contact with a well-developed subculture of users, dealers, and police, as well as a network of facilities and programs to treat addiction, including methadone clinics. The use of heroin had become institutionalized.

A new element in the Chicano heroin market is the Mexican Mafia, a strongarm organization that developed inside the California prison system (see Chapter 5). The Mafia self-consciously patterns itself on the Italian Mafia as it is described in the media, and uses extreme violence as a substitute for barrio ties. This Mafia is believed to be attempting to monopolize heroin marketing in East Los Angeles, but given the pluralistic nature of this market, it is not likely they will succeed.

The Structure of Heroin Marketing in Chicano Los Angeles

This brief history of heroin and gangs brings us directly to the structure of heroin marketing from 1950s to the early 1970s. It is tempting to draw an elaborate chart, because this is similar to the public relations efforts of the many (and often competing) police agencies who use charts to explain the complexity and expense of their work. In fact, in Chicano Los Angeles the basic relationships are those of a group of men from certain barrios, certain fighting gangs, and certain prisons, who are related by blood and by enduring friendships of many years. There is no reason why their working relationships and responsibilities should resemble management charts; it is very likely that they do not. In terms of management responsibilities, heroin is an amazingly casual business. And it is probably easier to get into the heroin business profitably than into other kinds of businesses. Heroin is actually easier to deal in than pills, because the latter require a considerable volume before a reasonable profit is possible.

Elaborate structures have been described for the marketing of drugs in other cities. Preble and Casey (1969) and Hughes and Crawford (1974) detail the structure of heroin dealing in New York and Chicago, respectively. Their rather similar pictures are echoed by Feigenbaum for New York in 1973 (in Kaplan and Kessler, 1976). The New York structure is supposed to be a composite of the entire city; the Chicago structure is a portrait of a particular and localized copping area. Both models describe rigid pyramidical structures, in which the heroin flows from one major source, through successively greater numbers of people. Those at the top are never addicted, and those at the bottom always are; there is an increasing likelihood of addiction as the pyramid is descended. Before we contrast this with the Los Angeles structure, a little more background is necessary.

We noted earlier that when the European sources of supply dried up in World War II, Mexico became a significant producer of heroin (cf. Preble and Casey, 1969, p. 5). Yet as recently as 1972, Mexico was regarded as the smallest among six worldwide illicit producing areas (India producing about 100 metric tons compared to Mexico's 10 to 20 metric tons, World Opium Survey, 1972, 1973). At that time (also the time of the New York and Chicago studies), the vast bulk of heroin in the U.S. was produced through the French connection with Turkey, most of it coming directly to New York. Some was transshipped through Canada, Latin America, and Mexico, but it was estimated that only 25 percent of the heroin moved into the United States was either shipped through or produced in Mexico. Thus at the time of the Chicago and New York studies, heroin was coming to those cities largely from French connection sources. We hypothesize that at that time in Los Angeles Chicano dealers were acquiring their heroin from Mexican producers and distributors, rather than through European sources. The illicit poppy fields are located in Northwest Mexico, close to Southwestern U.S. ports of entry.

The nature of the ultimate source has an important impact on the market structure. The French connection is a near-monopoly (cf. Moore, 1970). Ianni (1974) details the struggles of black and Puerto Rican narcotics dealers in New York to escape the limitations imposed on them by the Italian dominance of the local markets, down to the block level.

What is striking about the Chicano structure is that it was difficult to monopolize at the source. Some of the Los Angeles Chicano connections may be to Mexican distributors who are merely transshipping through Mexico, but at least some are definitely Mexican producers, even operating on credit through friendship networks. A more pluralistic source of supply for Los Angeles means that it is possible for relatively small dealers to make relatively small connections with Mexican growers or distributors, compared with the more tightly controlled market of New York or Chicago. (See Redlinger, 1969, for a description of the pattern in San Antonio.)

A second point about the structures delineated for Chicago and New York is somewhat more difficult to communicate and also more speculative. Control of the source of supply means a certain degree of quality control—that is, a reasonably predictable level of purity. This is important because the hierarchy of dealers outlined in detail for New York depends on the ability of each stratum (connection or dealer) to be able to cut the heroin enough to make a profit. The Preble and Casey chain starts off with 80 percent pure heroin and winds up with 3.3 percent pure heroin after it travels down the full length of the dealer hierarchy. If the original heroin received by the importer were only 40 percent pure, it could not be cut by as many people without the risk of selling "pure sugar." According to drug enforcement officials, French chemists consistently produced heroin that was 90 percent pure. Mexican brown heroin, by contrast, is more variable in quality and usually only about 65 percent pure (*Los Angeles Times*, August 1, 1976). This means that the elaborate structure described for New York cannot be constructed in communities dependent on less well-refined original supplies.

The East Los Angeles marketing arrangement has little to do with rational and predictable long-term organization. It has much more to do with what the dealers call "insulation," or safety from the "heat" of law enforcement. Our street and prison sources note that in Chicano dealing in East Los Angeles, there are no more than five steps, or cuts, in the heroin. Yet each dealer wants as many layers of insulation between himself and the street addict as he can possibly produce. The street addict is discounted: it is assumed that he will not only inform but also work with law enforcement agencies to set up his connection for a buy. As one former dealer said, "It's one thing for people to say you're dealing. That doesn't mean anything for a bust. It's another thing for people to see you dealing. And it's another thing for people to buy from you." These are three levels of risk of evidence faced by every heroin dealer, because most narcotics law enforcement operates through the informer/set up system.

Every level of dealer tries to minimize the risk of informers and of set ups by dealing only with reliable people. For the larger-scale dealers, there is the risk of being cheated by lower-level distributors, but that is less important than snitching or setting up. For both reasons, one works with people who are known to be reliable. These must be homies whom one has seen in a variety of test situations from adolescence through adulthood. This is true even at the lowest levels of street dealing: one confines one's dealing to people one has known for years, usually fellow gang members, fellow ex-prisoners, or people vouched for by mutual gang or prison acquaintances. The risk is highest at the street level, for the street addict is the most vulnerable to police pressure and the least able to afford legal protection. The dealers higher up the distribution ladder work less often with unreliable addicts. In addition, they can pay for adequate legal services.

At the level of the addict-dealer, it is almost impossible to talk in terms of entrepreneurial motivation—or at least in terms of entrepreneurial success. At best, he normally sells only enough heroin to finance the purchase of an equal amount of heroin the next time (for example, an ounce); the rest he consumes. He tends to consume more and more as time passes, and pintos estimate that he is generally on the streets no more than six months between one incarceration and the next. There are periodic dry spells, or panics, in the Los Angeles heroin supply. The street dealer then reverts entirely to his short-run interests as an addict rather than as an entrepreneur, holding back what heroin he has on hand and refusing to sell. This is a self-defeating strategy, since he then does not earn enough money through sales to make another buy, and must soon (within a week) turn to other activities—usually criminal—to sustain his habit. He has used up his operating capital, and sinks a notch lower in the marketing system by becoming purely a consumer.

Narcotics dealing in East Los Angeles was an outgrowth of the Chicano gang structure and reflects the nature of the supply. In recent years, authorities have estimated that Mexican heroin is becoming increasingly more important on a national level; New York police said that in 1976 60 percent of that city's heroin was of Mexican origin. Ianni argues that blacks and Puerto Ricans have begun to move in on Italian-controlled organized crime, with special difficulties in the drug market. Preble and Casey, by contrast, argue that "the syndicate" "officially withdrew from the market" in 1957, creating a "relatively free market" (p. 6). Regardless of the contradiction in these two accounts, it is very likely that Preble and Casey's bureaucratized structure has changed a great deal since their study.

Our final point is critical for understanding the structure of heroin dealing among Chicanos in Los Angeles: doing business with Mexican connections does not require "an organization." The initial source, the opium poppy, will produce a crop within ninety days of planting. It is grown in virtually inaccessible mountain fields in the Sierra Madre mountains of Mexico. The turnaround time from delivery in Los Angeles until the importer has his profit, while longer than with barbiturates, is still very short, only two or three weeks. Fields may be burned one year and produce the next; dealers can go out of business almost immediately if they feel heat. It is, in fact, critically important to be able to go out of business almost immediately. One small-scale dealer went into business simply because he met the right friend in a bar and the friend knew a man in Mexico. Another moved into the hierarchy simply because he decided to drive from Los Angeles to new customers in San Fernando, a distance of about twenty miles. And always, of course, the city of Tijuana (once a major distributing point) is an easy half-day drive from the barrios. There is no necessary continuity for an organization. None of its components need to be retained from one deal to another.

Thus heroin marketing in Chicano Los Angeles started not from a monopolized source, but from many sources. It was entrepreneurial and decentralized, in both Mexico and Los Angeles. Suppliers and dealers can—and do—go in and out of business with relative ease. Probably there are proportionately more street dealers than in the more organized cities. The smaller number of levels within the organization (created, at least in part, by the lower purity of the original heroin) may account for the Chicanos' high arrest rate.

In general, the marketing of heroin greatly resembles many other aspects of life and business in East Los Angeles. Drug dealing is a grassroots enterprise that is an established part of the prevailing social structure, particularly in the youth gangs. It is based on the survival habits of the barrio market, in which an individual deals directly with other individuals, rather than with an organization. Its casual nature and emphasis on kinship and friendship ties fits perfectly into the barrio economy, and makes it unlike the structured organizations observed in New York and Chicago.

Heroin marketing techniques grew naturally out of the barbiturate trade; this can be clearly seen in the history of Chicano gangs in East Los Angeles. Aggressive law enforcement simply reinforced the existing emphasis on personal relationships. The whole process is not only natural, but is predictable when viewed against the background of barrio life.

5

Prisons and the Barrios

OBVIOUSLY, many Chicanos who are involved in street gangs or in narcotics marketing wind up in prison. The Chicano prison experience is important because, like other American racial minorities, Chicanos have been consistently overrepresented in the jails and prisons. Drugs have long been associated with this overrepresentation. Furthermore, their prison experience sharply underscores the significance of the three factors outlined in Chapter 1. These factors never dominate life more than in the prison experience.

As in their home barrios, Chicanos in prison are caught up in an illegal economy as well as their legitimate but low-paying economic life. As in their Los Angeles neighborhoods, Chicano prisoners are defined, and define themselves, as a racial minority. And as in the city and county of Los Angeles, their lives are constrained by the operating requirements of a people-processing bureaucracy.

Economy, Race, and Institutions in Prison

The prison economy—a complex web of barter activity in contraband food, drink, drugs, weapons, and the like—has interested criminologists who study inmate subcultures (cf. Williams and Fish, 1974). Sometimes, but not always, it is seen as related to the low rate of pay for prison work, just as the illegal economy of the barrios is sometimes, but not always, related to the dead-end jobs dominating the secondary labor market.

There has been substantially less interest among traditional criminologists in race as a factor in prison life. This may be, at least in part, because minority prisoners are frequently not very cooperative with institutionally based research. (This appears to have been notably true with Chicanos. Bowker, 1977 cites Rudoff, 1964 and Kennedy, 1970 as representing two such instances at two California institutions.) To some extent this long-standing neglect was more than rectified, at least in the public view, by the appearance of literature written by black prisoners or former prisoners (for example, Malcolm X, 1964; Cleaver, 1968; and Jackson, 1970), and also by the identification of many prison uprisings, especially at Attica in 1971, as related to the problems of black prisoners.

It is the prison as an institution that is the primary focus of this chapter. This has interested criminologists in at least three guises. First, there is the question of differences in the behavior of inmates as a function of the institutional orientation—that is, whether the staff is oriented toward custody or to treatment. Second, there has been a long-standing interest in what one of the first students of prisons (Donald Clemmer, 1940) calls prisonization (or, more colloquially, institutionalization), the long-range tendency for inmates to become more oriented to prison survival than to the outside world. Third is a more abstract and process-oriented version of prisonization that stems from Goffman's work (1961) on "total institutions." It is abstract in the sense that Goffman sees prisons as one of a class of institutions (such as mental hospitals) which for a period of time totally encompass all of the social life of the participants. It is process-oriented in that Goffman is interested in the details of the acculturation of the participants, such as the identity-stripping rituals that take place on the inmate's entry.

A Total Institution?

It is the prison as a total institution that primarily interests us in this chapter. We must begin by noting that the extent to which prison, is in fact, experienced by any inmate as a total institution (functionally eradicating his or her pre-prison identity) is a controversial subject in criminology. Some experts argue, for example, that the prisoner culture is not endogenous but rather represents a congeries of imported subcultures (cf. Irwin and Cressey, 1962). This controversy is relevant to us because we are tracing linkages between types of experience that are usually conceived of as opposed, such as legal and illegal economic activities. In particular, we want to trace the continuities between prison and pre-prison experiences with a view toward identifying those normalizing influences which may be drawn upon both within prison and outside prison.

But to ex-prisoners who were involved in this study, this controversy seems meaningless. To be sure, they were angry at the degradation ceremony at their entry into prison and are usually fully aware of the debilitating effects of dependency on the prison routine. Many are also aware of the seductive nature of making it inside prison. Yet in their view, prison is experienced as a climax institution of the Anglo world as it impinges upon the barrio. Prison exaggerates many of the familiar features of outside Anglo institutions. Even more important, social relationships in prison are familiar because the Chicano's fellows in prison are the same people he sees on the streets of Los Angeles.

In this chapter we will discuss the continuities between barrio and prison experiences in generalized fashion. Critical aspects of the prison social structure or the prisoner mix will be mentioned, but our focus is not the social types in prison that have intrigued so many researchers. And although the material here was developed with men who were in many different prisons, our descriptive referent is San Quentin in the mid-1960s. We choose this place and time because of its relevance to the self-help movement, described in the next chapter.

It must be understood from the beginning that this account is derived from, and largely written by, Chicanos who have lived in prison. Many of the topics that arouse popular interest about prisons do not appear here because they did not seem important to these collaborators. There is little interest, for example, in homosexuality—perhaps because relatively few Chicanos are involved. Nor is there much interest in the specifics of prison violence, perhaps because the Los Angeles Chicanos who go to prison anticipate violence and anticipate being able to cope with it. For most Chicanos (and for most other prisoners), their interest is pragmatic: to find resources inside and outside prison, especially those that may help with release. It was this topic that we dealt with in our questionnaires, administered inside four prisons, which are summarized in the last portion of this chapter (see also Appendix C).

Thus our primary concern is finding how barrio influences and social relationships continue to operate within the prison, how they help men cope with prison as an institution, and deviations from this pattern. Secondarily and indirectly, we are concerned with the racial effect—that is, Chicanos as a minority group within prison. But it must be emphasized again that our account is developed by Chicanos, who are perhaps less interested in certain aspects of the Chicano experience than outsiders. Nonetheless, in the next chapter Chicanismo will appear importantly, but not exogenously and as imposed by the institution.

Chicanos in Prison: A Historical View

General Overrepresentation

Minority overrepresentation is one of the truisms about prison, yet minorities almost always means only blacks. In its decennial census of institutional populations, the U.S. Census did not even enumerate Mexican Americans, but counted them as "white." Therefore it is something of a task in itself to document the actual extent to which Chicanos are overrepresented in the prison population.

Overrepresentation is indicated in consistent data over a hundred years. Between 1876 and 1909 more than half of the inmates of the Arizona Territorial Prison were Mexican (Jeffrey, 1969), while only about 30 percent of the population of the territory was Mexican.[1] Among the foreign born in the U.S. in 1910, the Mexican born had the highest ratio of incarcerations per 100,000 population—5 percent of all persons committed (U.S. Dept. of Commerce, 1918). In 1929, almost 11 percent of California's prisoners were Mexican; Mexicans then comprised 4.6 percent of the state population (Taylor, 1931). In 1934–35, about 5 percent of the 11,000 federal inmates were Chicanos, at a time when only a tiny fraction of the U.S. population was Chicano (U.S. Bureau of Prisons, 1936). By 1973 the percentage was up to 18.4 percent (U.S. Bureau of Prisons, 1973).

Table 3   **Ethnic Characteristics of the California Prison Population, 1959, 1964, 1969, 1973**

Ethnic Characteristics	1959 (%)	1964 (%)	1969 (%)	1973 (%)
White	58.3	54.9	53.6	49.1
White, Mexican descent	16.8	16.8	16.4	17.2
Black	22.6	26.6	28.5	32.0
Other	2.3	1.7	1.5	1.7
Total N (= 100%)	(15,843)	(20,591)	(21,240)	(16,886)

SOURCE: California Department of Corrections, 1959, 1964, 1969, 1973.

In more recent years in California, overrepresentation has not been as gross, but it is still present. In 1959, Chicanos comprised 16.8 percent of the California prison population, and 9 percent of the state population. In 1969, 16.4 percent of the prisoners were Chicano, compared with 11 percent of the state population.

Between 1959 and 1973, there was comparatively little variation among the twelve California institutions in ethnic composition, but there were sharp variations in age, from a low median of 23.5 years in Deuel Vocational Institution (Tracy) to a high of 39.4 years in Folsom (1973 figures). The median age in San Quentin was a little higher than that of the system as a whole, at 31.2 years.

How does this compare with overrepresentation of blacks? Using slightly different statistics, del Pinal (1973) estimates that incarceration rates for black men in California aged 25–44 are about seven times that of white men of the same age. Chicanos have about twice the rates for whites. Thus things are not quite as bad for Chicanos as for blacks.

Chicano Offenses

For what crimes are Chicanos imprisoned? The most common offense is narcotics. In 1929 the narcotic was marijuana, then believed to be associated with "atrocious crimes" (Taylor, 1931). In recent years it has been heroin. Narcotics are a far more significant cause of incarceration for Chicanos than for any other ethnic group in California. This is shown not only by the offenses for which inmates are committed in California, but also by surveys of incarcerated men.[2] By the mid-1970s, roughly a quarter to a third of all state and federal prisoners had used heroin at some time in their lives.[3] By contrast, recent surveys of Chicano prisoners far surpass these figures. Fifty-five percent of Chicanos surveyed in Michigan prisons admitted heroin addiction (Pachon, 1976. This survey omitted Muskegon, the narcotics hospital of the Michigan prison system.) In our own survey, about the same proportions of men incarcerated in two California institutions admitted having been addicted to heroin. Of the inmates in the federal facility at Lompoc, 72 percent admitted heroin addiction (see Appendix C). Thus at least twice as many Chicanos as prisoners in general admitted heroin use. At the least, these data suggest that the experiences of imprisonment in Chicano communities would be vastly different without narcotics involvement, or if heroin use and marketing were not illegal.

One final note: because of California's harsh minimum sentences for narcotics offenses, the average sentence served by narcotics offenders tends to be substantially longer than for most other crimes. Chicanos serve longer time for opiates offenses than do members of other ethnic groups, possibly because they may be second- or third-term narcotics offenders, whose mandatory minimum sentences increased with each conviction.

The Official View of Chicanos

How do prison officials view Chicanos as prisoners? In 1970 the principal author interviewed men who were current or former leading treatment personnel at San Quentin. Several points emerged, the most important of which is that Chicanos were seen as alien (speaking a foreign language), and thus represented a problem to English-speaking custody officials. Treatment personnel felt they were best understood in light of ethnographic studies of Mexican village life that emphasize such cultural themes as machismo, personalism, mutual suspicion, and a tendency to violence connected with factional struggles for power. They were seen as making two basic types of adaptation to prison—either total withdrawal or extreme militancy.

A few years later the predominant cause for attention to Chicanos was interprisoner violence. Alarmed at the increase in violent incidents in the prisons, the California Director of Corrections commissioned a task force in 1973 to investigate the matter.[4] The investigators quickly disposed of the notion that black/white racial tensions were the prime cause of violence. Only 14 percent of the aggressors in 1972 were blacks, although they were 32 percent of the population. (By the last half of 1973 this aggressor figure rose to 26 percent.) Chicanos were 49 percent of the aggressors in 1972, although they were 17 percent of the population. (Their share declined to 35 percent by the last half of 1973.) The authors of the report saw Chicano violence as attributable largely to "organized gangs" which they identified as "tightly organized units . . . that have stable leadership, high cohesiveness and dedication to a set of principles" (p. 2). Although only about 10 percent of the incidents between inmates are acknowledged as "related to gang affiliation," the gangs that transcend barrio loyalties (the Mexican Mafia and Nuestra Familia) still get the credit for Chicano violence. No data on Chicano violence before 1972 is given, but the authors speak of a "consistent pattern" of violence over time.

Continuities between Street and Prison Life

Prison is an omnipresent reality in barrio life, and contact with it is continuous and drastic, affecting nearly everybody in the barrio. In 1950 the Census counted about 350 boys aged fifteen to nineteen in the two census tracts that include the White Fence barrio. From our data on the first three cliques of the White Fence gang (Table 2), we can estimate that between 15 and 20 percent of those neighborhood boys ultimately spent some time in prison. While we do not have comparable data for the other two barrios studied, we have no reason to believe that the proportions are much lower.

Prison adaptations are seen by convicts themselves as variants of adaptations to street life. For the Chicano pinto (prisoner), it may be easier to generalize about adaptations to prison, because the barrio is self-consciously important to him, especially if he is involved with heroin. Generalizations about Chicano experiences, with appropriate modifications, may also apply to other minority group prisoners. Although the barrios emphasize family and family-like relationships more than many ethnic communities, all poverty areas in recent years have experienced similar relationships with institutional agencies and with the tripartite economy.

Familism in Prison

The first generalization about Chicano prisoners is that they are extremely familistic. Chicano barrios place an unusual emphasis on family relationships. The families are large: the convicts interviewed had as many as fifteen or twenty aunts and uncles (each with large families of cousins) and as many as seven or eight siblings. (At one recent funeral of a pinto, nearly three hundred relatives attended.) The wife of a pinto has as many close relatives as he does, and during his incarceration both of the families are asked to help.

In addition to blood relatives, there are two other structures that have some of the characteristics of a family. First, the barrio gang assumes family-like qualities, among both the members and the families of members. In youth the member is known not only by the gang members but also by the families of the gang members. These relationships are strengthened by kin-like obligations that have consequences in prison. Thus, when a younger brother of a barrio friend and gang member shows up in prison he becomes the charge of the older pinto.

Second, barrio ties are consolidated and formalized through the *compadrazgo*, or ritual godparent relationship. Although the *compradrazgo* may be only a residual influence in the more affluent segments of the Chicano community, in the world of the barrio and the pinto, where needs are urgent, a young man cements a firm bond of obligation if he stands up as best man in the wedding ceremony of a friend or "baptizes" his child.[5]

In prison the significance of outside familistic networks is obvious when anyone from the pinto's home barrio appears on the scene. Prisoners routinely watch the bus bringing new prisoners and immediately identify a barrio carnal (homeboy): "It was like you were a celebrity, either way, if you're coming in or going out. Either way, it was a celebration." They offer him help and such necessities of life as cigarettes, snacks, and razor blades; in turn they get the latest neighborhood gossip.[6] The new addition to the barrio inside the prison is both an obligation and a source of information about the family and happenings in the outside barrio.

Wives, the Barrio, Welfare, and Money

The gossip that the pinto acquires from new prisoners is enormously significant in his life. With all of its malice and its distortions, it is often the only source of information about his wife and children. If familistic barrio ties are an important psychological support to the prisoner, his own nuclear family is, predictably, a source of intense anxiety. Part of the difficulty is caused by a historical accident: most California prisons were built when the bulk of the population was living much further north, in a state nearly one thousand miles long. Chicanos in prison tend to be a long way from home; there is no allowance for the transportation of relatives to prison, and many of northern prisons prohibit conjugal visits.

The pinto's wife often resents her husband's "desertion" to prison and her own total lack of preparation to cope without a protective guide. While "the welfare" is usually a fall-back source of support, it is, like most institutions, generally hostile to the pinto.

If the lines of communication between the pinto and his wife and children falter, and the pinto attempts to get information about his family through institutional sources, he is almost invariably frustrated. The county-based welfare system has no interest in a man incarcerated in the state prison system; county and state bureaucrats appear not to work routinely with each other. To the welfare worker, the convict is a non-person. His wife is often advised to divorce him. The welfare worker will not respond to queries from the convict about his wife and children without the consent of the wife; the prison counselor is usually equally unresponsive. The pinto cannot get information. Nor can he help in any way.

It is in this context that barrio gossip becomes vital to the convict. Marriage ties rarely survive the median three or four years of incarceration, and the prison yard is full of brutal teasing about marital infidelity. Sometimes the pinto's wife resolves her problems by transferring her dependency needs to her own family—and homies bring in the news. But very often she transfers those needs to another man. Some prisoners even learn of the collapse of their marriage when they see their wife's picture in the cell of a recently arrived prisoner.

Another problem for the large Chicano families is that the maximum money allowance from welfare is never more than that allowed for a family of four. Thus the available money often falls short of meeting basic needs. There is very little that the pinto can realistically do. One possibly damaging consequence of the frustrated pinto concerns about family and money is that they are strong inducement to smuggling or other illegal activities in the underground prison economy.

Usually a woman with school-age children is urged by her budget-conscious welfare worker to get a job. Yet there were few reliable child-care facilities in the Chicano areas of Los Angeles even in the mid-1970s. A few case workers may encourage the wives of the convicts to go to school, but this is rare.

Over the years, the woman's capacity to deal with the institutional system of East Los Angeles tends to increase. She begins to rely upon the welfare check as her independent income. Meanwhile, the capacity of her pinto husband is severely curtailed. Predictably, when the two people meet again after the convict leaves prison, their efforts to get together again are rarely successful.

Since little is done to maintain the convict's family and sense of responsibility for his wife or his children, many pintos develop defenses.

They actively block out the outside world, jumping into a game of hand-ball or dominoes when they begin to worry. All of the pintos periodically serve what is called hard time, but futile brooding does not sustain their sense of responsibility when all outlets for the exercise of responsibility are systematically blocked. From a theoretical point of view, it seems this blockage would hasten the process of institutional dependency and encourage regression into pre-adult modes of behavior. From our point of view, this represents a major discontinuity.

Experiences with the Prison Economy

In prison, the shortcomings of the educational system become more critical and more consequential than on the streets. Few Chicanos who drop out of school in the tenth grade to enter the working world ever find out how poor their education really is. Very few ever learn dramatically the consequences of illiteracy. Chicanos who go to prison make both of these discoveries.

Dropouts who go to prison are often shocked to discover at the Reception Guidance Center that their actual educational attainment is far below formal grade attainment. The eleventh-grade dropout frequently tests at the fifth-grade reading level. In San Quentin in the mid-1960s, the Chicano population had a median fourth-grade attainment—and this had important consequences for their treatment in prison. At that time, an eighth-grade scholastic achievement (and a low custody rating) was required for most vocational training. (Among Chicano convicts, the realization of the very poor level of their formal education was one of the reasons behind their efforts in San Quentin to establish a bilingual basic education program. This was the beginning of the Chicano self-help movement in prisons, to be discussed in Chapter 8).

The pinto's low level of educational attainment is reflected in their prison work assignments, despite a recent California correctional policy to establish ethnic parity at each pay level (basic pay levels run from three to twenty-four cents per hour). The jobs assigned Chicano prisoners are almost always at the bottom levels of the system, in such work as tier tending. Some Chicanos are unclassified—that is, they have no work assignment whatever (see Appendix B). It is important to realize that this unpleasant experience represents a continuity for the Chicanos in prison. Back in their home neighborhood, poor jobs and inadequate training are an old reality. For a pinto who returns to the streets, unemployment may mean an early return to prison. The dreary round of welfare, education, and jobs still exists, and is exaggerated, in prison.

Another continuity is the importance of narcotics. Not only are narcotics a major reason for incarceration and long sentences, but outside the California Rehabilitation Center, addiction is still treated as a crime rather than as a medical problem. In the thirteen major prisons of California, addiction has neither been treated by the medical staff, nor noticed by the administration, except as a means to exclude addicts from many jobs and from most vocational training. This exclusion was one of the first targets of the Chicano culture groups, along with their interest in education. Finally, even in prison, drugs encourage the convict to engage in illegal activities. Hustling is a means to get what the Chicano convict could get on the streets, including drugs for the tecato. The profits encourage others who are not addicted to smuggle and deal within the prison as they did on the streets. This, of course, is best done within the familiar framework of the Chicano gang, which is very much alive and well inside the prison—and even more important than on the streets of the barrios.

Continuities Inside and Outside Prison

Up to this point we have attempted to demonstrate the continuities between street life and prison life. There are familiar support networks of friends and familistic networks. There is the familiar poverty cycle of the private troubles that are minimally assisted, neglected, or exacerbated by the barrio institutions operated by Anglo Los Angeles. There is the familiar low-status low-pay position in the legal economic structure, thanks to the lack of education and involvement with narcotics. There is the familiar illegal economy, in which an astute prisoner can get anything he wants except a woman. Thus, in exaggerated form, the prison is a climax institution representing the same forces that the Chicanos of Los Angeles have felt all their lives.

The barriers are the same. The consequences of failure to pass these barriers are underlined and exaggerated in prison. The same systems work or fail to work. The agencies that manage educational and job opportunities and the opportunity structures that can provide money in default of work have their counterparts in prison. The Chicano prisoner finds that the educational, occupational, and money-making activities are at least as limited in prison as on the streets; therefore, many prisoners are attracted to the illegal money-making activities inside the prison. More important yet, street agencies continue to operate dysfunctionally for the convict. Usually their effect is to undermine the family networks that might provide incentive for resocialization to a square life. Responsibilities as conceived by an agency are not always seen as responsibilities in the barrio. Little is done either for the prisoner or for his family to strengthen the traditional values and existing networks that might operate in favor of his assumption of a non-criminal way of life. In prison, as on the streets, the barrio and *la raza* become the primary psychological and social resource. The institution continues to operate in the context of a familistic style that itself represents the major continuity.

Prison as the Climax Institution

Even if the Chicano man experiences prison as a familiar set of systems, there is, nonetheless, a sense of surprise among many Chicano convicts that the muddle of deprivation and misunderstanding inside a maximum security prison is so familiar. This time they expected it to be different. In the minds of most Americans, the general notion of the criminal justice system is concocted of impressions gained from mass media melodrama (which includes courts, police, and prison), buttressed by occasional first-hand contacts. Los Angeles Chicanos (despite their far greater exposure to the realities of the criminal justice system than middle America) to some extent share the notion that Justice with a capital "J" is at stake. And (to make a broad speculation for a moment) there may well be enough of a self-exculpating as well as a self-blaming tendency in most felony arrestees to create a strong sense that somehow, if only the full individual and the full circumstances were known and understood by the criminal justice system, there might be some way to construct a meaningful, rather than a moronically brutal, future out of the shreds of the past. This need for reconstruction is frequent among even the most "hard-core" barrio first offenders. In actual experience, pintos can see their lives as a set of recurrent, accelerating interactions with Anglo institutions that inevitably climaxed in the disaster of prison.

The Lifelong Journey to Prison

For those who wish to conceptualize the criminal justice system for purposes of policy, the beginning point is usually arrest. This is followed by court processes, incarceration, and then a return to the community. Each step of the journey draws upon relationships with agencies of the criminal justice system that each individual has taken a lifetime to establish. This strongly suggests that the welfare, educational, health, and economic agencies function in parallel in prison and on the streets.

For the young Chicano growing up in a barrio, contact with the police begins at an early age. The Los Angeles Police Department maintains a continuously updated file of gangs (identifying some sixty Latin gangs in 1973). The Sheriff's Department (with jurisdiction in Los Angeles County outside the city proper) keeps an even more accurate estimate of both the names of the gangs and their territories.[7] The ongoing hostilities have generated traditions among both youngsters and policemen.

> In school they taught us that the law was there to help us and that they were servants of the people, so they said. Yeah, that's what they said. Everytime we'd be standing on a corner a police car would come by and they would stop and get off and grab us by the neck, turn us around, and search us, and if you tried to talk back you'd find yourself with your back to the floor, and they'd slap upside your head, call you "Punk" and what have you.
>
> Every once in a while you'd see a young rookie, usually with an older cop, you could see his eyes, they were saying, "Hey, I wonder what's he hitting him for?" Six months later you'd see the same rookie and his eyes real hard and he had another rookie. That's the way they used to train them, I guess, to be beating up on young Mexicans.

These contacts, of course, greatly reinforce the ties of the barrio gang. Even an overnight stay in Juvenile Hall means that a young Chicano must find his own homies and fight with the members of other gangs. Parental controls are weakened both by the obvious impotence of the parents against the system, and by the ever-increasing amount of control exerted by the system. (This lack of parental ability is symbolically underscored when a boy is placed in a foster home.)

> My father, I knew he was a man, he wasn't afraid of fighting. He had gotten into several fights, even in his old age.
>
> Well, anyway, every time this happened my father wouldn't say anything, just sit and listen with his head bowed, it tears down the image of my father, it did to me. I used to think, well, you know my father didn't talk back to the judge or to the school officials or whatever, even a honky cop used to come to the door and yell, "Where in hell is that kid?" and my father would not say a word, he could have broken them in half. So it becomes a fear instead of a meekness, and then defiance—you gotta hit back, one way or the other.

For many men, the first prison sentence is preceded by progessively longer sentences to the county jail for petty offenses.[8] In addition, the cohesiveness of barrio addicts was reinforced by the policies of the Sheriff's Department (until the late 1950s) of segregating addicts into their own tanks. There, barrio hostilities were nonexistent and mutual aid for detoxification and for material needs became an established pattern.

It is important to remember that the juvenile and municipal courts and the county jail mete out justice by bureaucracy. Attorneys appear very rarely. There is very brief attention to individual cases. In general, everyone concerned is a passive participant in a well-established routine. In fact, the criminal justice system operates much like the welfare and medical bureaucracies, particularly in the lower levels of the court system.

All of this appears in sharp contrast to the American ideal of the equality of all men before the law and the intrinsic worth of the individual. Mexican Americans are as impressed by these ideals (as expressed on television and other media) as any other segment of America. The jury trial, for example, is so well established in American ideology as a just process that the reappearance of the familiar bureaucratic routines is a bitter disappointment for the first-time felony defendant. Instead of telling his full story and winning the understanding of a group of peers in a jury, the defendant usually sees only a judge, in a bureaucratic process that is reminiscent of the lower courts.[9] The major concern is the convenience of agency officials. There is little interest in the individual case. The defendant's final shock is that, regardless of whether the judge appears understanding and humane, he does not set the actual sentence. It is set by the Adult Authority, within certain statutory limits. This was the procedure until 1976, when changes diminished the importance of the indeterminate sentence.

It is strange that a sense of summary treatment or even a sense of being victimized is so slow in coming to many new pintos. Many not only keep their faith in the processes of trial, but believe in the professional diagnosis that occurs at the Reception Guidance Center, where all the rhetoric and authority of professional educators and psychologists is summoned. First-termer convicts are impressed by the personal attention and the professional backgrounds of the counselors. But once again the prisoner learns, sometimes slowly, that the needs of the institution, not his welfare, are paramount. The final diagnosis results in a choice of prison and a custody classification. Many convicts report that they hoped that their educational and other deficiencies would at last be corrected. Irwin (1970) has commented on the six weeks of study at the center, and the consequent sense of injustice and disillusion among inmates. It seems reasonable to many Chicano youth that they have offended society, which results in a willingness to be studied by the doctors and to be corrected. This sense of penitence and confession appears to be strong among Chicano offenders; it may possibly grow from a traditionally Catholic sense of morality. (The notion of cleansing oneself by confession and penitence is often used deliberately by Los Angeles police officers in the process of interrogation.) For a while, many new pintos believe in the rightness, usefulness, and honesty of the work done in the Guidance Center.

Prison is the climax in a series of dealings with progressively more punitive institutional agencies, all of which depersonalize and compartmentalize the individual. All of them force long waits for inadequate services that are recognized as such by the client. So the journey to prison is not discontinuous with previous experiences. The crisis of imprisonment is not small, particularly in the barrio family network. But prison is no very big change for a man who walks a lifelong slack-wire between the highly personalized and emotionally consuming worlds of the barrio and of the institutional agencies.

Barrio Norms in Prison—and Some Abnormalities

We have shown that the concept of a total institution that strips the incoming prisoner of his identity is invalid, at least for the Los Angeles Chicano. Here we will show that prison operating norms are also familiar, and that they are enforced by familiar significant others. As one pinto has put it: "You deal with your own. You know from the outside who's who and where you fit. You are also known. You have your place when you go in. You don't go in trying to fit into an unknown status system." The same people, the same institutions, the same preoccupations, and the same norms of conduct, mutual evaluation, and self-esteem prevail.[10] Later we will note some exceptions, but the nature of pinto norms inside the prison are our first concern.

The barrio is the base of pinto norms. Both the prison groupings and the observable norms reflect, first, the preoccupation with leaving prison, and, second, the pressure of the homeboy peer group. In addition, pressures from the family and the women outside gives the pinto a strong sense that he is being watched, that his behavior inside prison will be judged and will have consequences for his fate after release.

Barrio Prestige

Each individual barrio has its own reputation, or prestige ranking in the prison. This is at least partly dependent on the size of the barrio. For Los Angeles, the gangs of Maravilla (El Hoyo, along with a half-dozen others) tend to dominate numerically and to form an alliance. The conflicts on the streets with gangs like White Fence tend to continue in the prison. In the youth prisons (Tracy, as an example), White Fence boys are often involved in incidents of violence. Sometimes these involve individual feuds. But more often the incidents involving White Fence men are a result of the street reputation of the barrio as a whole. EPT (convicts from El Paso, Texas) is another solid clique within the California prison system. Pintos from small towns often have no real homies in the prison; they are accepted or rejected on an individual basis. But generally, it is barrio homies who affected the convict in the past and will affect him in the future. These are the people who were crime partners or were jointly involved in the use, sale, and trafficking of narcotics. And they are people who can help or hinder the convict during his time in prison.

But the idea of barrio goes beyond merely a neighborhood, to include the entire *raza*. This is the concept of the Mexican American as a member of a special "race," with a distinctive heritage and a special destiny.

Mexico and Mexicanism is not far from the pinto. The rule of silence (the familiar convict code that forbids snitching) is already part of the street adaptation of Mexicans and part of their special experience with Anglo authority in the American Southwest. From this experience, many pintos have a strong sense of nationalism that often approaches a romanticization of Mexican culture. And then, among themselves, they have an equally strong sense that bringing down the flag, that is, bringing loss or disrepute to either the home barrio or *la raza*, is immoral. (Interestingly, many convicts' experiences in the armed forces clarify and intensify this feeling.)

Inmate Status

Barrio-based norms are also a significant source of inmate status. "You are known" from the barrio streets, and your reputation follows you into prison. In addition, the prisoners from each barrio are expected to help out others from that barrio. The ability to help and to provide resources becomes an asset in prison. These resources may grow from a position attained in the prison resource network, from particular skills (writ-writing, described in Chapter 6, is an example), or from access to outside resources.

Status-related behavior in the prison is also related to the crime pattern. For example, the very few professional criminals among Chicanos rarely mix with the Chicano population. The professionals tend largely to keep to themselves, doing their time "with the least amount of suffering and the greatest amount of comfort" (Irwin, 1970, p. 68). For prisoners with some prestige in the world of organized crime, prison is a time for laying low, for avoiding attention from the authorities, and for spending energy on getting out.

In contrast to the relatively petty scale of their typical crimes, the state-raised youth tend to assume a high visibility in the prison world. They wheel and deal. They dress better (because they care about appearance and have prison connections to get better clothes) and they may have a cluster of younger men who do their bidding without apparent question. These are personal, rather than barrio-related, cliques of younger men who are obligated to their leader for one reason or another. Such men often acquire the facility (rare among the average barrio-oriented Chicano convict) of relating to non-Chicanos, both in the administration and among the convicts. This is an asset in establishing connections in the prison.

But these men have little to hope for on the outside. Their youth has been spent learning to optimize their environment inside the camps, youth facilities, and prisons but nowhere else. This optimizing is very visible; to the outsider, they appear to be "influentials." But the barrio-based norms continue, and the ultimate grim fate of the state-raised youth is underscored in a series of sayings in Spanish that emphasize the implacability of the prison destiny.

Thus norms based on the barrio continue in prison for both social control and the allocation of respect. The outwardly influential appearance of the prison-wise convicts, who are usually state-raised, is one of the abnormalities of prison life.

Barrio Norms in the Institution

Of course, the operations of the institution modify the operation of barrio-based norms. The system is pervasive. It creates dependency, uncertainly, and the loss of important social skills (such as vocabulary) and a style that permits self-confident communication with squares and particularly with women. Convicts are trained into an incapacity to deal with the routines of normal street life and with real money, as apart from the barter economy. The management of anxiety about what is happening in the personal world of the convict outside of prison often combines with the constraints of the system to produce unrealistic, regressive, and dysfunctional adaptations that persist upon release. If everything else is held constant (which it is not), these adaptations will present serious problems after the release of the convict.

Barrio norms become more or less important from one time and place to another in the prison milieu (cf. Irwin on the stages of prison career during incarceration). Prison authorities try to minimize the operation of anything but institutional norms, but they are not very successful, at least with Chicanos. While most convicts are more likely to prepare for their appearances before the Adult Authority Parole Board by emphasizing a relationship with the appropriate institutional referees, the Chicano is always careful to reassert his barrio contacts—even though he is understandably anxious to impress the authorities that he is a good risk for parole. Transfer to another prison or release on parole is a time for the barrio to reassert its interest in communications and normative controls. The parolee is deluged with messages to and from the homies who are more aware that they are being watched, because their behavior will be reported to those outside. This pattern means that there is a periodic strengthening of barrio norms in any given spell of incarceration.[11]

As far as daily and weekly routines are concerned, there are in-between times and places where the prison administration has no effect whatever on the prisoner's behavior. It can give him a custody rating, which limits his access to other homies. A high custody rating means limited access.

But the convict's most important place is his own cell, and his most important person is his cellmate. The convict is locked up with his cellmate for twelve hours a day, from 6:00 P.M. until 6:00 A.M., unless he is attending prison-sanctioned evening functions. (Few Chicanos were programming in this fashion in the mid-1960s, the period we emphasize here.) The cell is tiny. If the cellmate is untrustworthy or even incompatible, life can be agony. Under the more stringent conditions of lockup (a condition that prevailed in most California medium and maximum security prisons during the mid-1970s), even longer periods are spent with the cellmate.

The prison atmosphere is tense. No exercise of prisoner social controls can do much to minimize this basic fact of life. A short period of the week—one day in the weekend—is the only time that can be anticipated as a period totally alone, a relief from the feeling of being crowded and the violation of personal space. But the cellmate can control this period. Cellmates negotiate which day, Saturday or Sunday, one man can go to the yard while the other stays in the cell for some much-needed privacy. This safety-valve can be disrupted by an inconsiderate "cellie."

The most desirable cellmate is a man that is known and trusted from life before prison. This would be a homeboy from the barrio or someone else with whom trust has been established. Cell changes can be negotiated with the administration by mutual request, but the process may be complex and slow. A man may change a cell by changing his programming (which automatically involves a shift in location in the prison), but he may have to use other resources, such as bribing an inmate clerk or making a direct complaint.

The famous yard at San Quentin (combined, the two yards are roughly the size of two football fields) has been an important place for establishing and maintaining social relations. For those convicts who have no work assignment (probably about 10 to 15 percent of the pintos, according to the LUCHA survey reproduced in Appendix B), the entire day is spent on the upper yard, gossiping and playing dominoes. Others are in the yard all day either Sunday or Saturday, and for up to an hour after breakfast and lunch every day.

It is in this place and at those times that the neighborhoods establish their territories and discuss the behavior of members. For some of the cliques, territories are guarded. A man from El Paso reports:

Any pinto who has done time in Quentin will tell you there was a place in the big yard "reserved" for EPT. No one, and I mean *no one*, was allowed to loiter there with us when we were there, and even when we were not there no one would stand in that particular place. It was known as "el ojo" and was situated along the North wall, right next to No. 4 guard shack.

Privacy of discussion can be maintained, however, even if a particular barrio does not claim territory, and policy decisions can be reached. White Fence, to name one group, was a minority barrio in the mid-1960s, with only about twenty members incarcerated. It was in San Quentin's upper yard that White Fence agreed not to engage in behavior that might cause the entire barrio to get involved in conflicts which could keep members in for longer periods. They agreed to back each other up in case of trouble, but not to create or exacerbate situations. It was in the lower yard that the discussions that led to the formation of the first Chicano culture group took place.[12]

The work setting is another place for both social interaction and development of resources. The kitchen, the laundry, any job that involves crossing the wall (such as the clothing factory), and the few clerical jobs held by Chicanos provide such resources. Custody ratings constrain access to such jobs. In spite of the generally high custody rating of the San Quentin population, a certain proportion of the prisoners held low custody ratings and did the work necessary to the prison in the off-reservation detail. Some of these men, for example, tended the gardens of prison officers who lived on the grounds but outside the walls of the prison.

To a lesser extent (because so few Chicanos were programming), the educational setting also provides a place for the operation of barrio norms. But the most important place and time for organized norms to operate is in the culture groups, which meet as voluntary associations in the evenings. (Chapter 6 gives a full account of this self-help movement among Chicano prisoners.)

Variations among Prisons

Yet more information about the salience of barrio norms comes from contrasts between prisons. Four prison culture groups answered a questionnaire that permits such a contrast. Three Southern California prisons, representing three of the five culture groups still functioning in mens' prisons by March, 1975, and one federal facility near Santa Barbara, responded (see Appendix C for details). There is no clear indication as to what kind of sample of pintos these data represent. The culture groups try to attract all Chicanos regardless of their geographical origin or other characteristics, but culture group officers acknowledge that they are most successful with the older, the more aware, or the convicts serving longer terms.

In two of these prisons (CRC, the civil committment center for addicts, and CIM, a pre-release and short-time prison), there is a fast turnover of inmates. In both prisons (Table 4) it is notable that com-

Table 4   Reference Group and Preoccupations of Culture Group Members,
               by Prison, 1975

Reference Group and Preoccupations	Prison			
	CRC* (%)	CIM† (%)	CCI‡ (%)	FCI§ (%)
How much are you staying with your own home group?				
Most of the time	49	30	62	66
Very little	43	60	32	19
Not at all	8	10	6	15
Total N (= 100%)	(31)	(20)	(34)	(32)
Greatest worry this time‖				
Family	58	64	57	63
Money	44	9	43	41
Prison officials	14	0	17	3
Doing time	11	18	20	16
Programs	8	9	23	3
Sex	8	9	6	0
Violence	6	9	14	3
Other	11	32	9	12
Total N (= 100%)	(36)	(22)	(35)	(32)

*California Rehabilitation Center, Corona, California, MAYO executive board.
†California Institution for Men, Chino, California, COPA members.
‡California Correctional Institution, Tehachapi, California, MACHO members.
§Federal Correctional Institution, Lompoc, California, PUMA members.
‖First two mentions combined. Some prisoners mentioned only one "greatest worry."

paratively few of the prisoners reported "staying with their home group" most of the time. However, in CCI (a minimum-security facility at Techachapi) and the federal maximum-security prison at Lompoc, two-thirds of the Chicano prisoners reported staying with their homies most of the time. It is also noteworthy that the inmates report that family and money are their two major preoccupations, an important corroboration of our suggestions about the continuities between barrio and prison. (Our earlier material comes from the maximum-security prison of San Quentin.) Continuity rather than discontinuity, barrio rather than prison, are the critical themes for understanding the effects of prison for a large proportion of the Chicano inmates. Variations in continuities or of the salience of the barrio norms can be understood in terms of prison setting and the prisoner career in that setting.

In any event, the Chicano inmate solidarity appears high compared with other prison populations. Carroll (1974) cites Clemmer's (1958) findings that only 18 percent of the prisoners were affiliated in primary groups, and Wheeler's (1961) finding that 43 percent of his sample were so affiliated.

Exceptions to Continuity

There are two types of prisoners who are relatively difficult to reach through the barrio social control system and its norms. The first type is state-raised youth (cf. Irwin, 1970).

State-raised youths represent a complete failure of all of the socializing institutions of the family and the neighborhood, as well as the state. These children of the state of California are a recognized social type in the prison population. Institutionalization begins at an early age for them, through a series of constantly changing foster homes, numerous trips to Juvenile Hall, supervision by probation officers, special treatment in special schools, and a special visibility to the police. All this is followed by nearly continuous residence in the facilities of the Youth and Adult Authorities.

The prison adaptations of the state-raised prisoners are conditioned by their fragile ties to the outside world of both the family and the barrio. Long institutionalization deprives them of some of the linkages to barrio groups that offer both moral and economic support to most pintos. When we talk about the continuity of prison and street life, we refer to norms that shape pinto behavior and are derived from gangs and the context of familistic Mexican neighborhoods. This is our heuristic norm, and what we believe to be operative norms for most Chicano convicts. However, for Chicano convicts who are state-raised, this norm is often perverted by long institutionalization. Their "barrio" is the prison faction, not the normal intermingling of square and deviant that we will discuss in Chapter 7.

For the normal barrio resident, the goal is to return to the barrio. Usually, no matter how remote the chances, he hopes to get a stable job, get married, have children, and assume a square identity. The normal pinto is painfully aware of the internal and external obstacles to such a goal, but he has real exemplars of the goal in his life on the streets. The state-raised youth has few such exemplars: he claims membership in a barrio gang that comes to life only in prison, and the normalizing influences of life in the free world are unreal to a man who has spent most of his life in institutions.

Generally, the state-raised youths lack the personal resources or the motivation to fit anywhere but at the bottom of the formal prison system. Often they are hostile to educational or training programs.

On the streets their poor education qualifies them only for the worst jobs, or unemployment. They are, however, prison-wise. As indicated earlier, the entrepreneurial among them can make out because their goals have been displaced from street to prison and their "bonaroos," or tailored and pressed prison uniforms, become a symbol of success.

The state-raised youths also represent a major source of violence among Chicanos in the prison. For them, the violence is related to the fact that they represent a deviant variation of pinto and barrio norms. Prison, rather than the streets, is their normal situation, no matter how little they like prison. In prison their immediate need is to make a reputation—and this may have deadly repercussions in the prison communities. The state-raised prisoners know how to maximize their resources inside, although they are rarely able to do this on the street. They know the correctional system thoroughly; they can manipulate the bureaucracy and find their way around convict gatekeepers. They also tend to follow styles of leadership from earlier years in state youth institutions. In these institutions, which are violent even compared to San Quentin, styles are based more on muscle than in the street gangs. In turn, they tend to find a ready group of followers among younger state-raised youths who are accustomed to this style. Thus their violence is related to norms that are based on a virtual lifetime of incarceration.

It is critical to note here that institutional bureaucrats and others outside the barrio network seldom distinguish between the state-raised pinto and the man whose involvement with gang activity is street-oriented. The treatment officials interviewed at San Quentin in 1970 were clearly aware of the differences between the EPT and other locality-based cliques in the Chicano population. But they do not distinguish between state-raised and barrio-raised youth. It is possible, in time, that this faulty perception may become a reality in the population mix of the prison and therefore, of the barrio itself. Tables 1 and 2 show that increasingly large proportions of gang youth are spending increasing lengths of time in juvenile institutions. Perhaps the state-raised orientation, rather than the barrio orientation, will mark the Chicano prisoner of the future. In any event, this will further increase the impact of the prison system on the barrios.

The second type of prisoner that is difficult to reach through the barrio social control system is what prisoners call the "psycho."

Men convicted of crimes of violence are sent to San Quentin. But a crime of violence can be many different things; a man convicted of murdering his wife is not likely to do it again. The prison system keeps the violent label for all future incarcerations, so the label may describe a man incarcerated on a narcotics charge, because his first felony conviction was for manslaughter.

But it may also include men whom the prisoner culture recognizes as psychotic; men from every ethnic background, some who were transferred from mental hospitals, and some who are periodically held for two or three months in the "psych" ward of the prison hospital. In the mid-1960s the "psychos" were routinely released into the general prison population until they showed signs of extreme disturbance. In recent years, tranquilizers have been used more frequently. The "psychos," who represent a source of unpredictable violence, are largely outside the influence of interpersonal networks. They contribute to the atmosphere of tension that most San Quentin ex-convicts report as almost tangible.

Mafia and Familia

In the 1970s, the California prisons saw the growth of two Chicano groups that the correctional system calls "inmate gangs": the Mexican Mafia and Nuestra Familia (cf. "Profile/California" *Corrections Magazine*, 1974). Both groups are composed primarily of state-raised men, the Mafia from Southern California and the Familia from Northern and Central California. Both are strong-arm gangs that use extreme violence in pursuit of power and economic control. It is very unfortunate that in both public and professional thinking they are confused with constructive Chicano prison groups.

Perhaps such carelessness is excusable in the Los Angeles press, but it is not excusable among professionals. One criminologist identifies them as the only national Chicano prisoner group "organized around race and ethnicity," and lists them coequally with such other destructive groups as the Aryan Brotherhood and constructive groups like the Black Muslims (Bowker, 1977, pp. 109–110). The author notes that the Mafia and the Familia are the only national groups to produce "sustained violence." Apparently he is unaware that the constructive Chicano self-help groups attempted to give themselves a uniform name—EMPLEO—but were not permitted to do so by the correctional system, and so thereby became local groups. Ironically, the corrections officials reasoned that to have culture groups with the same name in each prison would enhance tendencies toward militancy. Clearly neither the Mafia nor the Familia needed even the minimal official sanction that the culture groups required. Nonetheless, the culture groups managed to survive through the mid-1970s and were generally modelled on one organization (this is described in more detail in Chapter 6).

The origin of the Mafia and the Familia are perfectly understandable in the light of the Chicano prisoner cliques. They are composed of strong, barrio-oriented cliques, loners from smaller areas, cliques of state-raised men, and psychotic prisoners. The Mafia arose among state-raised youths and "psychos" because of the relative weakness of some cliques of outsiders in the underground prisoner economy. The Mafia's success stems from the prison-centeredness of the state-raised prisoners.

The key question is, of course, why does the California prison system produce an underground economy? First, simply because money is scarce. Even for the San Quentin prisoners who work, the rate of pay is extremely low, especially for the poorly educated, many of whom are Chicanos. Many state-raised men and "psychos" receive no funds from the outside world whatsoever, because their families (if they still exist) do not send money. Yet money is absolutely necessary to buy personal items like cigarettes, toilet articles, snacks, drugs, and liquor. It is needed to bribe convicts who can supply some prison amenities. Finally, money is often urgently needed for the family outside. Second, California prisons have a corruptible staff who send and receive illegal goods. Third, there are compliant convicts (not actually involved) who can be employed to hold money or cigarettes (or other goods important in the barter economy) to ensure their availability for the purchase of goods outside the immediate sphere of the prisoner's operation, for the payment of transportation, and for emergencies.

These economic activities are, in fact, little more than an extension of the outside world of the pinto. Those pintos with fewer resources from family or other outside sources tend to have a greater investment in manipulating the prisoner economy. Resources are the major preoccupation of resource-poor state-raised men, and the main foundation of their influence in cliques of other resource-poor inmates. However, there are always some men who are excluded from even these cliques.

The Mafia and Familia began when a group of state-raised men from Los Angeles and some "psychos" began to strong-arm Chicano loners and Chicano prisoners from small towns and rural areas who did not belong to strong barrio cliques. In response, older Chicanos from Los Angeles and northern California joined to protect the victims. The "M" (or "Eme," originally meaning "Mafia" but soon to be glorified as "*El Mejicano Encarcelado*") accepted this as a challenge and stepped up their attacks. The men from the northern and rural areas formed Neustra Familia and the war was on. Normal barrio controls were ineffective against this new organization.

By the mid-1970s, the Adult Authority was segregating men from each gang—the Mafia into San Quentin and the Familia into Soledad—and even sending them in separate waves to the pre-release center.[13] On the streets, the Mafia attempted to use its prison-based organization to move into the narcotics market in East Los Angeles, and also, reputedly, into some legitimate pinto-serving community agencies.[14]

Both the Mafia and the Familia began in the prisons, their origins are rooted in the practices of American prisons, and they grew strong among men who have been imprisoned most of their lives. Their tactics of intimidation and the predictable countermeasures of the prison authorities began to dominate Chicano life in the prisons. The more barrio-oriented prisoners simply became as inconspicuous as possible in order to avoid involvement.

Although both "super gangs" are Chicano, there is little ideology behind their activity. Indeed, members of the surviving culture groups view these groups as destructive of their legitimate goals of persuading inmates to build up strength for a square outside life. Many of the victims of Chicano prison violence are themselves Chicanos. The Mafia motives are pecuniary—dominance of the underground prison economy and, ultimately, of the illegal economy of the streets. No serious culture groups could condone such ends.

The California correctional system describes its various attempts to deal with the "violence of Chicano gangs," but it does not mention their roots in the prison economy, nor does it note the membership of state-raised convicts. Davidson (1974) makes the link to the prison economy, but in a simplistic manner that glamorizes the Mafia as a movement-oriented group (see the prisoner critique, Chicano Pinto Research Project, 1975a).

At present there is no basis for estimating the size of these groups. Some newspaper and magazine articles suggest 150 full members and "about 700 or 800 hangers-on" (*New West*, Dec. 19, 1977), a figure probably obtained from the corrections system. Because most Chicano convicts (and Mafia members) are heroin addicts, Chicano ex-prisoners think it very unlikely that, once released, these addicts can be disciplined by the Mafia, no matter how efficient they may be inside prison where they are relatively "clean." It will be difficult to build a "killer bureaucracy" on the model of the Italian Mafia if "hangers-on" are unstable, unreliable street addicts. It is worth noting that the "super gangs" won no significant following in federal prisons as late as 1975. Yet the federal prisons hold the much more important "big time" Chicano drug dealers. They show very little activity in the underground economy and here it appears that prison policy does make a difference. Federal prisons give prisoners "real pay" and thereby change the meaning of prison for even the resource-poor state-raised youth.

The Search for Resources Inside Prison

In a general way, we have noted the continuities between prison life and barrio life. If there are real and important continuities, then their extent can be traced in some specific questions about resources that were asked the Chicano culture groups. Our material up to this point has been based largely on documents from pintos and on discussions and focussed seminars inside and outside prison, but concentrating on the specific milieu of San Quentin. We can now broaden our consideration of barrio influences by drawing on data from questionnaires administered in four prisons by our project (see Appendix C for details).

The first set of questions concerned two types of problems, concrete and personal, inside prison. Then we examined the prisoners' expectations about resources that will be available when they leave prison.

Cell and Job Assignments

Inside prison, the problems of getting a cell change and getting a more desirable job placement are critical to the prisoner. We noted earlier that the institution itself constrains the search for resources. We will limit ourselves to the effects of two factors: type of prison and length of time served. These factors recognize the importance of the individual prison milieu and the "prisonization" effect (i.e., time served).

Most of the convicts were repeaters—only a quarter of them were serving their first sentence, if one counts time in Juvenile Hall or Youth Authority prisons (see Appendix C). Yet it is still necessary to learn one's way around a particular prison. Obviously, a number of other factors than prison and length of time served go into the prisoner's resource search—his particular barrio connections, his involvement with hard drugs, the norms of the particular barrio with regard to suspicion of outside resources, and age.

However, it is clear that the length of time served has a strong impact on resource search with regard to cell change and job placement (Table 5). The institution tends to diminish in usefulness, especially for the cell change, as does the inmate's sense that "nobody" can help him. He finds his way around the inmate network, largely among the convict gate-keepers ("other inmates" and "exchanging goods"), but also tends to find barrio friends useful in his search. This is especially true in the later years (five or more years on the current sentence).

The prison effect is less clear. Each prison has its reputation. The federal institutions (like the one at Lompoc, in the survey) are reputed to be cleaner, less tense, and less violent. Men can earn money toward their release date and are not burdened with the recurrent drama of the Parole Board hearing created by the indeterminate sentence in effect in California at the time of our study.

The state prison reputation tends to reflect some of the rehabilitative intent of the system, ranging from the deadly bleakness of Folsom (the prison of old men), to the drugged depression of CMC East, to the wild violence of the young men in Tracy. Each prison is intended by the administration to create a different milieu: age grading and offense are intended to separate the hardened habitual criminal from the youthful offender, and the violent from the less violent. (This follows Suther-

Table 5   Percent of Culture Group Members Who Perceive Various Resources as Helpful in Meeting Prison Needs, by Time Served on Current Offense and by Prison, 1975

Sources of help	Time served on current offense			Prison			
	Less than 1 year (%)	1–5 years (%)	5 or more years (%)	CRC* (%)	CIM† (%)	CCI‡ (%)	FCI§ (%)
Obtaining a cell change							
Nobody helps	16	10	9	3	14	14	19
Barrio friends	9	8	21	3	5	25	19
Other inmates	19	25	47	33	41	46	9
Exchanging goods	6	5	15	0	14	26	0
Institution	53	55	31	44	23	51	50
Job placement							
Nobody helps	12	12	6	3	4	14	19
Barrio friends	38	18	30	22	4	29	47
Other inmates	19	30	43	28	41	43	19
Exchanging goods	6	5	15	0	14	26	0
Institution	28	30	25	28	18	46	16
Total N (= 100%)	(32)	(40)	(47)	(36)	(22)	(35)	(32)

*California Rehabilitation Center, Corona, California.
†California Institution for Men, Chino, California.
‡California Correctional Institution, Tehachapi, California.
§Federal Correctional Institution, Lompoc, California.
NOTE: Figures represent the number of men who checked a resource as "helpful" as a percent of the total number of group members.

land's theory of differential association, but has some unintentional effects. The Adult Authority youth institution at Tracy has a horrendous reputation for violence, because the youngsters with no pinto experience endlessly act out their notion of prison life. One of the project staff from White Fence recalls being asked to transfer to Tracy when he was in his thirties in order to help influence some of the younger people from his own barrio to reduce the violence.)

Among the institutions surveyed, the federal institution near Santa Barbara at Lompoc (FCI-maximum facility) and the state institution at the mountains at Tehachapi (CCI-minimum facility) are reasonably normal representatives of their respective systems. CIM and CRC, however, are both anomalous. The California Institution for Men at Chino is largely an institution for transients, most of whom have done the major part of their sentences at other institutions and at the time of our study expected a relatively short stay before their release to parole in Southern California. Some inmates were serving their full sentences at CIM, but they tended to have specialized skills, such as meatcutting, that are necessary to run the institution. In addition, at the time of the survey the prison held a number of "ninety-day dry-outs," addicts and alcoholics who were returned to prison from parole for a ninety-day observation. The nearby California Rehabilitation Center is the "hospital" for addicts, where sentences for civil commitments vary from time to time as the correctional system struggles to make some kind of rehabilitative sense out of the absurd laws that put addicts into their custody. At the time of the survey most inmates were in CRC for six- to nine-month terms.

The theme of peer-group reliance is reiterated when we look at prison variations in resource search (Table 6). The effect of the federal system is notable in the responses to the question about cell change: a very high proportion of prisoners at Lompoc turn to the institution. This is also true at Tehachapi, but an equally high proportion at that state prison find help from other inmates and barrio friends, which is not true at Lompoc. Except at Tehachapi, barrio friends and other inmates almost supplant the institutional sources to get placed in prison jobs. This is true even at the short-term CRC, where repeated incarcerations are common enough to allow the convict to adapt readily to inmate culture.

Personal Problems and Stress

Turning to personal problems, the reliance on barrio friends and other prisoners for help increases notably with time in prison (Table 6). We note especially that inmates tend to stop handling their problems by themselves (turning to "nobody") as their time in prison increases. It means that true relationships are formed and the personal reticence of the first year gradually tends to break down. Only a quarter of the men

Table 6 Percent of Culture Group Members Who Perceive Various Resources as Helpful with Personal Problems and Most Important in Stress, by Time Served on Current Offense and by Prison, 1975

Sources of help	Time served on current offense			Prison			
	Less than 1 year (%)	1–5 years (%)	5 or more years (%)	CIM† (%)	CRC* (%)	CCI‡ (%)	FCI§ (%)
Personal problems							
Nobody helps	53	35	28	42	27	31	41
Barrio friends	28	22	40	25	23	40	34
Other inmates	12	18	21	11	14	31	12
Exchanging goods	9	2	6	0	9	17	0
Institution	12	18	15	6	27	23	9
Total N (= 100%)	(32)	(40)	(47)	(36)	(22)	(35)	(32)
Stress							
Friends	45	54	36	33	32	37	53
Drugs	23	35	36	36	5	31	16
Psychiatrist	0	3	10	3	0	6	6
Clergy	12	7	5	11	0	6	3
Group therapy	8	10	0	8	0	6	0
Total N (= 100%)	(26)	(31)	(36)	(36)	(22)	(35)	(32)

*California Rehabilitation Center, Corona, California.
†California Institution for Men, Chino, California.
‡California Correctional Institution, Tehachapi, California.
§Federal Correctional Institution, Lompoc, California.
NOTE: Figures represent the number of men who checked a resource as "helpful" as a percent of the total number of group members.

serving five or more years continue to try to handle their problems by themselves. Institutional sources of help are insignificant at any point in the man's sentence. In response to another question about the functions of therapy in prison, only about 15 percent felt it helped with problems. The overwhelming majority felt that it either does nothing "or is designed to make you conform to the institution."[15]

Stress is a different matter. Stress refers to the real personal crises almost all prisoners experience some point during their stay in prison. In coping with stress, even among the newer inmates, "friends" or "drugs" are the overwhelming choices. This preference shifts only slightly in importance among those who have done more time and as reliance on the institutional resources of group therapy and clergy tend to decline. Some of the inmates with longer time admit using psychiatric help. These admissions are hard-won, indicating that the man has reached the limits both of self-reliance and of the abilities of his *raza* and barrio friends.

Differences between the prisons are not easily explained, except that for ordinary personal problems, the barter economy can help in the two regular California prisons. It is noteworthy how often the convicts at isolated Lompoc prison turn to each other when under stress. The availability of drugs at CRC and Tehachapi is also remarkable. Even at Lompoc, more prisoners turn to drugs for stress than to psychiatric help. Although our question did not distinguish between illicit drugs and tranquilizers, both types are available in these institutions.[16] This reliance on drugs is a damning indictment of the prison system, especially in view of the high proportion of these men (50 to 72 percent) who have histories of heroin addiction outside prison.

The Search for Resources Outside Prison

Our respondents were active members of Chicano culture groups in the four prisons. At the very least, this means that they wanted to prepare themselves for an adequate (drug- and crime-free) life outside. Prison tends, however, to have reinforced their long-range skepticism about institutional resources, so they turn to the inmate culture rather than to institutions to meet their personal needs. These tendencies increase with the length of sentence served, and vary only slightly from one prison to another, despite vast differences among the prisons in programs and general ambience.

Looking forward to the outside is difficult for a prisoner. He tends to become immersed in fantasies about his future life, even if he has experienced the shock of failure and reincarceration more than once before. Making realistic plans, and realistic organization of means to reach those plans, is difficult. More than a quarter of the prisoners said that they did not know what goals they wanted to pursue in prison to prepare themselves for the outside. We chose two sets of problems: finding a job and getting moral support. These are counterparts of the prison problems of cell and job assignment and personal and stress problems. And we asked what resources they felt would be most useful to them when they left prison.

Job Search

What emerged most strikingly is the overwhelming reliance of the pintos on family and friends to find them a job—and their faith that someone will help them (Table 7). The length of time served on their present sentence has little clear effect on their expectations. There is one exception; the longer the incarceration, the less a man depends on his parole officer to find a job. The scattering of responses to this question probably reflects the resources of the different culture groups, rather than the reality of the job market. Each group has an official who is responsible for job development. His contacts are limited, being confined to those outside groups which are willing to correspond with him. At the time of our study, only one or two community groups did correspond or go inside with any regularity. Thus it seems reasonable that the pintos should rely considerably on contacts available to the culture group to supplement their own personal sources because, in fact, the culture group is usually the only direct contact. Further, the pattern of response probably reflects the hopes and efforts of culture group members (or respondents) who are trying more strenuously than most convicts to relate realistically with the outside world. It is plain that for most convicts, this world has ceased to have much reality.

In studying the differences between prisons, we must remember that CRC and CIM are filled with men near their release time. It is at CIM that the men were most actively searching for jobs. Their generally low opinion of the available sources of help probably reflects a greater awareness of the very poor job situation that they, as well as other convicts, face. However, it should also be noted that their low opinion of family as a source of help is related to the fact that relatively few pintos have outside ties (see Appendix C). It is also notable that the men at CRC believe more in the helpfulness of the parole agent than do inmates at other prisons. These are special units where the men have "outpatient" status, making it likely that they receive more understanding from their parole officers than do most ex-offenders.

Moral Support

Moral support is important to the newly released convicts, as most of these men know from direct experience with the transition from

Table 7 Percent of Culture Group Members Who Expect Various Resources to be Most Helpful in Obtaining Jobs, by Time Served on Current Offense and by Prison, 1975

Most important expected source of help	Time served on current offense			Prison			
	Less than 1 year (%)	1–4 years (%)	5 or more years (%)	CRC* (%)	CIM† (%)	CCI‡ (%)	FCI§ (%)
Family	57	57	55	58	18	54	72
Friends	31	37	21	25	18	34	37
Community agency	41	35	53	44	36	54	34
Convict serving agency	37	30	51	47	27	40	37
Parole officer	25	20	17	36	9	23	3
No one	3	22	2	8	4	3	19
Total N (= 100%)	(32)	(40)	(47)	(31)	(20)	(34)	(32)

*California Rehabilitation Center, Corona, California.
†California Institution for Men, Chino, California.
‡California Correctional Institution, Tehachapi, California.
§Federal Correctional Institution, Lompoc, California.

prison to the free world. It is particularly important for the heroin addict. Family and friends are the major expected sources. The longer the time served, the more they tend to rely upon friends—and this is realistic, for them (Table 8).

When prisons are compared, the drug offenders at CRC (many of whom are on short sentences after periods of addiction in the recent past) show the least reliance on their families. (This may be caused by a combination of factors. The high recidivism may mean they have exhausted family resources. They may also have an addicted wife who is actually a threat, rather than a support, to morale.) The high proportion at Tehachapi (CCI) who rely on their friends is consonant with earlier responses. This is the prison in which a very high proportion of pintos stay with their homies "most of the time." At the time of our survey, the culture groups at Tehachapi were very cohesive. Peer group support thus may have been especially important in this isolated prison.

The Total Institution Reconsidered

There is no question, even after the necessary cautions for our survey, that these men rely more on their peer and primary group resources than on the resources given through the correctional system. These institutional resources are expensive, and the men in the survey are probably the most sophisticated Chicano users of the available resources. Even more significantly, reliance on peer and primary groups tends to increase with the length of sentence. This tendency varies somewhat from one prison to another, but it is consistent. This parallels other findings that show increased orientation to the prisoner subculture with longer confinements (Bowker, 1977, pp. 20, 55).[17]

The pintos in the survey are men in self-motivated culture groups who stimulate and encourage each other to "do good"—to avoid criminality in their own lives and to help other Chicano convicts and the Chicano people in general. It is not possible to interpret their peer group dependency as a persistence in bad associates. Rather it appears to be the inevitable social consequence of their lives in the world of the barrio and the abnormal prison situation. For them, the self-help movement discussed in the next chapter provides a constructive and fruitful approach. It draws on normal peer group dependency and is—or was—unequivocally rehabilitative in motivational intent, no matter how petty its operations may have seemed.

Our view of prisoner adaptations (or the prisoner subculture, if this term is preferred) complements the tendency in recent criminological analysis to focus on prison as an inextricable part of the social system, rather than as an isolated (if expensive) adjunct to the society that has

Table 8   Percent of Culture Group Members Who Expect Various Resources to be Most Helpful in Moral Support After Release, by Time Served on Current Offense and by Prison, 1975

Most important expected source of help	Time served on current offense			Prison			
	Less than 1 year (%)	1–4 years (%)	5 or more years (%)	CRC* (%)	CIM† (%)	CCI‡ (%)	FCI§ (%)
Family	78	72	75	58	68	74	94
Friends	22	35	45	17	32	60	25
Community agency	37	22	28	39	14	20	31
Convict serving agency	28	18	26	31	4	23	28
Parole officer	9	15	4	22	9	3	0
No one	6	10	4	14	0	0	9
Total N (= 100%)	(32)	(40)	(47)	(31)	(20)	(34)	(32)

*California Rehabilitation Center, Corona, California.
†California Institution for Men, Chino, California.
‡California Correctional Institution, Tehachapi, California.
§Federal Correctional Institution, Lompoc, California.

impact only on the individual prisoner. We are interested in the valid but usually unavailable collective life experiences of men in prison.

Two recent prison studies by white anthropologists are badly flawed methodologically.[18] But they raise major substantive issues in the older criminological controversy as to whether inmate culture is imported or is endogenous to the prison. Carroll (1974) summarizes the arguments:

> The major premise of the deprivation (i.e. endogenous) model is that inmate subculture and social organization are collective functional responses to the deprivations imposed by incarceration. Sykes and Messinger identified five such pains of imprisonment: loss of freedom, deprivation of material comfort, loss of autonomy, denial of heterosexual contact, and physical insecurity. To this list McCorkle and Korn have added rejection by society. . . . Inmate solidarity is one means by which the pain may be reduced for the greatest number. . . . Implicit in this model is a conception of the prison as a closed system, a total institution impermeable to influence from the outside. The inmate culture emerges through the interaction of prisoners within the walls and new prisoners are socialized into it. Predisposing inmates to the socialization process is a ritual series of degradations that is part of the formal induction into the prison. Through such defilements pre-prison identities are extinguished. (P. 3.)

To this view Carroll contrasts what he calls the "importation model," most clearly expressed by Irwin and Cressey (1962). This approach argues that the inmate culture "is imported into the prison through the interaction of people from similar backgrounds in the face of common problems to which they must adapt" (p. 4).

Carroll's interest is in race, and race relations in a specific type of prison. He argues generally that solidarity of white inmates historically had been a response to the prison itself (i.e. endogenous), and had been eroded by a new treatment orientation, but that the solidarity of black prisoners was an importation, largely through black consciousness-raising or revolutionary groups.

Although he acknowledges the importance of previous crime partnerships, Carroll is primarily concerned with the effect of ideologies on race relations in the prison, rather than with more routine kinds of pre-prison relationships and expectations among blacks as these impinge on the prisoners' reconstructions of a survivable world. Both Carroll with blacks and Davidson with Chicanos present prison as a society of strangers.

In every respect except his emphasis on ethnic identity, Davidson (in a book that is largely accepted by such white criminologists as Bowker, 1977) assumes that the convict social structure is endogenous to the prison, and that prior roles and norms are irrelevant to Chicano pinto behavior. Davidson dismisses ties to the barrio as no longer viable or important at the time of his study.

Partly because of this book, we focussed our San Quentin analysis on that same time period when he was visiting the prison—the 1960s. Apparently Davidson was talking to Mafia founders and to other state-raised youth, then far from a majority. He grossly misinterprets the Mafia as being both benevolent and effective. It is odd that he also almost dismisses the position of the convict in the formal social structure (job assignment, program, proximity to release) as important in understanding the convict social structure. Davidson sees the pinto social structure as confined to the prison, and having endogenous values and norms of conduct.

Some people associated with our project who were in San Quentin at the time were also Davidson's informants. They remember him as useful to some cliques, but to others he appears as a funny, frightened, and rather obvious butt for outrageous stories. (The pinto critique of Davidson is detailed in Chicano Pinto Research Project, 1975a, and is predictably angry.)

American Urban Gulag

One of the most interesting and frightening implications of our research is the very real possibility that, for stable urban populations with high incarceration rates over a period of time, there is a gulag situation. Solzhenitsyn (1974–75, pp. 626–7) comments, "We Soviet people stepped upon the soil of the Archipelago spiritually disarmed . . . already tinged by it out in freedom, and we strained from the old camp veterans 'how to live in camp.' " With few modifications, many Chicanos and blacks can say much the same today. The dimensions of prison are at least as well known prior to incarceration as are the trials and hazards of going to Europe among young middle-class Anglos. This is clear from the interviews of gang members gathered by our researchers. And, ultimately, an urban gulag is the unmistakable implication of the academic interest in the dispute about prison continuities versus endogenous culture.

Continuities and Parallels

Just as Ianni (1974) emphasizes the pre-prison male networks, we have traced the continuity of the same kind of male networks out of the community and into prison. Ianni's interest is mainly in what he believes to be the emerging hegemony of minorities in the drug rackets of New York. Our interest is different, although the Mafia and Familia super gangs at times seem to take Ianni as their guide, and although there is little doubt that even less ambitious criminal coalitions are often generated or reinforced in prison. We are concerned with longer and deeper continuities that go back to conventional, or square, identities.

Unlike other students of prisoner life, we feel that something beyond the male networks should be considered. It is at least as interesting theoretically and even more important from the point of view of policy to account for *conventional* as well as the criminal norms of conduct among men and women convicted of felonies. For prisoners of Latin descent, especially the Chicano, the street continuity is further enhanced by the importance of the *compadrazgo* relationship (ritual godparenthood), and by the entire community and near-familistic context within which the male networks function on the streets.

Finally, we must consider racism. More than half of the inmates in the California system are non-Anglo. Much has been written about racism in prison (Jackson, 1970; Cleaver, 1968; Wright, 1973), almost entirely from the perspective of the black prisoner. Yet the extent to which racism and racial or ethnic identity is an issue of serious proportions for the Chicano population of the Southwest and the Midwest (and the Puerto Rican people of the East and Midwest) is evident. Certainly the Chicano pinto's experiences with racism are overlooked, even among those studies dealing primarily with California prisons (cf. Wright, 1973; Irwin, 1970).

We suggest, therefore, that there are three important sources of continuity for minority—and especially Chicano—prisoners. The first of these is their strong affiliation with local neighborhood networks, primarily the localized fighting gangs, whose members provide anticipatory socialization for each other on the streets and serve as a primary group within the prisons. The second is some degree of normative continuity with the larger neighborhoods from which the gang members derive. Third is a degree of continuity with the special experiences of minorities with institutional agencies and racism.

Although we opened this chapter by considering certain parallels between street experiences and prison experiences, it is also true that parallels are analytically distinct from continuities. All Chicano prisoners take the continuities for granted. Yet in their thinking about the parallels, some of our ex-convict Chicano researchers went beyond questions of the individual coping with the prison, into collective modes of coping not only with prison but with post-prison experiences. This is the core of interest in the Chicano self-help movement, which we will discuss in the next chapter.

Chicano
Self-Help

THE CHICANO PINTO self-help movement appeared in the early 1960s in California prisons and lasted through the late 1970s, both in prisons and on the streets. To its members, it is called the pinto movement. We will examine in detail its forerunners, its early problems, the structure of the typical group, its continuing problems, and its effect on ex-convict life on the streets of East Los Angeles.

The pinto movement is part of both the larger Chicano movement (which it preceded) and the national prisoner self-help movement. Usually the pinto phase is ignored, probably because of a typical interest in broad political changes for Chicanos. (An exception is Moore, 1972, which ties the pinto movement into the broader changes.) The more general prisoner self-help movement among blacks received much publicity, while the Chicano counterparts of such groups as the Black Muslims and the Black Panthers (or even the Puerto Rican Young Lords) were almost unnoticed. Eloquent as they were, the Chicano protesters failed to reach the mass audiences of Cleaver, Jackson, and others. It should also be noted how strongly the self-help groups confirm our argument in Chapter 5 about the importance of imported prison culture. Born in prison, and rooted in the square continuities of pre-prison life, the self-help movement was to move out of the prisons and back into the streets.

What is Self-Help?

The Chicano self-help groups are all too frequently confused with other types of Chicano (or black) organizations. Neither the Mexican Mafia nor the black Symbionese Liberation Army is a self-help group, although both began in prison.

Inside prison, the self-help groups are officially recognized as organizations that meet at specified times in the week in order to pursue individual and collective self-improvement goals. Both the goals and the means to the goals are established by the prisoners. Thus there have long been self-help groups in prison, but it is only recently that minority prisoners like blacks and Chicanos were allowed to organize on the basis of minority identity. Minority self-help groups consciously emphasize ethnic themes to draw in and motivate individual prisoners. In most prisons they are called culture groups to distinguish them from those self-help groups (like Dale Carnegie) that are based on nonethnic principles.

On the barrio streets there have been ex-convict self-help groups operating without funding, and funded organizations that operate on self-help principles (the former type is discussed in Moore, 1972). Funded organizations working on self-help principles are like the familiar poverty agencies, but with some important differences. They serve Chicano addicts and convicts, and not only employ ex-convict counsellors, but set policy with a degree of decision-making input in the administration or the board of directors. There have been many addict-serving groups which hire pinto counsellors, but do not allow them access to decision-making (cf. Bullington, 1977, and Munn, et al., 1972, on the operations of such an agency in Los Angeles).

The important points about self-help groups, either in prison or on the streets, are: they are legitimate; they use ethnic solidarity and ideology in the service of self-development; and they require that prisoners and ex-prisoners actively participate, by making decisions, in their own rehabilitation (see Goldfarb and Singer, 1973, on the consistent incapacity of the correctional system to provide this last, essential service). It is true that self-help groups have occasionally come to be dominated by illegitimate subgroups with revolutionary or criminal intent, but none of these are pinto movement organizations. This is a critical distinction because both the correctional system and the complex bureaucracies that serve East Los Angeles have played consistently on the general public ignorance of such organizations—and their own confusions—to oppose both the establishment of self-help organizations and their continued existence.

Documenting the Self-Help Movement

It is easy to understand why the self-help movement among black and Chicano prisoners has been neglected in prison studies (cf. Bowker, 1977) and popular books (cf. Mitford, 1974; Wicker, 1975). There are obvious problems of access and serious problems of meaning. A typical prison meeting might consist of a dozen or two dozen men struggling through parliamentary procedure, hearing committee reports on, for example, how an upcoming Chicano holiday is to be celebrated, or the details on getting a band for some upcoming event. The meeting may be sharpened by an outside visitor, who reports on how an organization is working in the barrios. If the prisoners are lucky, the visiting group may include one or two pretty Chicanas who will flirt with them over coffee. It does not appear exciting to the outsider.

But for many of these men such a meeting represents a major change in life style. Barrio gang boys are not trained in public speaking, in parliamentary procedure, or in the writing of reports—especially not on their own volition. Such activities are viewed as boring, rather effeminate and "Anglo," and also totally beyond the capacity of the gang-oriented Chicano. The next step (and an important incentive) in some prisons has been to permit this internal training to be put to public use. The McNeil Island federal prison, for example, had teams of prisoners lecturing in Seattle high schools, especially to young Chicanos.

Thus the prison self-help groups offered a major, self-initiated change in life style, within a legitimate public context invariably turned to altruistic purposes.

The linkage with the Chicano movement already in full swing outside in the barrios gave many prisoners a full, and often important, participating role. Possibly for the first time in their lives, it gave them a participant role with square people. One example will suffice. After the bloody riots of August 1970 in East Los Angeles, there were plans to cancel the traditional Mexican Independence Day celebrations on September 15 and 16 because of the tension in the community. Then a pinto organization intervened. The group offered to provide security for the Grito (the evening celebrations of the fifteenth) and for the parade on the 16th of September. Then the group marshalled the services and organized some 150 to 200 ex-convicts in the community (all of them vouched for by personal acquaintance and also by their participation in prison self-help groups). Without their work as monitors, the parade would not have taken place. This incident dramatically emphasizes the kind of participation and recognition that the pinto movement provided for its members. Many men's lives were changed by this kind of activity.

This rather dramatic effect of the prison self-help groups is worth discussion in itself, but there is also an important analytic purpose. We argue at the close of Chapter 5 that it is just as important to analyze the sources of conventional behavior as it is to analyze the sources of deviant behavior. Following this point, we see that the self-help movement represented a major desire among Chicano prisoners for their constructive potential to be recognized and developed. The movement is an effort to find a way of attaining conventionality.

Forerunners of the Pinto Movement

The Writ-Writers

The Chicano jailhouse lawyers or writ-writers (as they are known in prison) are the predecessors of the more generalized pinto movement. The growth of this activity is worth some attention.

Once incarcerated, many convicts begin to think clearly about their legal cases, and the quality of their legal representation, for the first time.[1] In general, the discussions with other prisoners focus on such issues as the violation of constitutional rights (for example, illegal police methods ignored by the trial courts, and the disregard of individual rights for the sake of judicial convenience), the persistent practice of sentencing on the basis of prior records, and the pervasive feeling that the severity of the sentence is disproportionate to the seriousness of the crime. These are longstanding themes, especially among minority prisoners.

While prisoner grievances are often diffuse, many are specific and legally viable. In the 1960s and 1970s, the nation's courts began to respond to writs charging mistreatment of prisoners and miscarriages of justice at the time of trial and sentencing (cf. Goldfarb and Singer, 1973, chapter 8, for one of the few detailed general treatments of prisoner legal activity).

By 1975 the efforts of prisoners to free themselves by filing writs had become a major activity. Chief Justice Burger of the U.S. Supreme Court noted that by 1974 three-quarters of all convicted persons in the nation's prisons were appealing their cases.[2] They accounted for 18 percent of all civil actions filed in federal district courts. This is a notable increase over the one-third that had been appealing ten years earlier (*Los Angeles Herald Examiner*, April 6, 1975). Many writ-writers feel that the inspiration for prisoners in California came especially from the example of Caryl Chessman, who fought his case for ten years during the 1950s while he was held in San Quentin's death row. Certainly the vast increase in the number of cases reflects a greater receptivity on the part of the courts. This happened in 1969, when a landmark decision (*Johnson* v. *Avery*, 393 U.S. 483) released a Tennessee inmate writ-writer from solitary confinement and, through a series of subsequent cases, won prisoners the right of access to law books and the right to help each other in obtaining access to court. This decision was critical, because prison administrators generally counter the activities of writ-writers with punishment, ridicule, harassment, and by providing inadequate facilities or no facilities at all. They also place obstacles to filing writs (for example, withholding correspondence privileges). In the mid-1970s, the *Johnson* v. *Avery* decision still was not followed in many state and federal prisons, and writ-writers continued to face ridicule and depreciation. In 1977, the Supreme Court ruled that prisons must provide either law libraries or personal legal assistance to inmates seeking legal relief.

Chicano writ-writers became visible to the national law enforcement community through the familiar Miranda warnings, which are based on a successful pinto appeal.[3] So writ-writing long preceded the Chicano self-help groups. At each prison there may be several Chicanos among the writ-writers, each of them with several research assistants. Later it became directly related to the self-help movement. Often Chicano culture groups will have a legal component which channels and manages potential appeals. One such appeal from McNeil Island (Salvador Pulido, 298 F. Supp. 795) resulted in the release of a man illegally convicted for a twenty-year term with no parole. Pulido served ten years of the term before the court responded to the out-of-time appeal by appointing counsel to represent him and ruling that he had indeed been convicted illegally. It ordered that the indictment be dismissed and Pulido released.

Writ-writing has a number of positive effects, especially for minority convicts. First, it tends to counter some of the alienation of the repeater convicts, who may be particularly susceptible to a passive acceptance of their fate.

Second, the men doing legal research must upgrade themselves educationally. Often this education (and the motivation for education after release) is really the only benefit, but it is still important.

The third positive function is concerned with issues of social organization of convict life. Although writ-writers may start their work with the single selfish motivation of seeking their own release, they are also helping other convicts help themselves, and have firmly established the idea that self-help is useful and practical. Lengthy incarceration does not offer much incentive for developing a new life style. There is, however, an incentive to seek release by petitioning the courts. The writ-writers who undertake this long and tedious chore learn both the legal process and self-discipline. It gives them a sense of self-worth, accomplishment, and purpose.

The writ-writer's sense of self-worth is echoed in his prestige in the convict community, and by the constant ridicule from the prison administration. Although writ-writers usually take lower-paying prison jobs (because they take up less time), and rarely have time for socializing with fellow convicts, a code of ethics has developed to match their paraprofessional prestige. Good writ-writers refuse pay for their services, are selective in their cases, and otherwise behave remarkably like the legal professional in the outside world.

Both the work and the importance of the writ-writers generally escapes the attention of the general public and those who study convicts (Goldfarb and Singer, 1973, represent a rare exception). Writ-writers are known only to the courts, to lawyers, and to the men who keep them in prison. Most professionals depreciate their work as unprofessional, forgetting the adverse circumstances and the limited resources of prison life. There is also some degree of vested interest in this depreciation; writ-writers exist because many convicts feel their legal counsel was inept. A proportion of these writs are successful, and the very effort of preparing them is constructive; this challenges both legal professionals and the ability of the correctional system to meet its own standards.

Although writ-writers work across ethnic lines, helping one another and their clients, their existence is of special interest in the Chicano prison population, which has a very low educational level. The Chicano prisoners (perhaps even more than the black convicts, with their history of civil rights activism) tend to be extremely suspicious of the extent to which constitutional rights apply to them. Because the writ-writers link barrio helping relationships with the legal system, they represent a structured base for self-help groups. It is precisely the same helpfulness shown in watching for newcomers to prison from the home barrio, taking care of their first needs when they arrive, and providing protection, emotional support, and normative criticism throughout their stay.

System Self-Help Groups

The California correctional system encourages attendance at certain kinds of self-help groups, including Alcoholics Anonymous, the Dale Carnegie course, the Gavel Club, and Yoke Fellows club. (In addition, self-improvement is possible in formal classes and vocational training for those individuals who are motivated and who meet the minimal qualifications.)[4]

Before the late 1950s, when Chicanos initiated the activity that led to the formation of culture groups, few Chicanos participated in such groups or in the formal self-improvement programs. There are technical reasons for this—their inability to speak English well and their low educational level. In addition, the social isolation of many barrio Chicanos led to uneasiness and lack of confidence in the presence of non-Chicanos.

But the ethnic factor should not be dismissed with a simple remark about lack of self-confidence. Mexico and Mexicanism is still very close to the Chicano prisoner. For some, this means that they simply get nothing out of the non-Chicano self improvement groups. Participation in establishment self-help groups is akin to collaboration with the enemy for many Chicanos. It tastes of assimilationism, a willingness to disavow cultural heritage and to acquiesce in what many pintos see as a systematic depreciation of their heritage. Prisoners who do participate are subject to ridicule and to harassment from barrio homeboys. There is an analogy here with black prisoners. Several authors have commented on the tendency of correctional personnel to equate the reform of black offenders with their rejection of the black heritage.

Thus the availability of system self-help groups did little to help the Chicano prisoner. It was not until the spread of the Chicano version of self-help—the culture group movement—that the developmental potential of the barrio ties of most Chicano prisoners began to find a channel that would supplement their supportive functions and provide a self-conscious base for positive change. But first there were many obstacles to be overcome.

Establishing Self-Help Groups in Prison

Predecessors of the Culture Groups

The first Chicano culture group was EMPLEO, formed in San Quentin in 1966. This group climaxed several years of organizational effort focussed around the attempt to establish a bilingual basic education program for Chicanos. Such a program was deliberately chosen by the Chicanos after several periods of activity built around other projects. The concentration on an educational issue rested, first, on the fact that the low educational level of many Chicano inmates excluded them from most vocational training in the prison and, second, because the basic education courses then available in San Quentin did not meet the needs of Chicanos, many of whom had difficulty with English. In addition, the convicts felt that education was a project that could win administrative support. The group devised a formal proposal for a Bilingual Basic Education Program. It was submitted directly and through mediators several times. After several rejections, it was finally implemented through the sponsorship of the high school principal.

Why was acceptance so hard to obtain? To some extent, the answer lies in the mobilization of the administrative culture regarding Chicanos. At the time the administration resolutely opposed organization along ethnic lines except for staff-initiated projects for special groups like the small number of American Indian alcoholics. Interviews with officials who were at San Quentin during this period indicate that Chicanos were the "most feared" inmates to the staff and to the other inmates—both because they spoke "in code" (that is, in Spanish slang), and because they were seen as a tightly-knit group with an extremely efficient communications network that extended outside the prison walls. Furthermore, prison officials saw the Chicanos as an "all or nothing" group that made either no demands or strong demands they would not back down from. Even then they were seen as responsive to Mexican national symbols and potentially "revolutionary." Thus there were special reasons for distrusting organized groups of Chicanos in addition to the normal opposition to ethnic organization.

Manipulation of Race in Prison

Former prison staff members comment that the custodial staff often manipulates racial and ethnic differences, both for public relations purposes (to distract public attention from institutional malfunctioning), and for inmate control (the divide and conquer principle). The appearance of black and Chicano prison movements in the mid-1960s (Eldridge Cleaver was then a San Quentin inmate) began to provide a non-criminal, non-institutional basis for identity and action. In fact, it seriously threatened the correctional system's claim to a monopoly over the efforts of the inmates, as well as to rehabilitative efficacy. Thus both the strategies of public relations (particularly with state legislators) and the strategies of control evolved to meet a new situation.

Several strategies were used. Residential units were desegregated, effectively keeping Chicano (and, usually, black) convicts from representation on elected inmate councils, because they never formed a large enough voting bloc. Also used were crude detective and spying intrigues to monitor and undercut ethnic leadership (Toch, 1969), as well as blackmail and favors—an informal network of communication through inmates that serves to discredit ethnic leadership and to convey what the administration will accept or resist. This network is also used to set up (frame) inmates and dissident staff members.[5] Convict leaders were harassed, especially with respect to their annual appearances before the Adult Authority Parole Board.

It is important to realize that this is not a specific reaction against ethnic self-determination. The issue of inmate self-determination is generally controversial. Some years later, the California Assembly Select Committee on Prison Reform and Rehabilitation asked for a rationale for denying inmate control over the $4.7 million Inmate Welfare Fund. The response, which neatly illustrates the institutional view, denies that the inmates have a moral claim to the money, denies their legal competency, and claims that such control is unnecessary because they are kept informed. Most of the letter argues that inmates are unable to make plans, have no regard for property, and would use the fund to establish positions in the prison economy that would lead to warfare. It also asserts that prisoners would stock straight razors and hazardous items in the canteens. The fund would suffer losses because of their irresponsibility and deprive the inmates of movies, thereby generating disturbances. According to the Adult Authority, a representative system is not possible because "elected members are often not the real leaders" (letter to Assemblyman Richard Alatorre from Walter L. Barkdull, Sept. 25, 1974).

This is the administrative context in which the Chicano Basic Education Proposal appeared. This context also included notions among prison educators and psychologists that Chicano prisoners are hard to reach. Like their counterparts on the outside, the treatment personnel were concerned that Chicanos were underrepresented in educational programs and unresponsive to conventional therapy techniques.

Correctional Careerists and Outside Staff

Part of the answer to our question about the rejection, and subsequent acceptance, of the proposal lies in the structural division within the treatment staff. This staff includes correctional careerists who transfer from one prison to another, and often ultimately to the correctional headquarters in Sacramento. At this time some employees of the Marin County school system had contracted to provide teachers for the prison high school. Correctional careerists tend to be confined to social networks that include top-level treatment and custody personnel who are correctionally oriented. Many even live on the prison grounds. By contrast, the outside employees tend to retain social and professional contacts outside of the correctional world.

The Basic Education Proposal was first presented to the teachers and counsellors who were prison careerists. It was rejected largely because the careerist mode of expressing concern with Chicanos precluded working with the convict structure. In form, it took the shape of distrust of its author, Eduardo Aguirre, who had been labeled by custody as dangerous, militant in philosophy, and having some influence over other convicts. To have acknowledged Aguirre's leadership by implementing his proposal would have flouted the recommendations of custody, which the treatment careerists were not willing to do.

On purely professional grounds, the proposal made sense as a means of reaching the Chicano convicts; but it also entailed a segregated class of Chicano inmates. This was another violation of prison policy, even though it made pedagogical sense, since Spanish was a dominant language only for Chicanos.

The staff members who ultimately implemented the proposal were not careerists. They saw its pedagogical merits and viewed its advocate in professional terms—he was a good student and influential among Mexican Americans. The then-principal of the San Quentin high school tells the story:

> We always had trouble getting illiterates in. Our teaching staff was weak in that area. The illiterates were hard to reach and there were very few Mexicans. Ed [Aguirre] and I were talking one night and I said, "A lot of black guys are surpassing the Mexican Americans. What's wrong?"
>
> Coming from a suburban elementary school, there were things I didn't realize. He explained the suspicion of the program and that many of them didn't know English. I asked him how to reach them. He said, "You get them; I'll talk to them." I docketed sixty men who had low reading scores. Only about a dozen of them ignored the docket. Ed spoke to them in Spanish. He had their respect. It is very rare for an English-speaking administrator to have an inmate talk in Spanish.

To evade the policy barring segregated classes, the principal "low-keyed" the innovation as an "extension of the basic literacy program," with inmate teachers' aides included but not named as such. The course was scheduled when there was a watch change, so that the guards' attention would be distracted. By including lecturers from the outside, the course began to take on broader educational functions, foreshadowing the linkages with outside organizations that characterize the culture groups.

Prison treatment careerists will usually subordinate professional goals to custody evaluations. The outsiders were structurally free to utilize professional norms, both in the goal and in evaluation of the means. They were not socialized to the prison culture regarding Chicanos, and were outside the gossip network regarding individual inmates. They took a risk in implementing the program, but their position in the outside world meant that the risk could be undertaken without permanent jeopardy to their careers, their friendships, or their self-concept. For them, the prison experience was a peculiar aspect of an otherwise outside-oriented career.

Few careerists (whether or not Chicano) are free to act on their risk-taking potential. There is always ambivalence, suspicion of inmates, and the possibility of severe and personally degrading sanctions from the prison administration. For a period of time after this new program, working through the inmate structure became partially legitimated among treatment careerists as an appropriate tactic. Culture groups were at least outwardly encouraged, although custody considerations still always took priority.

EMPLEO in San Quentin

The Bilingual Basic Education Program was a conscious tactic of a small group of Chicanos. For them the critical element of the program was the placement of key pintos as teachers' aides, or inmate teachers.

Changes in the educational administration, coupled with the threat that inmate teachers represented to the precarious professional identity of prison careerists, led to its termination in 1965. In 1966, a class was established (Communication Problems of Spanish Speaking Adults) to bring the Chicano to an understanding and acceptance of the Anglo way of life.

But the class was not actually taught to meet these objectives. A sympathetic instructor, Fred Persilly, permitted the students to focus on problems Chicanos face and methods that the students could use to help. The class project became the development of EMPLEO (*El Mejicano Preparado, Listo, Educado y Organizado*).

The organization, initially directed by the class, grew rapidly, until all but a handful of the Chicano prisoners in San Quentin had joined. One month after granting approval for the formation of EMPLEO, the warden received a request to hold a meeting for five hundred members.

Spread of the EMPLEO Concept

The EMPLEO group was the first. Many of its members—especially those who participated in its development by learning organizational procedures in the class—ultimately were transferred to other California institutions. Others who, like most pintos, were involved with narcotics, wound up in federal prisons or another California prison within a short period from release. The original members undertook to establish EMPLEO wherever they went.

Within two years (by the end of 1968), every state prison in California (and a federal prison in Chihuahua, Mexico) had a Chicano organization modeled after EMPLEO. Requests to use the name EMPLEO were routinely denied by prison administrators, who feared the establishment of a single large Chicano inmate organization that would spread across corrections. (See Appendix D for a list of the variety of names given Chicano prisoner organizations.) By 1975 we could identify approximately twenty-five Chicano culture groups operating in federal and state institutions in the United States. All developed in the racist and generally hostile environment of prisons. All operated on variations of the original EMPLEO constitution, bylaws, committee and governance structure.

The Objectives and Structures of Chicano Self-Help Groups

The prison culture groups express the principle that it is through Chicanismo—the easily-awakened group identity of the Mexican American people, and their sense of obligation toward their people—that constructive change for addicts and ex-convicts can be achieved. This principle demands that prison administrators accept the fact that some minority persons reject assimilation, and that the cultural autonomy expressed in the culture groups must be respected. This presents obvious problems to the prison administration. Pintos themselves felt that the culture groups are in the prisons to stay, with or without administrative approval, and that they provide (as does no other prison group) an opportunity for prisoners to interact with each other and with free people from their own community in furthering self-developmental goals.

Self-development, education, discipline, training in public speaking, cultural awareness, self-esteem, and pride are the almost uniform emphases of all Chicano culture groups. Each of these phrases implies a program, which differs from one institution to the next. In addition, by consistently instilling the philosophy of carnalismo/Chicanismo (brotherhood), they attempt to create unity to work within the system for the improvement of prison conditions and to stop inter-Chicano violence. The relationships with outside community groups give the prisoners links to motivational resources, concrete resources for help after release, and outside organizations related in some fashion to the concept of the Chicano movement.

The groups operate under the conventional forms of constitutions, bylaws, elections, parliamentary procedures, committee structure, and the like. Some also have screening committees for new members which test for appropriate motivation.[6] (Some groups make every effort to recruit the *vato loco* or alienated gang youth as clear cases of fellow Chicanos who can benefit from self-development.) Strong efforts are made toward unity, which means, of course, that the group must reach across barrio ties.

In some of the culture groups there is an implicit understanding that the *mesa directiva* (executive body) is to be balanced according to barrio representation. In state prisons this means including men from both Northern and Southern California and from warring barrio gangs, thus averting factionalism. An interesting effort at unity was begun by the Chicano culture group at Tehachapi prison in 1973. It was made after the killing at Tehachapi of a newly transferred prisoner, and occurred at a time when California prisons were dealing with violence by lockup. (Thus, the Mafia were locked up at Soledad and the Familia at Folsom. The opposing gang was kept in the main line.) The human relations staff of the Corrections Department had visited several prisons to speak with Chicano culture groups about peace negotiations, with little progress. At this point the Tehachapi culture group, MACHO, proposed a summit conference aimed at peace negotiations. Culture groups at all of the prisons were to be involved, along with members of the Mafia and the Familia, in a carefully staged series of negotiations. The superintendent at Tehachapi transmitted the proposal to the Department of Corrections with the following comment:

> I feel that MACHO here is sincerely interested in an end to the violence. It is also my belief that CCI [Tehachapi] might have had serious repercussions following the killing of Inmate Arias a few months ago, were it not for the stabilizing influence of MACHO among other factors. Whether the "summit conference" idea is practical or not, any positive suggestions by inmates deserve hearing and acknowledgement. 2/2/73, J. Enomoto.

The case is particularly interesting because MACHO was willing to appear along with corrections staff in the peace negotiations—an unusual concession testifying to their intense concern about the threat that the Mafia-Familia conflict represented. Five years after that effort, the Department of Corrections (then directed by J. Enomoto) had yet to come up with an effective means of dealing with the Mafia-Familia violence. The culture groups were seriously undermined during these years.

Culture groups must have a sponsor who is a member of the prison administration. Most groups try to interest a staff Chicano. This is often difficult, given the ethnic composition of most prison staffs. It is also often difficult to overcome the limited vision of administration Chicanos, who often originate in small towns near the prison and who imagine that helping other Chicanos implies their release into small towns like Ontario, Soledad, Represa, Susanville and other remote California towns. Visitors from organized groups in home communities like Los Angeles are particularly important under such circumstances, because they establish to the administration, as well as the inmate, the existence and legitimacy of the self-help principle in the complex metropolitan world. This combination of administrative and rural attitudes increases the need for a realistic relationship to metropolitan resources.

The culture groups (as a system-linked but authentically Chicano network for change that is solidly rooted in normal barrio norms and networks) can often operate successfully to create individual change. Such personal changes can be the base for a permanent change in role structure for the pinto, if the outside doors are open. We note in the next chapter how this can happen. The self-help groups can literally transform a criminal identity into a square identity without violating what is common to both—the barrio identity. There is no similar mechanism available in prison. It might have been, in fact, a mechanism invented by such criminologists as Cressey (1955), who argues that "if criminals are to be changed, they must be assimilated into groups which emphasize values conducive to law-abiding behavior . . . [by changing] anti-reform and pro-criminal subcultures so that group leaders evolve among those who show the most marked hospitality to anti-criminal values, attitudes, and behavior" (p. 118).

It is clear that prisoners coming from distinctive street subcultures like the Chicanos can only rarely be transformed by artificial and prison-specific groups. We have argued that Chicano adaptations to prison are variations of their adaptation to street life, rather than totally new role sets. It is for this reason that studies like Davidson's, which treat the prison as both a total institution and a totally discontinuous institution, are so deeply misleading. If research assumed continuity, we might more clearly distinguish the effect of the institution per se. If this argument is valid, then the period of incarceration is, theoretically, most fruitfully concentrated in the familiar but non-criminally oriented world of the culture groups, where the group supports personal efforts at change.

The problem is that this is totally alien to institutional logic, especially to the institutional preoccupation with defining convicts solely as probable troublemakers in prison and almost certain recidivists on release. This stance appears clearly in the discussion of the Inmate Welfare Fund. It also appears in the response to the first efforts at developing a self-help group at San Quentin in the early 1960s, which underscores the fact that custody preoccupations prevail in prison. There is probably no more frustrated occupational group in the nation than California prison treatment personnel.

Continuing Problems of Prison Culture Groups

Even under the best of conditions, not all Chicanos in prison want to join these groups. Activists often have trouble motivating the young state-raised *vatos locos*. And there are always loners who are engrossed in some personal preoccupation. A few Chicanos opt for assimilation, still want to be "Spaniards," or fear that participation in the group may cause them to be labeled as militant and jeopardize their release date.

In the mid-1970s, after a short period of comparative tolerance, prison administrators (especially in state prisons) reverted to the policy of suppression. Analysis of the fate of the Basic Education Proposal shows clearly the institutional dynamics underlying such a policy. But there is always a rationalization to the public in terms of current events. In the early 1970s in California, one of the most significant was the attribution of the extremist Symbionese Liberation Army (of Patty Hearst fame) to a black culture group origin. This is probably erroneous, but it reiterates the custody fear of ethnic groups (organized or not) as breeding grounds for revolutionary disruption.

In the middle and late 1970s, prison officials rationalized the policy of suppression of Chicano groups by pointing to the existence of violent

Chicano gangs (Mafia and Familia) as outgrowths of Chicano organizations, despite clear evidence to the contrary (as shown in the Tehachapi incident described earlier). Culture groups were accused of being branches of these organizations and of smuggling narcotics.

The tactics for suppression include: outright suspension of the group; transfer of leaders or members of the group's executive board to other institutions as agitators, as inciting to riot (some Chicanos have spent months, and even years, in solitary confinement for this); co-opting leaders; turning a group into a "rehabilitation" social group (an overdose of cooperation), and in some cases, appointing correctional officers as honorary members to make most decisions affecting the group; and discouraging officers from being sponsors or getting involved with the group's functions. Some institutions do not have a group, because the interested Chicanos could find no sponsor. Finally, some administrators have imposed so many inconsistent rules and guidelines for operation that it amounts to sheer harassment. A 1975 letter from a pinto incarcerated in a California prison indicates the net effect:

> The main obstacle to the group is administrative antipathy. They put so many regulations on the groups and throw up a wall of red tape that it is difficult for the groups to do anything constructive. It seems as if most of the energy of the group leaders is expended in trying to get around these obstacles.
>
> The first thing the administration does is to impose the rule that no political activity is allowed. All they really want is a social group where the Chicanos can sing a few songs and drink soda and discuss what Spanish-language movies we would like to see, and the administration picks the sponsor that will see that the pintos don't get too much done in addressing themselves to the root problems of exploitation, racism, and class struggle. This tends to frustrate those members who are more aware and the elected leaders who have not been co-opted so that they feel it is pointless to continue hassling with the administration, the sponsor and the co-opted members of the executive committee.
>
> I think that the only way a group in here will ever be effective is to have active outside support. Much like the outside steering committee we had at McNeil Island. This will hamper the administration's manipulations and repressive tactics.
>
> The groups are sorely needed because that is the only place that the pinto will be able to learn his place in the socio-economic-political scheme to which the system has assigned him. He must know the true nature of Capitalist exploitation and how he is not only a victim of this oppression, but how he is manipulated into becoming the unwitting tool of the system in his own and his people's oppression. However, all this comes under the heading of politics which is a taboo subject as far as the administration is concerned. I personally have

heard the sponsor tell the group that they will have to do things his way or else there will be no group. This was bad enough but what really turned me off (as well as a lot of other dudes) was when the co-opted elected leaders defended the sponsor's position against those of us who were trying to show how wrong he was.

I think that most groups have this problem although it may be more pronounced or not depending on the institution. This institution is pretty bad in that respect. Unfortunately, the outside people around here aren't much better. Well, maybe things will change a bit but I doubt if this joint will.

Self-Help Groups in the Barrios

Unfunded Groups

The Chicano pinto self-help movement spread, not only to other prisons, but also to the streets. This happened first in San Francisco. Here the San Quentin EMPLEO began to serve as a bridge for newly released pintos, to develop the support of the Chicano community, and to help implement certain prison reforms recommended by EMPLEO inside. Attempts were made to form a "outside" EMPLEO statewide, but this failed. At about the same time (1968), a number of pinto self-help organizations began operating in Los Angeles: LUCHA (League of United Citizens to Help Addicts), ALMA, La Junta, and one might include the Brown Berets. Operating almost entirely without funds, LUCHA was founded and staffed by pinto volunteers (cf. Moore, 1972). Its director, Eduardo Aguirre, had been instrumental in lobbying for the bilingual education program at San Quentin that preceded EMPLEO, and many of the volunteers had been directly involved in the San Quentin groups. LUCHA was very visible in the Chicano movement of the late 1960s, with wide community support in East Los Angeles, and spoke with authority to the many elements of the larger Los Angeles community seriously interested in the Chicano problems of drug use and gang fighting. During the now-famous riots of this period, LUCHA (along with ALMA) opposed the more radical Third World elements of the Chicano movement, which La Junta and the Brown Berets supported. As a militant, though ideologically moderate, force, it was highly controversial in the movement. Ironically, as a culturally nationalistic organization of ex-convicts it was viewed with considerable doubt by many elements of the Los Angeles Anglo establishment.

With other movement organizations, LUCHA became one of the founders of the Chicano Coalition, an organization of Chicano agencies in Los Angeles which was highly influential during its roughly five-year life. LUCHA's special role was to emphasize the importance of the Chicanos in prison, especially in legal issues, along with the Chicano

Legal Defense Fund. It concentrated on transportation, job offers, and emergency housing (in its office space) for pintos coming out of prison. It detoxified addicts cold turkey, either in the office or in members' homes, and spun off such other self-help organizations as the Committee for the Rights of the Imprisoned (CRI).

MAYO, the self-help organization of the California Rehabilitation Center for narcotics addicts, made similar attempts in Los Angeles to establish a street counterpart. So also did COPA, the self-help group at the California Institution for Men. All of these street counterparts of prison groups have had successes and reverses. Almost all of them operated without any but the most transient funding. During the same period of time, evangelical "Christian" congregations of addicts began in East Los Angeles, the most prominent known as Victory Outreach. Their work is clearly important as a religious counterpart of the pinto self-help movement. Furthermore, in two-year community colleges and on many campuses of the state universities, pinto programs were developed to help ex-convicts with problems in their educational efforts. Staffed by volunteer ex-convicts, they successfully fought legal restrictions barring the use of work-study money for ex-offender students, for example, in addition to more routine counselling.

Funding and Problems of Establishment

LUCHA ultimately received the largest and most consistent funding. Many believed the agency would demonstrate the possibility of the Chicano self-help movement becoming as well-established as other social service agencies. Yet it was eliminated some six years after initial funding. The process of its decay and downfall is worth some attention.

As background, the poverty programs in both Watts (south-central Los Angeles) and East Los Angeles allowed a wide range of so-called community-based programs. Under OEO, no Chicano ex-convict serving agency was substantially funded, although LUCHA was able to win a small grant (cf. Moore, 1972). Under the Model Cities program, however, its Chicano planners were intent on developing a convict-serving agency that would reflect the substantial prison accomplishments being publicized both through the movement press and through the actions of former members. The planners examined both Anglo models such as Seventh Step (cf. Goldfarb and Singer, 1973) and Chicano models, and ultimately directed their efforts through LUCHA.

It was predictably difficult to carry LUCHA through the various decision-making levels of the Model Cities program. Ex-prisoner input was the crux of the matter: at least half of the board of directors were to be ex-convicts. The new organization was incorporated in 1971 as Community Concern Corporation, and approval of the plan was achieved after lengthy and stormy work with conservative community groups and the city bureaucracy. Even when approved by the Los Angeles City Council, legal action had to be threatened by the new corporation in order to release funds. The basic plan was simple: to maintain liaison with prisoners through visits and correspondence with individuals and culture groups. It would provide resources to prisoners' families, newly released prisoners, and ex-convicts on the streets.

Yet there were still problems. Eighteen months after initial funding in mid-1973, a well-publicized scandal among some of the administrators led to its disfunding, even though no serious fiscal mismanagement appeared to be at issue.[7] For a short period the remaining staff worked again without pay on the original self-help principle, to keep the concept alive. Meetings were held throughout the community and in the prisons to regain political support for the pinto self-help idea.

After a two-month period of uncertainty, funds were restored to the agency. In the process, a number of pintos who had attained substantial jobs in a wide variety of community agencies banded together to form the Pinto Caucus, later to become CEPA, the Chicano Ex-Pinto Association, which endured for about two years as an unfunded political association, its members representing many of the existing community action agencies. The active members of CEPA were "graduates" of prison self-help groups.

Community Concern finally lost its funding in 1977; the last remnants of the LUCHA self-help influence had vanished two years earlier. How did this happen? Early in 1977, Get Going, a halfway house in East Los Angeles directed by an ex-convict, had been the focus of a series of exposes of alleged Mexican Mafia penetration of agencies in the Chicano community. The Los Angeles police tried to link this situation with a long series of unsolved but suspected Mafia murders that police felt were part of the Mafia attempt to push into the East Los Angeles drug trade. It had been rumored for some time that Community Concern had also been taken over by the Mafia. Thus it happened that an Anglo city councilman, trying hard to keep political control in a heavily Chicano area, charged that Community Concern had become "a base of operations for the Mexican Mafia . . . with reports of narcotics traffic, employee kickbacks, illegal diversion of funds and extortion of local merchants" (*Los Angeles Herald Examiner*, May 18, 1977). The irony that a prison-spawned criminal group was having a destructive impact in the streets of the barrios while the vast potential for rehabilitation of the self-help movement was being suppressed occurred to nobody in authority. This is submitted as the final argument about the continuity of experience for Chicanos in prison. It is equally possible for the Mafia, a destructive prison group based on state-raised Chicano youth, to feed back into the barrios.

In Los Angeles, there were yet other factors. The loss of funding occurred in the middle of a major local press campaign in which both the Mexican Mafia and the "illegal alien" issue or "invasion" kept the problems of Chicano Los Angeles very much in the public eye. A new organization, the "Hispanic Anti-Defamation" group, organized to counter some of the negative publicity. Yet by the end of 1977, the bad press about the Mafia had gained national importance, with an article in the *Reader's Digest* (November, 1997) repeating the correctional system's usual charges, plus some new alleged linkages between the Mafia and some newly-legitimated Chicano political leaders on the state level. It became clear that the press campaign directed against the prison-born Mexican Mafia was, implicitly, directed against all Chicanos. If there is any positive result, however, it may be the first realization for at least some Los Angeles Chicanos that the problems of ex-offenders are rooted in a basic minority problem—pervasive racism.

Aftermath

It should be made clear that the self-help movement involved people who were changed by their involvement with other people. Thus they were able to begin serious consideration of how they could help themselves in their own barrios. It is, of course, a desirable outcome, but there is nothing very unusual about this. We will show in the next chapter that it is a predictable outcome of the very mixed nature of square and deviant in the barrios. The Mafia is an artifact of the three-part survival economy of the barrios and the vicious underground economy in the California prisons. It seems obvious that the square-oriented self-help movement, despite its troubles with the complex of agencies working in East Los Angeles, still offers enormous possibilities in pinto rehabilitation, not to mention many other forms of constructive barrio development.

In 1978, the only Los Angeles street agency still operating with a pinto director trained in the self-help movement was located in the San Fernando area (*El Proyecto del Barrio*). This group was apparently remote and self-contained enough to permit a highly sophisticated version of the barrio-oriented programs initiated in the Los Angeles area ten years earlier.[8]

It is also important to note that the reaction of funding agencies to the crisis in the Los Angeles ex-convict organizations is similar to the reaction of the correctional system to ethnic groups. Unable to learn the criteria for distinguishing one subgroup from another, they stereotyped all ex-convicts. These things happened in spite of the ten-year experience of these agencies in dealing with grassroots organizations of the minority poor. In the end, these agencies were unable to develop non-traditional criteria for dealing with a non-traditional situation. The crisis was met, once again, with the ancient distrust of the ex-convict and the self-serving rubrics of racism.

7

Square and Deviant in the Barrio

THE SELF-HELP MOVEMENT among Chicano prisoners shows a search for conventionality—built on forms and patterns brought into the prison from the barrio itself. In time, the pinto movement returned to the barrios of East Los Angeles and gave its participants a legitimate community identity.

It is also plain that the gangs of East Los Angeles, while innovating and changing in a manner that is at least partially deviant, are also closely related to conventional adult life in the barrios. The drug markets, while clearly illegal, also illustrate the peculiar mixture of conventionality and deviance in the illegal economy of the barrios. Casual dealing in stolen barbiturates is a counterpart of the easy prescriptions available in better neighborhoods. Except for specialized barbiturate bootlegging operations, pill dealing in the barrios is a relatively small-scale and individualized hustle by people who are predominantly conventional. At lower levels of heroin marketing, addicted pushers are committed *de facto* to the illegal market because of their addiction and associated circumstances, the most obvious of which is imprisonment. But at any level except the very top, it has been rare for Chicano heroin dealers to see their business as a lifetime career commitment to a deviant role.

We have emphasized the importance of the continuities between barrio life before prison and the prison adaptations made by most Chicano prisoners. Although these continuities are primarily concerned with their barrio homies, the family and other square outsiders are important also. The importance of the square aspect of barrio life appears strongly in the prison culture groups and the outside self-help groups. When the pintos (inside and outside prison) appeal to the values of Chicanismo, they are trying to make an honorable alliance with the squares—and ultimately to establish their own square identity.

The conventional and the deviant are inextricably mixed in the barrios. This was implied in Chapter 1 in our description of the three-part economy of the barrio, and the necessary practice of commuting from one sector to another. A broader and even more interesting question is just how the residents of the barrio adapt—in general and as individuals —to the simultaneous presence of illegal and legal, deviant and square, in their communities. How do they deal with the most disruptive manifestations of deviance?

When we use the term square, we are consciously adopting the terminology of the gang, ex-convict, and addict segment—the deviants. It is a term describing people who are not involved in either the *vida loca* (crazy life of the wild adolescent or addict), or the illegal markets of the adult pinto-tecato. To almost anybody living outside the Chicano communities, the term square may seem pejorative. It is even difficult to say "he is a square" without imputing a sneer. However, for the gang-oriented person in the barrios, it is a simple term of description, often used with a degree of respect that acknowledges that many squares are decent, compassionate and honorable people. Of course, it also can be that many squares are not such people. Similarly, pintos and tecatos can be righteous in the same manner—or not. Throughout this chapter, we will be using the term square to refer to those people who view themselves and are viewed by others as having a predominantly conventional personal life style. By deviant we mean the usual objective matters, such as felony conviction, heroin addiction, and the like. Outside of terms like pinto, tecato, hard core, and barrio, there seems to be no one word used by people we call deviants to refer to each other. Square is a general category to gang-oriented men; deviant is not. Squares and deviants are not in a state of mutual warfare. It is not an either-or contrast. The stereotype comes from academic literature, probably because of the fragmentary view of life in poor urban areas. There are comparatively few documents (like Liebow's *Tally's Corner*, 1967) that even try to portray an inside view of such neighborhoods. Far more common is the view that such neighborhoods contain a mixture of lower class (deviant) and working class (square) people, with a vast distance between the two types. Relationships are portrayed (e.g., by Banfield, 1974), as mutual contempt and rejection. Perhaps the sharpest delineation of this view that square and deviant are polarized and mutually hateful is Lee Rainwater's study of the Pruitt-Igoe housing project, "Fear and the House-as-Haven in the Lower Class" (1966), which portrays the squares as victimized and terrified by the deviants.

But it is not necessary to see these two types as mutually polarized. We suggest that both the processes of social control and the processes of social deviance go on in these poor communities, as in all other settings. Exemplifying these processes of square and deviant tendencies, both conventional and unconventional people coexist in the lower-class urban ethnic neighborhoods, within the neighborhood, within the family, and even within the individual. Urban ethnic neighborhoods are simultaneously extensions of primary groups and gathering places for the anomic and the rootless. This mixture is a primary condition of life in such neighborhoods. This has been true for many years; undoubtedly it will be true for many years to come.

Legal and Illegal: Barrio Views of Problems and Solutions

Our first set of questions is nothing more than a sociological version of the middle-class question about barrios and ghettos: How can people live in neighborhoods with so many problems?

We gathered the evidence for our answer by interviews in the three barrios of Hoyo Maravilla, San Fernando, and White Fence. Interviews were conducted with a probability sample of a total of 136 householders, both men and women. For obvious reasons, we could not ask sensitive questions about their own participation in the illegal sector of the economy. We also felt it would be nearly impossible to ask if the respondent's family included an addict or a convict, although we did ask if any adolescent children were involved in gang activity.

Attitude Factors

Rather than face the problem of family involvement, we asked people whether or not they perceived serious neighborhood problems of crime, gangs, violence, personal safety, addiction, and the presence of ex-convicts who had difficulty adjusting to community life. We also asked them how they felt about such problem people, what they thought would be the best solutions to these problems, and how they evaluated existing institutional solutions. The questionnaire data were complex and quite long, containing a total of some two hundred questions. There were both open-ended questions that gave people a chance to speak off the top of their heads, and structured questions on the same topics. (See Appendix E for an analysis of pinto and non-pinto interviewers in the barrios.) After preliminary analysis, these questionnaire responses were clustered into three major groups using the technique of factor analysis. (Details are given in Appendix F, along with the responses to each question.)[1]

No Uniform Attitude

The first finding about attitudes is quite simple: there is no single barrio attitude. As shown in Figure 2, the respondents range widely on all three factors. As many people perceive problems as deny their importance. The specific questions ask, for example, if crime in the

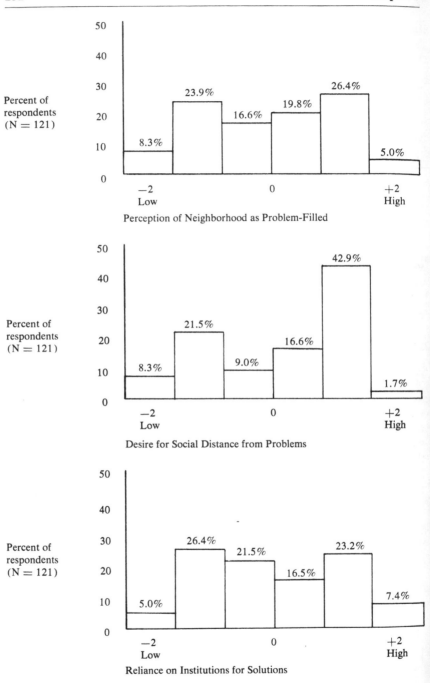

Figure 2
Factor Scores

streets is a problem, whether or not people worry about personal safety, and whether there is gang activity and theft in the neighborhood. Interestingly, no matter how negatively these barrios may be viewed by nonresidents, there are many residents who don't see them as problem-filled.

Conversely, a relatively high proportion want to establish distance between themselves and such barrio residents as ex-convicts, former addicts, and the like. Thus for many a solution to problems is personal distance between themselves and the problems. But there are many (about a third) who are willing to accept such deviants into their neighborhood and homes.

Finally, respondents were asked about the desirability of more police to help with narcotics and gangs, the positive and negative consequences of imprisonment, and the effectiveness of the local political system. Our respondents disagree greatly about the extent to which these institutional sources can be relied upon or avoided.

In sum, the first point is the considerable diversity in the barrios on the perception of problems, the reaction to problem people, and to conventional solutions to problems. There is no one answer to the question, "How do Chicanos in the barrios live with the problems around them?"

Personal Traits and Attitudes

If there is no one attitude, what kind of people hold one or another attitude?

At the beginning, it seemed reasonable to suppose that the attitudes of barrio residents might be related to some broad background characteristics, such as age, degree of acculturation, familiarity with the Los Angeles scene, or the extent of neighborhood attachment or linkage. We examined twelve such characteristics, and found that they are related, although not in any very obvious manner. We will give the results of this analysis in a patchwork of profiles of barrio people with different attitudes.

By use of these profiles we can broadly typify people who see their barrio as filled with problems. These people are more likely to be older, longer in Los Angeles, more likely (if women) to visit with neighbors, would not want to move, and would believe that barrio problems will improve in the long run. Conversely, those who do not see problems would have opposite characteristics.

Thus, those who believe their barrios are filled with problems have been around more, are more observant, and care more about their communities and their social milieu, while those who do not see problems simply do not care very much. The key indicator is the willingness to move. To a middle-class rationality, if you see your barrio as filled with crime, gangs, violence, drug addiction, and theft, you should want to move—or at least you should not firmly deny any wish to move. This is not the rationality of the Chicanos we are studying. It is not even realistic, because they know from experience that another Chicano neighborhood within their income will simply transfer their problems. (Many have gang members or addicts within their own family and know they cannot escape.) Those who want to move are people who don't care enough about the area to pay much attention to specific problems. Nor is there, in fact, much time out of the daily business of simple survival to worry about abstract problems of the neighborhood.

People who are tolerant of deviants (convicts or former addicts) are likely to be older, to be women, to have lived longer in Los Angeles, to visit (if men) with neighbors, and to be migrants (from either Mexico or other parts of the U.S.) who came to Los Angeles as adults. Those who are intolerant (or wish social distance) are likely to have opposite characteristics and to have been born in Los Angeles. Even though the scores on these types are not correlated with each other, the "intolerant" Chicano looks remarkably like the "no problems" Chicano. Possibly the comparatively young (and perhaps still aspiring) native Angeleno who sees no reason to associate with losers (some of whom he surely knows as peers) can be compared with relatively older, perhaps more resigned, and generally more accepting women who will tolerate and possibly even help the losers in a neighborhood of adoption, in which their families are more socially integrated.

Finally, those in the three barrios who are less willing to trust officials or institutions are more likely to be older, to have lived longer in Los Angeles, to be migrants who came to Los Angeles as adults, and to visit (if women) with neighbors. Again, those who would trust officials would fit an opposite description. Remembering that scores on these groups are not correlated with each other, we see that we are picking up the same two types. Accordingly, we can make some speculative generalizations from these data.

Adaptations as a Function of Minority Status

In the broadest sense, our data suggest that these adjustments rest ultimately on some broad adaptation by barrio people to their lives as members of a poor minority group inside a powerful and wealthy dominant system. Wealth in Los Angeles is particularly visible, because, coincidentally, much television and movie filming is done in the city. Yet Chicanos are very barrio-bound compared with other segments of the Los Angeles population. This tendency to be unfamiliar with areas outside local neighborhoods is even greater than for the black ghetto residents of Watts. (On a comparative scale, the Anglo residents of the wealthy community of Westwood are the most, and Chicanos of East

Los Angeles are the least, familiar with other areas of Los Angeles. Orleans, 1967.) What does this imply for the barrio Chicano? Does he desire unceasingly the success goals of the larger system, and reject the problems around him as hateful? Does he turn his back on the larger system and concentrate on his own barrio?

Our data show two major types of adaptation, or responses to these questions. The first is that of many native-born Chicano Angelenos, and particularly the younger men in these dusty, poverty-stricken barrios: the "I'm all right, Jack" approach. By this we mean that they consciously disavow interest or responsibility for the people around them, so they can concentrate on their own precariously satisfying way of life. This is an easy and perfectly natural psychological defense. It could be a refusal to relate their own discontents to collective problems of the Chicano minority, and even to group problems in the immediate locale. They may find neighborhood problems to be uncomfortable reminders of their own relatively helpless status as members of a minority. The denial is also realistic, as we have suggested. Moving to another barrio is simply moving to another set of pressures. They may be able to maintain their households, and their satisfactions in those households, in neighborhoods they just happen to be living in until something better appears. It is perfectly possible that they can recognize the neighborhood as deteriorating; some of them are all too aware of the difficulties of their old schoolmates who have gotten involved with narcotics and the law. They can avoid having anything to do with such people themselves—and reaffirm (though not very vigorously) their belief that the institutions of that powerful society out there are benevolent enough to take care of things.

The barrios also contain older people, many of them reared in much harsher environments, who exhibit a second broad type of adaptation. These were Chicanos who moved to Los Angeles from Texas and the rural Southwest, where discrimination is much sharper and more overt, or from Mexico, with its greater poverty. It can be said that their progress in Los Angeles since their arrival as adults is not spectacular. Yet their life style may be much superior to that of their origins. They may view these Los Angeles barrios as their ultimate destination, rather than as launching pads, and they like the good things offered by barrio life. They are aware of the problems in the neighborhood—the gangs are quite conspicuous and so are the police. But it is their neighborhood: a limited but real sphere for expansion and self-expression. They have no reason to trust the larger institutional system. If they are Mexican-reared they probably carry the marked anti-Americanism and anti-establishment attitudes prevalent in Mexico. Even if they are reared in discriminatory American environments, it is easy to substitute barrio and ethnic group identification for identification with the larger society (cf. Garcia, 1973, and Acosta, 1972, for problems of dual identity for Chicanos). With this background they may be more willing to absorb the deviants as deviants indeed—but as *their* deviants. This rather fierce and defiant acceptance of some types of law-breaker as a persecuted member of *la raza* appears in many aspects of barrio life—in the *corridos*, for example. These long popular ballads do not necessarily condone murder or robbery; they simply view the hero as at least partially a victim of bad circumstances or racism. The *corrido* tradition appears to have died out in Los Angeles in recent years. But in San Antonio the *corridos* have reappeared as *contrabandos*, or drug running songs, and are played regularly on the Spanish-language radio or at Saturday night dances (Patoski, 1977). An extremely popular *corrido* of a generation ago ("The Ballad of Juan Reyna," recently reissued) celebrated a Chicano fugitive in East Los Angeles who killed a policeman and died a "suicide" in San Quentin.

In considering the barrio adaptations to the mixture of square and deviant, it must be recognized that very few square people spend much of their time thinking about social problems or their own minority status. Survival in the barrios is time-consuming. Even when somebody happens to have an overt example of a general problem in his own family, it may be seen as a particular family problem, and not as a problem for *la raza*. (Several aspiring Chicano professionals from barrio backgrounds have commented to the senior author that they are actively not interested in gangs and narcotics because "I have an uncle/cousin/brother who is an addict/ex-convict/gang member and I don't even know how to deal with the chaos he/she has caused in my own family. I don't want to spend my professional life on this bad problem.")

Barrio views of barrio problems reflect people's adaptations to their minority status. We have tried to outline the two broad adaptations that appear to underlie the attitudes expressed in our findings. But the broader implications lead us directly into some critical questions of alienation and attachment.

Attachment and Alienation

When the alternative system of the barrio and *la raza* is compared with the system of the larger society, we are forced into a fairly complex critique of what has come to be the common sociological concept of alienation. From his experience with Third World urban shacktowns, Morse (1971) sums up one side of this critique. He argues that the concept of alienation as developed in American sociology assumes alienation from a form of social relations found only in the primary sectors of advanced societies. Especially, Morse argues, the concept of anomie (as developed by Robert K. Merton) discusses normlessness only in terms of how people deal with the gap between middle-class values of success in an advanced society and the means available to a lower-class striver. Morse questions this by saying that it

> assumes societies in which life chances depend on the efficacy of internal police mechanisms, euphemistically called "personality organization." The hallmarks of good self-policing and therefore success are the sociologists' familiar indices of education, occupation and income. Such a society is thought of as the sum of its members, not as something "external" to large numbers of them.

In short, Morse argues that life chances in American society *do not* depend solely on self-policing, the proper socialization to achievement, or an attachment to success goals in the larger system. On the contrary, he argues that many people feel external to that larger system.

We would extend his argument greatly by suggesting that many minority people in the United States are simply *not attached* to such norms of success. Of course, some are indeed attached and some are alienated. But some are attached to what is explicitly seen as an alternative system. It is nonsensical to view and measure them as alienated from the Anglo system, which they never accepted.

This idea is critical. Without it, we cannot understand a large group of people living in Chicano society in the United States. More concretely, we suggest that the second type of adaptation to barrio problems represents people attached to *la raza* and the barrio as an alternative system complete in itself. The older, adult in-migrant types (low Social Distance and low Institutional Reliance scores) have not internalized the success goals of the Anglo system. Their interest is in the narrower world of Chicano life. They are willing to face up to local problems as part of their real world orientation.

Squares and Deviants as Individuals

Four Career Types

This and yet other types of adaptation to barrio problems should be seen as lifelong career paths, not simply one-time responses to a set of questions. People assume their adaptations to other people, goals, and norms over the course of a lifetime. We suggest that they do so through alternative reference groups and work and emotional-sociability roles that assume critical salience at different stages of the life cycle. In developing this idea, we will focus on the three stages of adolescence, young adulthood, and maturity-middle age. There are institutional forces in each stage.

We suggest four ideal-type career patterns. The types of career paths are empirically based. The first two are abstracted from the survey data. The third type comes from the materials on Chicano gangs given earlier, as well as on life histories and personal experiences. The fourth is added partly to complete the logic, and partly because the barrios have indeed produced a number of mobility-oriented and achieving persons. Career histories of all four types derive from personal involvement, interviews with Chicanos from a wide range of backgrounds, and yet other survey data.[12]

There are at least two types of squares currently living in the barrios. The first is exemplified by the new immigrant to East Los Angeles, for whom making it may simply mean establishing himself in Los Angeles and becoming attached to a Chicano community. He accepts the community, lives in it, and sets his goals inside the barrio. He is oriented primarily and actively to the barrio-*raza* system. In adolescence he develops in response to reference groups that may include some highly localized networks in the rural United States or urban or rural Mexico. Work roles include migratory agricultural labor or possibly venture jobs in a preliminary effort to settle in urban areas. The work role is highly salient.

In young adulthood, he begins to establish a base in Los Angeles with very low level, part-time jobs. The family may—or may not—be brought with him to the new area of settlement. His sociability is done through newly-established groups—community dances, bars, and churches.

In maturity and middle age, he tends to consolidate his Los Angeles base; he is buying a home, relating to neighbors, and extending his sociability radius on the basis of a reasonably stable work role, possibly including some form of small entrepreneurship.

The second type of square is the native of Los Angeles who cannot make it in the dominant Anglo system. He is not particularly attached to the barrio, but lives in it *de facto*, perhaps in a highly individualized, family-oriented life style. He is oriented primarily, but not actively, to the barrio. In adolescence, he develops in response to reference groups within the extended family, in his roles as son, brother, and cousin. There is adequate, but not salient, performance in the segregated but regular schools, and he takes part-time or entry-level jobs. His social life is important, and includes the use of alcohol and various drugs at parties with, predominantly, other squares.

In young adulthood, he moves rapidly into marriage and more or less stable work in the secondary labor market. His sociability centers on his family and on other Chicanos at the same family life cycle stage, but he is basically male-centered.

In maturity and middle age, his family roles as husband-father and son-brother (especially in relationship to his aging parents) are more salient. He is an established and stable laborer or semiskilled worker, or he may operate a small local business. He owns his own home. His sociability is increasingly family-oriented.

Our third type, the barrio-oriented deviant, has already been discussed at length. He develops in response to reference groups that include the traditional barrio gang in adolescence, and barrio factions in the special schools, Juvenile Hall, probation camps, and Youth Authority facilities. His work career develops around opportunities at the very bottom of the illegal market, with casual dealing in pills and marijuana. While his social life is focussed around the barrio gang, he goes to parties that include squares as well, and tends to be indiscriminate in his use of alcohol, barbiturates, and marijuana.

In young adulthood, he moves into veterano status in the gang. His reference group includes Chicano factions in prison. He has begun to use heroin, with several short periods of addition, and his work role is that of the dealer-user. His reference group has expanded to include tecatos from other barrios, and his sociability is increasingly restricted to the pinto-tecato network.

In maturity and middle age, the gang remains a reference group, but his prestige in the gang drops. He becomes a lower-status veterano. He is now a dope fiend, with short periods of efforts at staying clean. Prison-based factions are important to him, after many years in and out of prison. He remains at the dealer-user level, although he is less trusted and has a harder time getting income. He may become involved in self-help groups. He may become an alcoholic as he ages. His sociability is confined to other convicts and addicts.

This career pattern is developmental, in that one stage tends to push the person toward the next stage, as shown in the diagram below. This is the career pattern that correctional and law enforcement officials tend to believe is the *real* pattern, because it is only the deviant roles that they see.

	Adolescence	Young adulthood	Maturity-middle age
Reference group	gang	Chicano prison faction	Prison faction
Sociability	gang	pinto-tecato	tecato

Of course, this is not the only career pattern, even for deviants. A few young Chicanos are picked up by large-scale organized crime and leave the barrio-based tecato-pinto networks. This is analogous to those upwardly mobile young men in the square system who go to college and make it outside the barrio. And a certain number of young Chicanos move upward in the narcotics network. Many do not get seriously addicted and begin to make substantial sums of money as middle-level dealers. There are other variations, also.

But the most important unrecognized element in this ideal-type career model is that it is ideal-type. In fact, the young adolescent also participates in the square reference groups. These are almost always family groups and even church groups, as well as the neighborhood gang. In fact, his deviant career is lived out to its end in the context of the square barrio system. (One of the variations on the deviant theme outlined above is for the young adult addict to control his habit and establish a family and a normal job—dealing, and perhaps stealing, on the side. This is a rare adaptation. Far more common is the middle-level dealer who maintains a full facade of squareness. It is important to realize that the facade is more than merely appearance.)

Finally, there is the square who is a native of Los Angeles who has left the barrio and entered the dominant Anglo system. In adolescence, he is strongly oriented to roles in his family and in the school. Peer reference groups are less salient. There is enough achievement (higher status roles) in school to serve as a reward and incentive. It is likely that the family maintains a self-concept of higher-class origin than do most people of the barrio. Voluntary associations, if any, tend to emphasize linkages with the dominant system, rather than the barrio system. Work, if any, may be in entry-level jobs.

In young adulthood, he may serve in the armed forces (often an important break with the barrio). His work roles will tend toward low to middle status in a group of mixed ethnicity in a career ladder job. Family formation may be slow, and may entail mixed marriage. Sociability is with mixed ethnic groups. There is often a change of residence to a neighborhood outside the barrio and into an area of either mixed ethnicity or predominantly Anglo residents. It will be chosen on grounds of its life style. *Sal si puedes*, or "get out if you can," is a common place name for Chicano barrios.

By maturity and middle age, he has moved—both physically and psychologically—outside the barrio. He is oriented to mobility in the social class system. Ironically, this mobility often entails work as a token Chicano, sometimes administering Anglo programs in the barrios, or otherwise building a career on ethnic specialization.

Use of Career Models

These four models are highly abstracted and oversimplified ways of presenting a great deal of detailed data. Though based on empirical reality, the career models represent no real individual. In fact, the abstraction deliberately exaggerates degrees of squareness, deviance, barrio orientation, and dominant-system orientation.

But these models allow us to grasp the critical fact that individuals participate *simultaneously* in each of the career lines. The deviant participates in square reference groups. In adolescence the square goes to school with, and may deal grass and pills at parties attended by, the deviant. In young adulthood the barrio-oriented square and the deviant may work side by side, may marry each others' sisters, may find themselves the same day in juvenile court to help out younger brothers, or in municipal court facing the same misdemeanor charges.

This simultaneous participation, both actual and potential, means that the deviant may at any time (at least while young) gain enough gratification from square participation to change direction. That is, his family and the chance of a stable job in a family-owned business might be satisfying enough for him to shift his primary identity to that of the square. It is possible that he might be picked up by some special community program (such as Upward Bound) that puts him onto the Anglo system track.

For the young Chicano, the options are broadest during adolescence. In gathering gang cohort data, our researchers found that a number of the fighting gang members went square at early stages in their life cycle —that is, they began to be influenced more by square institutional structures than by deviant structures. One of the gang members was heavily influenced by his military service. In fact, his life illustrates the usefulness of the career models quite handily.

Joe grew up in Hoyo Maravilla and participated in his family and gang as primary reference groups during his adolescence. There were occasional brushes with the law, and brief incarcerations tended to reinforce the gang membership. He did some small-scale dope dealing during adolescence. School was not an important experience for him, except as a source of bitterness toward the Anglo system. As a young adult, however, he joined the army and avoided the addiction of many of his gang friends. He re-enlisted, and when he returned from military service his career switched to a predominantly square pattern. He attained a responsible foreman-level job near the barrio. Although his marriage was not successful, he remained family-oriented with respect to his mother and his children. He became preoccupied with the problems of addicts, partly because of his addicted brother, a talented artist. Joe left his factory job for a job in a community agency serving ex-convicts. When the agency collapsed he returned to the factory, this time as an active unionist.

In essence, Joe participated simultaneously in all four structures. Thus the career model is used not to explain Joe's behavior, but rather to locate him in social space—to provide an interpretive framework for his behavior at different points during his life. Joe is unusual in that his simultaneous participation in each structure led to major life shifts. Others in his adolescent group narrowed their participation; after starting from the same point, becoming addicted, and going to prison, they more consistently followed the career of the deviant. Still others of his age group grew up in the barrio and remain there to this day. It can be presumed they were some of our respondents in the survey.

The Use of Career Models in the Self-Help Movement

Beyond explaining individual career shifts, this career model provides an interpretive framework for explaining the prison experiences of Chicano men. We have discussed not only the reinforcing influences of prison in confirming the defiant identity of the Chicano through barrio-based prison factors, but also the self-help movement. This is strongly based on the orientation that distrusts institutional solutions to social problems, but is willing to work with other Chicanos in improving local conditions. Because these men participate simultaneously in both square and gang networks, we know that some aspects of this square identity are firmly within the role repertoire of Chicano convicts. The self-help movement permitted these aspects to emerge—not in the creaky sense of reviving a past role, but rather as the pinto movement became an accepted part of a general Chicano movement, led not by revolutionaries but by respected community-oriented squares.

Indigenous Solutions to Local Problems

Turning to the degree of similarity between square barrio residents and those who have been labelled as deviants (i.e., pintos), we find the following answers to specific questions (based on the forty-two newly-released convicts from the three Los Angeles barrios).

Youth Problems

In general, both barrio residents and ex-convicts think in terms of solutions that they know about, or of policies already in effect. Most of the solutions proposed for barrio problems of gangs and drugs appear to be posed both in terms of the benevolence and malevolence of the agency concerned, and in terms of efficacy. Thus the barrio residents and ex-convicts overwhelmingly choose the educational system when they are asked what would be most effective to control gangs (Table 9). (This was true for barrio householders in both open-ended questions and when choosing from the list of alternatives shown in the table.

Table 9   Most and Least Effective Approaches to Controlling Gangs, First and Second Choices Combined, Barrio and Ex-convict Respondents, 1975

Approaches	Most effective		Least effective	
	Barrio residents (%)	Ex-convicts (%)	Barrio residents (%)	Ex-convicts (%)
Better job training in school	88	62	6	n.a.
Special programs for dropouts	48	50	4.5	n.a.
Parental guidance	20	14	27	n.a.
Longer jail terms for kids	11	0	67	n.a.
Social and athletic centers	20	21	12	n.a.
Community or street workers	11	24	10	n.a.
Social workers with family	6	2	9	n.a.
Car/bike clubs	3	0	22	n.a.
More police in neighborhoods	2	0	42	n.a.
Total N (= 100%)	(136)	(42)	(136)	(42)

QUESTION: "A lot of people have different opinions about kids and what to do about controlling gangs. Which three do you feel would be most effective?"
NOTE: n.a. = information not available.

Pintos were questioned only from the list.) Comparatively few residents (38 percent) knew of programs being operated for youth in their neighborhoods, and most such programs were evaluated positively. But the conventional social work approaches to gang problems—social workers with the family, car clubs, social and athletic centers, and street workers—are seen by neither barrio residents nor ex-convict veteranos as effective. Not surprisingly, the punitive approaches (more police, keeping kids in jail) are opposed. This is in spite of the fact that many barrio residents are deeply concerned about gang violence in their neighborhoods. The overwhelming concern is that the barrio gang kids be turned around, via education, into fruitful adult career lines.

This concern should be emphasized, because in every policy decision a group of vocal residents can always be mustered to ask for harsher penalties for youth involved in gang activities; for example, several hundred were so organized in one barrio by a local priest in 1977 (and several hundred youths were organized by an opposition group). Such organization is dramatic and attracts the newspapers, but it is far from adequate representation of the sentiments of the largely quiescent barrio residents.

The general community desire for professional help is also clear in responses to a question asking where they would be likely to send a young person for help with hard drugs. This response pattern may surprise those who stereotype ghetto residents as traditionalist, punitive, and naive. In Table 10, potential resources are arrayed on a continuum roughly representing the degree of their institutionalization. There appears to be a curvilinear relationship between institutionalization and perceived usefulness as a source of help. The uniformed police are avoided by a majority; probation officers and teachers are also avoided to a notable degree, and there is a good deal of variation in the willingness to turn to the priest.[3] Mental health and health professionals are seen as most useful sources of help. Avoidance rises again as the resources get closer to the fictional drug user, and—interestingly—a majority would "never" advise a kid to handle his drug problem himself. Clearly, a high proportion of these respondents are ideologically capable of utilizing professional resources, if they are available.

Table 10   **Sources of Help for Youth Involved with Hard Drugs, Barrio Respondents, 1975**

Sources of help	Very likely (%)	Maybe (%)	Never (%)	Don't know (%)
Mental health agency	59	19	11	11
Doctor	54	28	10	8
Family	50	28	16	6
Priest	29	32	28	11
School teacher	21	27	40	12
Probation department	21	21	43	15
Friends	17	38	38	6
Police (juvenile)	11	19	59	11
Nobody—handle it himself	8	26	53	13
Total N (= 100%)	(136)	(136)	(136)	(136)

QUESTION: "Suppose somebody you know has a kid that was involved with hard drugs. Where do you think you would suggest that he go for help?"

Drugs

Differences between barrio residents and newly-released ex-convicts appear when they were asked about policies appropriate to controlling drugs (Table 11). Within the limits of response options, barrio residents prefer community-based intervention, and avoid either increased law enforcement or permissiveness (for example, legalizing marijuana and heroin).[4] Ex-convicts (mostly ex-addicts), by comparison, are strongly in favor of legalization of marijuana and are much more opposed to police and jail. However, a high proportion of barrio householders see police and incarceration as ineffectual or bad and to be avoided. Education for the young and community programs for the addicted, rather than institutional intervention, are overwhelmingly the choice of barrio residents and ex-convicts alike in dealing with their local narcotics problems.

Table 11 Good and Bad Approaches to Control of Drugs, Barrio and Ex-convict Respondents, 1975

Approaches	Good, should be done		Bad, should be avoided		No effect		Don't know / no response	
	Barrio Residents (%)	Ex-convicts (%)	Barrio Residents (%)	Ex-convicts (%)	Barrio Residents (%)	Ex-convicts (%)	Barrio Residents (%)	Ex-convicts (%)
Community organizations to help addicts	87	83	2	2	2	2	9	12
Drug prevention programs in schools	87	86	4	0	4	5	4	9
School workers with the family	64	43	4	21	15	26	16	9
More methadone programs	48	55	12	31	2	5	38	9
More police	41	5	22	70	26	20	10	5
Keep addicts in jail	22	2	35	50	29	41	14	7
Legalize marijuana	14	64	57	7	6	9	23	19
Legalize heroin	7	26	74	50	2	7	18	17
Total N (= 100%)	(136)	(42)	(136)	(42)	(136)	(42)	(136)	(42)

QUESTION: "Here are some policies some people talk about with regard to controlling drugs. What would you say about: _____?"

This was put to the test at two separate points in the interview, when respondents were asked about the chances for a locally-based program to help addicts. The proportion agreeing that such a program was needed, in that neighborhood, and would work, were about 70 percent in each question (with about 20 percent don't know). Though this is lower than the 87 percent who felt that "community organizations" would be good policy, opposition or distrust of such a program was at a low 3 to 8 percent.

Parallels and Differences

There are variations based on differences in individual experiences, but it is striking that barrio householders and ex-convicts from the same barrios tend to agree on how to deal with neighborhood gangs and neighborhood narcotics. For gangs, they suggest education both in school and for dropouts as the most effective approach. Police and jails they see as the worst. Like barrio residents, pintos opt for community agencies and drug prevention programs in schools as the most important two policies for narcotics control. Both tend to agree in listing jail, police, and social workers as the least effective. However, unlike the barrio householders, the pintos select legalized marijuana and an increase in methadone programs as their third and fourth most approved policies. These may very well be due to differences in experience. The last two items drew a high "don't know" and "no response" pattern from the barrio residents.

But the response differences also reflect value differences, especially with regard to marijuana. The three policies most named as "bad and to be avoided" by the barrio residents were legalization of heroin, legalization of marijuana, and keeping addicts in jail. The three pinto counterparts for "bad" policies were more police, keeping addicts in jail, and legalizing heroin. It seems reasonably clear that the difference regarding legalization has to do with confused concern about the consequences of use of these substances. Some people fear that legalization will encourage use—which is generally defined as bad among barrio residents. Pintos rarely define marijuana as bad, but have been sharply exposed to police harassment and to cases of other prisoners who in the past served long prison sentences for marijuana use. Thus they are in favor of legalization of marijuana. But both pintos and barrio residents appear to view heroin as so vicious that only a few are in favor of its legalization.

Earlier, we noted that barrio people consider the benevolence and malevolence of proposed and existing practices as much as they consider efficacy. The barrios have long been voiceless victims of unintended negative effects of institutional policy, so it is inevitable that barrio people are cautious. We also noted earlier that policies are implemented in the context of ideas and traditions that have developed over the years at the local level, and that such ideas should not be overlooked. The clearest and strongest desire is for professional resources and local programs.

Barrio residents routinely live inside a tripartite survival economy. In open-ended questions about policy, the closest they came to acknowledging its importance was the consistent belief that jobs, and training for decent jobs, are needed for youths and ex-convicts. We have tried to go further here, and suggest (in Chapter 1) that such a search is bound to a degree of failure: there just aren't that may good jobs in the economy. The illegal economy, which in Chicano Los Angeles is dominated by the drug trade, is a serious obstacle to any rational development of the skills and resources of the local population.

8

A Policy for the Barrios

THERE ARE FEW FRESH IDEAS these days on the old problems of urban America; time and inertia have built a hard scab of conventional concepts and policy. To most Anglos, even those who live in Los Angeles, the Mexican American population is exotic and alien. Although gangs, addicts, and prisoners have existed for generations, they seldom appear in college textbooks or on policy agendas.

But the unknown experiences of this urban minority offer new ideas, particularly in light of current population changes. Chicanos, Puerto Ricans, and other Latin Americans will become increasingly important in the American cities of the next generation. Thus the Chicanos of Los Angeles merit serious attention in themselves.

Continuity the Keynote

This book presents the issues of barrio life in terms of the ideas and viewpoints of participants—the present and former convicts, gang members, and addicts of East Los Angeles who supplied their own experience, researched the basic material, and then criticized every sentence and nuance of meaning. Our collaborative methodology continues a tradition of naturalistic observation of the whole of life, as experienced by its participants. If the tradition has any value, it will especially in this age of funded research that is justified as policy-oriented.

Barrio people want to demonstrate the continuity of experiences that policy makers see as discontinuous. On the federal level, the continuity of experience is divided into departments: the Department of Labor rarely consults the Department of Health, Education, and Welfare or the U.S. Bureau of Prisons. On the state level, the situation is the same. In the academic world, the person teaching and doing research on criminology rarely teaches or does research on the family or urban sociology.

Major Factors in Continuity

The consistencies of life in the barrios stem from three factors: barrio ethnic cohesiveness, traditions, and emphases; institutional experiences at the barrio and the societal levels; and the tripartite economy and opportunity structure.

Barrio ethnic traditions in Los Angeles are quite different from those of blacks, and are even unlike those of Chicanos in other cities. Los Angeles has been the major destination of migrants from both Mexico and the more depressed or discriminatory parts of the United States. This means a continual turnover inside the poorest barrios that are the entry points for newcomers. This also means that the area's Mexican subpopulation actually exceeds the total size of most metropolitan areas in the U.S.—nearly one and one-quarter million persons. Thus the city served the traditional acculturation function for Chicanos while also establishing reasonably well-defined neighborhoods, each with different origins and traditions. Los Angeles has also suffered some violent racial traumas, notably the deportations of the early Depression years, the Zoot Suit Riots of the early 1940s, and the Moratorium Riots of the 1970s. Elected officials have consistently avoided any accountability to the large Chicano population, and there are no complaint mechanisms like those in larger Eastern and Midwestern cities.

Los Angeles' health, welfare, education, and criminal justice agencies are generally regarded by professionals elsewhere as relatively progressive and relatively functional. Yet in the experience of Chicanos, there is a consistent dark side to the image. Part of the friction stems from institutional resentment of Mexican nationals. It was the county's welfare department that arranged the deportations of the 1930s, and the local health and educational services are recurrently shaken by drives to eliminate or avoid the costs of serving illegal aliens. The criminal justice system is continuously alert to apprehend and deport undocumented Mexicans. Chicano experiences with the schools are similar to those of other minorities, with the expected high dropout rate.

For East Los Angeles people, status in the work world is confined largely to dead-end jobs in the poor-paying and marginal secondary labor market. Gaining status in the welfare economy is important for a large segment of the population. To become established in either of these economic structures requires separate endeavors. To enter the illegal economy is equally difficult.

These are the factors that build a continuity of experience in the lives (or careers) of individuals, and also in the lives of communities, gangs, drug marketing structures, and prisoner structures. For the participants, these structures are everyday, normal, and routine. From the point of view of most readers of this book, they are not. This is reasonable, since most middle Americans do not share the special minority experience of the Chicanos, do not experience failure-oriented public institutions, and are far less likely than Chicanos to experience either the welfare economy or the illegal economy.

This contrast must be emphasized. "Everyday, normal, and routine" middle American expectations are not part of the lives of the people of the barrios. Few elements of the American dream come normally to Chicanos. Equality, justice, and economic betterment are rather grim jokes. Even those barrio men who shift into a square career path often get there in an unorthodox way. Thus, while education is the most obvious route into the middle class, it can be acquired only after enormous struggle by most barrio men. Business investments may often draw on an illegal capital base. (This is not too rare in American history: there are capital bases and American fortunes built on gambling, prostitution, slavery, and illegal liquor. Many more legitimate fortunes have been built on such dubious foundations as defective merchandise, illegal price manipulation, bribery, and a host of ordinary crimes that are extraordinarily invisibile.)

The Three Themes in the Gangs

The special Chicano experiences (ethnic and neighborhood traditions and cohesiveness) are important for the barrio gangs. Possibly there were remote threads from the traditional small-town Mexican social organization of young males, but the barrio gangs were vastly strengthened by the vigorous Los Angeles racism. Although they develop autonomous traditions, the gangs are well in touch with adult social realities. Yet even here the institutional structure is significant. Barrio gangs are known and harassed by the police. The gang structure is strengthened inside the juvenile holding institutions. The younger cliques are in the process of dropping out and are in conflict with the educational institutions. The older cliques are the basis of the ethnic factions in prison. The influence of the search for economic resources is also evident: younger cliques are involved in the marketing of illegal drugs, both for personal use and for income. Gang members frequently draw directly on the governmental resources used in the gang programs that regularly sweep the barrios. The older cliques are, of course, the primary strength of the heroin marketing and use structure.

The Three Themes in the Drug Markets

The struggles to make it in the barrio economy are evident in our discussion of the barbiturate and heroin marketing structures. Yet these structures rely heavily on institutional roots: profits are large because the substances are illegal. Recently, the structures have been heavily modified because of the operations of the prison-born non-barrio Mexican Mafia. Yet since the law enforcement activities of the 1950s, the essential structure has been based on Chicano cohesiveness, particularly linkages to suppliers in Mexico. (It is also worth noting the culturally distinctive consumption patterns for both barbiturates and heroin. Chicanos still use reds at parties, a practice unknown in other, more affluent, parts of the city. Chicanos also remain more consistently loyal to heroin than do other addict populations.)

The Three Themes in the Prisons

The primary theoretical controversy in criminological literature concerns how much impact the institution has on the prisoner. We argue that "prisonization" is restricted for Chicanos—the institution is less than total—simply because Los Angeles Chicano prisoners are preoccupied with their homies and with other barrio-based groupings. But institutional impact is becoming stronger over time, because institutionalization is occurring earlier, and because state-raised men are far more prisonized than are barrio-oriented men. Of particular importance is the illegal economic structure of the California prison system, which fostered the development of the Mexican Mafia and its rival, Nuestra Familia. Neither organization developed in the federal penitentiaries, because administrative policies precluded the development of a barrio-like illegal economy. Enough resources are provided so that even state-raised men can survive without outside ties.

The theme of ethnic cohesiveness is superbly illustrated by the Chicano self-help movement in prisons. It appeared first in the prisons, and preceded the parallel *Movimiento* activities (such as those among Chicano college students in Los Angeles) by several years. It provided both a structure and an ideology for prisoners to participate in their own rehabilitation. Expressing the ideals of Chicanismo in the strongest possible fashion, it asserted that this ideology, and a linkage with other movement Chicanos, could provide a constructive alternative to crime, prison, and narcotics. The continuity of normal, rather than deviant, adaptations is critical here.

The Three Themes in the Barrios

We show that the three factors produce, as an ordinary condition of barrio life, a mixture of square and deviant opportunity structures, traditions, and social structures which barrio residents must adapt to. Obviously, their modes of adaptation are not random, although we have not been able to pursue this matter very far. We suggest a dualism, a simultaneous existence of square and deviant adaptations, as a property of the communities, the families, and the individuals in the barrios. This dualism, which is extremely perplexing for policy makers, is probably the most important matrix for understanding and dealing with the problems of the barrios.

A Major Dualism

The dualism, or tension, between square and deviant does not suggest in any way that the barrios have two moralities. This latter approach characterizes the work of many nonminority sociologists when they deal with deviance in the minority communities. Matza (1969), for example, implies that there is a lack of agreement on moral values between the middle and lower classes in his arguments about moral ambiguity, pluralistic moral definitions, and shifting standards of morality (p. 12). While there may be differences between the square and the deviant moralities, we are struck more by their similarities.

In the prison setting, our counterpart argument is that the most fruitful direction of study may be to search for the continuities of conventional behavior—to seek those experiences and processes that fix the deviant identity. This is because the square/deviant dualism persists even inside deviant prison groups. It is clearly rooted in the three factors we have emphasized.

Square and Deviant in Earlier Studies

Poor urban neighborhoods can simultaneously be extensions of primary groups and gathering places for the anomic and the rootless. This has been noted through many generations of study; students of American ethnic communities report it from the early 1900s. A classic study by Park and Miller (1921) was just as concerned with the Italian Black Hand and the counterforce of the White Hand as with the Italian church. Immigrant demoralization and the relaxation of community control were themes of the Park and Miller book. A generation later, in 1939, Whyte (1943) saw his corner-boys and racketeers as acting inside a normative frame of reference (in some respects) that also sent college boys out of the community and into the middle classes.[1] Even later, Herbert Gans (1962) was predicting the end of the persistent peer-group society. Simirenko's study of Russians in Minneapolis (1964) emphasized issues of community control. Thus again and again in ethnic community studies there have been statements about the simultaneous occurrences of processes of deviance and control, of square and deviant types, even though the nature of the square and of the deviant has varied among ethnic groups and among researchers.

Coexistence or Transition?

In other respects, however, this is a very new theme as we present it here. Although the facts were repeatedly discovered and discussed in these studies, most of the studies of older white ethnic communities see this tension between the processes of control and deviance very differently. It is not seen as a permanent formal characteristic (in Simmel's sense) of lower-class urban communities, ethnic or otherwise. Rather, scholars have tended to see it as a transitory problem.

First, the urban immigrant ghetto is viewed as a transitional area. The tension between square and deviant in such ghettos is seen as part of the transition from immigrant to American. This view assumes that, ultimately, assimilation will reduce the tension.

These notions were established by a series of ecological and cultural studies undertaken in Chicago in the 1920s. The notions were based on dual conceptions of the immigrant groups as going through phases, and of the city as a system in which certain areas almost inevitably served as magnets for the poorer immigrants. This magnetism was partly cheap housing, partly proximity to jobs, and partly because nobody cared about these areas. In Burgess' zonal hypothesis of urban growth and development (1925), they were zones of transition, into which not only immigrants, but also single working men and, occasionally, skid row bums, settled. Thus the first phase of immigrant settlement (the area of first settlement) happened to be in a section of the city that itself had weak social controls—as the immigrants were learning their way around the new society. The broadest example of this type of study was perhaps Louis Wirth's *The Ghetto* (1928), the saga of Jewish settlement from the ghetto of medieval Frankfort through the areas of first and second settlement in the city of Chicago.

The point of this paradigm is that the "disorganization" in the area of first settlement was temporary. Ward (1971) makes the point that these immigrant settlements in Northern and Eastern industrial cities were extraordinarily isolated. ("New immigrants from southern and eastern Europe . . . scarcely encountered the society and institutions of native born Americans"; p. 55.) This, he argues, was a consequence of the timing of immigration in the stage of development of the American city. New immigrant settlements were mostly near the employment opportunities of the central business districts, while native Americans were almost entirely vacating those areas in favor of settlement in the outer rings of the city. But this isolation was temporary, as each wave in turn vacated the original area of first settlement. Most individuals and families passed through these zones on their way to better (more square) lives.

Even the areas of *second* settlement came to be viewed as transitional, an example being Hamtramck in Michigan (Wood, 1955). The directionality inherent in these studies of immigrant communities is epitomized by Simirenko's (1964) distinction between Pilgrims, Colonists, and Frontiersmen among the Russians in Minneapolis. The Pilgrims were all new immigrants. The Colonists were those Pilgrim descendents who remained within the area of first (or second) settlement, and made claims on the symbols of both the ethnic community and the majority community. The Frontiersmen broke their ties with the ethnic community, although retaining occasional kinship ties. The Frontiersman operates within the wider American society, with the symbols and styles of life of the majority, claiming recognition only within the majority community. The important idea here is the directionality. Scholars were not concerned with the simultaneity of square and deviant, because the settlement and its internal dynamics were largely viewed as way stages to ultimate community dissolution. Warner and Srole's (1945) typology of ethnic groups provided a timetable for such dissolution when internal and external factors were considered.

Coexistence or Devolution?

When it was discovered that ethnicity was not such an ephemeral phenomenon, the studies of ethnic communities began to shift to issues of ethnic identity versus class identity. The problematics for studies were shifted accordingly. The ethnic revivialists take for granted the penetrability of the class structure, as well as ethnic survival in a highly differentiated society. Gans' study of West End Bostonians is a forerunner of this. It is epitomized by Sandberg's study of the Poles of Los Angeles (1974). More popularly, there is Michael Novak's (1972) paean for the Poles, Italians, Greeks, and Slavs (PIGS). Andrew Greeley's work (e.g., 1972) represents the more academic and empirical side.[2]

The difficulty in this tradition is the relatively naive conception of social class as purely social. The obstacles to absorption into the social class system as the primary source of identity are seen largely as cultural, motivational, or social-psychological. The actual nature of the opportunity structures on the bottom of the system are largely forgotten in this socio-cultural view. Recent careful studies show that these structures do not, in fact, work very well. In some cases they may effectively track, segregate, and smother absorption. Yet urban ethnic research is often focussed on identity, rather than the more basic structural question of what options actually exist for ethnics. The question of deviance tends to disappear when the alternative identities—class and ethnic—are both square.

Coexistence in Studies of Minority Communities

It is not surprising that the major dialectic survives in studies of black and Puerto Rican urban communities. Even as early as Drake and Cayton's study (1962) of the black community in Chicago, the authors were concerned with the illegal opportunity structure—the "policy" racket.

Disorder, anomie, fragile personal relations, and survival orientation are themes that run through books like *Tally's Corner* (1967), *Welfare Mother* (1975), and the like. Crime statistics show that blacks tend to victimize blacks—and in their own communities. In *Black Mafia* (1974), Ianni argues the increasing importance of the illegal market in New York's Puerto Rican and black communities. This new approach is a pendulum-like swing toward "savage discovery," in Ryan's (1971) terms. In his work, Kenneth Clark (1965) states flatly that "the dark ghetto is institutionalized pathology; it is chronic, self-perpetuating pathology" (p. 81). This emphasis on deviance to the neglect of the square has gone so far that it became an issue to some black sociologists, beginning with the counterattack on the famous "Moynihan Report."

In black and other community studies, the square/deviant dualism continues to be an issue, because the assumption of directionality has largely been removed. Black and Puerto Rican communities are *not* seen as transitional, but as permanent. They are seen as almost completely bounded. Therefore the focus on deviance or on the balance between deviant and square is much more evident.

It is odd that Chicano urban community studies make almost no reference to the pathology which has become the focus of study in other racial ghettos. Urban ethnographic studies in Texas and California (Rubel, 1966; Clark, 1959) assume continuities with Mexico; the problematic tends to be the extent to which certain practices (health, for example) have become syncretist (that is, how they reconcile or unite divergent indigenous forms with those of mid-twentieth century urban America). The large-scale surveys of Los Angeles and San Antonio done in the mid-1960s were based on samples of census tracts chosen on the dual bases of income and ethnic density. This allowed application of the class versus ethnicity paradigm in the analysis of questionnaire responses (Grebler, et al., 1970). Each factor in class and ethnic density appeared to be separately significant as a matrix for understanding variations in attitudes. Nonetheless this study (in which the senior author had a major role) totally eschewed any consideration of the tensions between the square and the deviant.

Implications for Policy

No researchers are neutral. It would seriously violate the intent of the original project (see the Introduction) if the project's policy implications were not stated frankly.

Research Format

The first implication is a question of process, rather than substance. We urge that the link between research and policy become more inductive and more pluralistic. This is a sharp contrast to the current vogue in research processes for deriving intervention models, which is predominantly deductive and monistic.

Our study followed a collaborative method focussed on three small neighborhoods, or barrios, within the Chicano minority in a particular city. We feel this approach added greatly to our general knowledge of Chicano gangs, drugs, and prisoners. Our next step would be to look at similar phenomena in other neighborhoods, other cities, and other states, and then to move to other minorities. This is inductive and pluralistic. The more common approach, however, is to identify variables from comparatively limited research, and then construct a model for the process of policy making. (This might be, for example, the spread of heroin use in a community.) This is predominantly a deductive process, and assumes a similarity from one subgroup to another. This means that heroin addiction among Chicanos in Los Angeles is understood in terms of studies of black heroin addicts in Washington, D.C.

Sociologically, we argue that the pluralistic and inductive approach will result in more realistic policies. Although it appears to be cheaper to build a model and then test it, the procedure involves the risk of omitting significant variables. This risk is so large that we have good reason to believe it affects all of the deviant phenomena reported in this book. Because these phenomena affect millions of Americans, the neglect of the reports on Chicanos is no small matter.

Similarly, we argue that the collaborative methodology can give us policy that is both more realistic and more acceptable to those affected by it. Obviously, there are biases introduced by street researchers. But there is no evidence that these biases are any greater than those of the average academic researcher—in fact (see Chapter 2), there is some evidence that biases are less important, at least in the data collection phase. We are by no means convinced that the discipline of the social sciences can overcome the built-in biases of the academics any more than we are convinced that academics are any less political than street researchers (cf. Moore, 1973).

Policy suggestions and changes do not occur in a vacuum. Much of what is wrong with the operations of the institutional agencies in the barrios is that they are incongruent with barrio operating norms. The incongruities never mesh into a harmonious synthesis, but rather continually produce frictions, hostilities, and mutual antipathies. Such systems are self-sustaining once established, and unbelievably difficult to change through minor modifications. Urban public schools are an excellent example. They effectively socialize new teachers, as well as new pupils. What Rist (1973) demonstrates for the schools in meticulous detail after many days of classroom observations can be extrapolated to police, the welfare system, and particularly the prisons.

Policy changes operate within the dual constraints of existing institutional arrangements and local community norms and expectations. They also operate within an ideological—or at least an ideational—context. Our survey of barrio residents and newly released convicts gives some very clear ideas about what these people want and expect. Building in collaboration at every step of the research process is another way of making certain that community norms and expectations are considered in policy agenda.

The Economic Factor: Heroin

This book argues that the income-generating opportunity structure of the barrios must be drastically modified to emphasize the square. It must de-emphasize the illegal and welfare economic structures.

Although drastic and difficult to implement, the most obvious conclusion is that heroin be legalized. The direct and indirect costs created by the drug traffic under current laws have grown to a point almost beyond comprehension. Assuming only 250,000 addicts (the lowest national estimate), the total direct costs of drug abuse were estimated in 1975 at over $4.25 billion. (Assuming 750,000 addicts gives costs of more than $5.5 billion. Rufener, et al., 1976.) These figures include medical treatment, law enforcement, the judicial system, corrections, non-drug crimes committed by addicts, drug traffic control, drug abuse prevention, and housing stock losses. The authors of this estimate also add the indirect costs of absenteeism, unemployability, and work loss through incarceration for a net cost to society of between $8.4 and $12.2 billion. Using a middle assumption of the number of addicts, they estimate that 62 percent of the total economic costs of drug abuse can be attributed to heroin.

Legalization would eliminate the major illegal economic opportunity of the barrios (for Los Angeles Chicanos), and would eliminate the Mexican Mafia as well. It is possible, of course, that the situation in the barrios of Los Angeles is simpler than the structure of heroin marketing in other parts of the nation, because the Los Angeles barrio economy generally lacks large-scale vice or numbers (policy) industries. There is little doubt that this one change would have a major impact, although the precise effect is still a matter of speculation. Bullock (1973), for example, argues that the total collapse of this single business in both the black and the Chicano neighborhoods of Los Angeles would plunge the city into serious disorders and riots (assuming no income-generating alternatives, of course).

Decriminalization of heroin might avert more negative encounters with institutional agencies. It is certain that the chaos of most drug programs has created loss of faith in both the professional solutions to social problems and the political readiness to face those problems. (Graham Finney, then commissioner of the New York City drug treatment and prevention programs, aptly titled his book *Drugs: Administering Catastrophe* [1975].) Like other poverty programs, drug abuse programs had their funding sharply reduced in the late 1970s—from $69 million in New York when Finney was writing his book, to $32 million by 1977. In addition, treatment modalities had moved away from one-to-one counseling programs toward the cheaper chemical solutions, primarily methadone.

Yet the decriminalization of heroin is unlikely, especially in view of the difficulties in many states (not least in California) of decriminalizing marijuana. Nonetheless, the Vera Institute concept of heroin maintenance is still being discussed. Legalization of heroin has been advocated by groups as diverse as the LeDain Commission in Canada and the Consumers' Union. A Ford Foundation project (Wald, 1972) followed the LeDain Commission in recommending the elimination of criminal penalties for the illegal use of drugs, as did a major study of addiction and crime (Baridon, 1976). We favor this approach, no matter how far from political reality it may be. Even the seeming unreality of this policy is part of its necessity; the drug markets in the barrios are too deeply entrenched for any measures short of radical change.

The Economic Factor: Prison

We have shown that the illegal economy of the prisons contributed to the rise of a particularly vicious criminal organization—the Mexican Mafia. We recommend that the state prisons adopt an economic incentive system similar to that of the federal prisons, and provide for normal labor relations with prisoners. The extremely low pay scale (three to twenty-four cents per day), the absence of either horizontal or vertical job mobility, and the absence of any reasonable due process in prison labor relations are termed "nefarious" by one group of economists concerned with post-prison job behavior (Lewin, et al., 1974). If prison is not truly rehabilitative, it should at least do no further damage to inmates.

The Ethnic Factor

Both common sense and sociological insight suggest that new social structures must be based upon indigenous structures. It is almost certain that imported structures "foreign" to the life and habits of urban Chicanos will fail. In a national climate of distrust for indigenous organizations (and a desire to save money), it is naive to expect a resurgence of support for nativistic Chicano movements. Yet it is essential that community-based alternatives either to existing remedial structures or to incarceration as a major treatment modality must go beyond the simple-minded policy of limiting the operational definition of "community-based" to "non-institutional." There are many possible alternatives. The Massachusetts experiment with alternatives to juvenile incarceration shows something of the possible range of success in establishing effective linkages between offenders and the community. This range can be redefined in terms of how well an offender can assume a square identity within the community—in community terms rather than in institutional terms.

For Chicano prisoners, the barrio identity is clearly the significant identity. But institutions like the California Rehabilitation Center will continue to experiment with endless variations of group therapy, hoping that a new variation will hit with their enormous Chicano population, rather than recognize that the Chicano inmate-barrio culture is serious and important, and could very well serve as the basis for institutional program development. Program building in the correctional system most nearly acknowledged ethnic autonomy when some street groups were funded on the self-help principle; but this happened only after much skirmishing and much distrust (cf. Moore, 1972). Although these groups were partially successful in nearly all instances, they were discarded for two reasons. First, they were not successful in all instances. Second, there were recurrent problems with individual administrators. In the barrios of East Los Angeles, any managerial problem arouses this latent distrust in the world of Anglo agencies. Even as this is written, the distrust has led to the destruction of the few organizations built on the Chicano self-help principle.

Yet there are a great many reasons for optimism. The mixture and coexistence of square and deviant found in the cohorts of the Chicano fighting gangs is an interesting discovery. It is entirely possible that the basic fabric of Chicano life can be used to carefully, constructively, and realistically encourage adoption of the square identity. Some of this possibility appears in the strange triumph and tragedy of the prison self-help groups that grew out and away from the prisons into barrio social movements, with very little help from traditional social agencies.

Even yet, barrio people endure with dignity, and hope for some fulfillment in American society. A small measure of understanding from professionals is long since due them.

Appendixes

Appendix A

Analysis of the
Natural History
of the
Pinto Project

IN THIS APPENDIX we analyze the collaborative process that occurred during the funded portion of the Chicano Pinto Research Project. We will deal with three major topics: first, the sources of strain and of collaboration that emerged when the collaborative model was implemented; second, the sequence of phases in the life of the project; and third, the consequences of the collaboration for the various pieces of the research.

Sources of Strain and Collaboration in the Collaborative Model

The unpleasant experiences of Chicano prisoners with institutional research are only slightly exaggerated versions of similar experiences of addicts, gang members, and residents of poor communities. Conversely, the positive experience of Chicano prisoners and the unusual role of the project director is by no means unique. The basic problem for all research projects with sensitive populations is always to create a collaboration that will permit optimal utilization of both the academic and the indigenous expertise. This means overcoming distrust and mutual stereotyping among the collaborating elements. It means enhancing the shared values about the need for good research to meet the social and intellectual ends held in common by all collaborating elements.

In our case there were four frames of reference. These were: the academic, represented by the project director and some of the graduate student assistants; the view of the convict-addict, about half of the research staff; the Chicano square community, represented in its middle-class guise by the administrative and clerical staff; and the organized outside Chicano groups, such as the prison self-help groups and the convict-addict serving agencies.

The primary research tasks were defined by a straightforward exploratory approach. We knew at the outset that a high proportion of Chicano convicts reach prison through one of two interconnected routes—gang-related activities and narcotics. The gangs in Los Angeles are neighborhood- or barrio-based. We concentrated on three barrios that were also the target areas for agencies serving convicts and addicts. We intended to survey the residents of these neighborhoods for their perceptions of local problems related to gangs and to drugs. The other principal data-gathering task was the interviewing of newly released convicts from these three barrios. It would be preceded by an effort to probe the extent to which Chicano convicts and addicts differ from the prisoners of other ethnic groups in their modes of adaptation to prison and to the world after their release from prison. The design called for a combination of structured instruments and some less structured, quasi-ethnographic data. It was deliberately kept broad, to allow possible modification in what was conceived of as essentially a pilot project.

All frames of reference had the common value of acquiring accurate and good data. The interpretation of the data would fall within a conceptual framework drawing equally on academic and indigenous sources. This conceptual framework did not exist at the beginning of the project; this book, in fact, is the development of this framework.

There were also divergent values, including at least four between the addict-convicts and the academic researchers. The first was a mutual distrust of project goals. Addict-convicts fear that academic research may further stereotype them and thereby reinforce already destructive institutional arrangements, for the ultimate profit of only the researcher. Academics fear that addict-convicts cannot identify with contributing to knowledge as a goal. (Obviously, these two divergent values are mirror images of the two sets of anxieties about the nature and uses of knowledge or information.) Second, there was a mutual fear of manipulation. Addict-convicts find it hard to believe in the sincerity of the academic researcher, and that any academic person can know anything of real value about the prison experience and the criminal justice system. Third is the common academic distrust (especially against addicts) of the convict's capacity to manipulate any situation to his own, potentially illegal or illegitimate, goals. Fourth is a mutual distrust of long-range commitments. The researcher is seeking a short-range benefit to himself, and sees little prospect of unfunded long-range followup of discrete projects. Many of these conflicts faded somewhat during the Pinto Projects, thanks to the peculiar mix of the individuals concerned; but they continued to be very real sources of distrust for both the academics around the project and for the convicts and addicts in the outside groups.

These are the value-based sources of stress. But there are also problems of mutual acculturation and overcoming stereotypes. The convicts found it hard to take the student staff's preoccupation with making it in the university. The university is a middle-class world in which the convicts would never play a role. The student staff found it traumatic when the violent life experiences of the pinto staff began to surface, and when they began to realize that the good attributes of the convicts (group loyalty and self-respect) were based in street and prison violence, betrayal, degradation, and oppression. Thus the students were greatly troubled by a member of the pinto staff who had become addicted to heroin at age twelve, and had spent all but the past two years of his adult life in the criminal justice system. At first the obvious disparity between the man's competent and considerate behavior and his easily stereotyped history produced reactions of pity. These were firmly squelched by the entire pinto staff. As these problems were worked through, students began to see how their own reactions (shock, pity, contempt) could be used to understand the difficulties of achieving a routine atmosphere of interaction between addicts and squares.

The pinto staff also underwent acculturation within its own ranks. As this was conveyed to the academic staff, it also contributed importantly to understanding the world view of the gang member, convict, and addict. The pinto staff included men from barrios who were traditional enemies and who held strong negative stereotypes about each other. There were differences in depth of involvement in the Chicano self-help movement. Dealers and addicts are natural enemies. Federal prisoners and state prisoners had differences in perspective. Two of the men were in methadone maintenance; some Chicanos hold such dependence in contempt. Friction between the pintos tended to be managed by pintos themselves, especially those who had done volunteer work in prison self-help groups or in unfunded street groups. In both such situations (as in the project), the pintos work for a collective purpose that brings no measurable personal reward.

Value conflicts, expressed by outside reference groups, seriously troubled the project almost at once. Rumor and gossip were the centripetal processes through which the reference groups worked. Rumors about improprieties were directed at nearly every pinto staff person. In keeping with the usual social functions of rumor and gossip, they did not reach the student staff, but were confined to pinto and community staff people and grew from these sources.

Everybody on the project realized that the management of rumors (especially those about the use and dealing of narcotics) was essential. Accordingly, the pinto staff discussed various management devices used in community agencies. Urine testing was vehemently rejected as a violation of the collaborative spirit, human dignity, and human rights. It was decided that the non-pinto had to understand—had to be socialized into—the nature and destructive impact of rumor. Thus the pinto staff (and the project director) assumed collective responsibility for rumor control. An emotional staff meeting followed, and the reaction of the non-pinto staff was illuminating. It was a shocked breakthrough in understanding the environment in which all pinto projects must function. There was guilt at the casual gossip—and a new and traumatic sensitivity to the importance of semantics. "Loaded" means many things to the non-addict. To the addict or to the authorities it means only one thing—the use of heroin. Casual use of the word can have devastating consequences.

Rumors about criminal activity are a great and obvious hazard to a pinto project. Gossip about individuals is less obvious and even more dangerous. In an atmosphere of mixed conceptions of normality, gossip is dangerous. The academic people suffered from rumors among fellow academics about neurotic motivations.[1] The community staff was accused of getting kicks out of ex-convicts. The pinto staff was accused of selling out to the establishment for personal profit. The charges were always accompanied by negative implications. Community gossip implied that both the pinto and the academic staff were using each other for unspeakable reasons.

Gossip is a social control mechanism that maintains the boundaries of subgroups. It was in the very nature of this project that the routine norms of subgroups should be grossly violated. In fact, to accept the goals and methodology of the project was to reject a normal mode of procedure for the reference groups of all staff elements. It was as difficult to prove the scientific intent of the project to academic reference groups as it was to convince pinto reference groups of its ethical soundness.

Implementing the Collaborative Model: Phase Sequences

Value conflicts and distrust between academics and pintos were at a minimum during the project's First Phase. Intrastaff acculturation was at a peak. The staff were all hired simultaneously and put to work on the clarification of some research tasks and on the development and testing of instruments. This became a time of mutual information exchange and value testing of the academic staff by the convict staff. For its part, the academic staff did very little testing. There was substantial, although uninformed, trust of the convicts. The convict staff acted predominantly as interpreters and held discussions in large and small seminars (including non-staff convicts and some visitors released for the day from prisons) about the structures and behavior of barrio gangs and prisoners.

The Second Phase (when actual work was performed and the questionnaires were taken into the field) served as a shakedown period. Performance, rather than mutual understanding, became the issue, and there were resignations and terminations. Within the convict staff, some internal conflicts were brought to the attention of the director. *Movimiento* concepts of "discipline" began to supplement the more informal controls of the convict subculture. When neither discipline nor informal controls worked, the project director was pressured to terminate deviants. With some exceptions, the student staff performed at an adequate level.

During the Third Phase, some data-gathering and small projects of an ethnographic nature were completed, and a new consensual conceptual framework appeared to be emerging. There was a harmonious, and apparently fruitful collaboration among all staff elements.

The Fourth Phase brought a crisis of major proportions. The trouble began with preparations for a conference (jointly with the American Friends Service Committee) near the end of the project. The preparation of an Advance Report for this conference (manuscript and production) split the staff into convict and non-convict factions. Even the strongest of the student staff were unable to commit their tentative and half-digested conceptualizations to paper, especially to a report that would be exposed to both professionals and pintos. Accordingly, the project director and the convict staff wrote almost all of this lengthy report.

This was a crisis of long-range commitment to goals. After this struggle the convict staff tended to write off the students. The students, after a series of tense confrontations, felt excluded. Their hard-won understanding was rejected as irrelevant because it had borne no fruit; they became alienated. During the final phase, additional research staff was hired to supervise data reduction, some preliminary data runs, and to analyze the convict questionnaires. One of these had been working in a nearby room but had not been involved in the understanding or the data-gathering phases, except when his nephew was arrested on a serious charge. He turned to the convict staff for advice. The other person was an ex-convict advanced graduate student.

This was a time of extremely high convict staff morale. First, the conference attracted a wide variety of community people and professionals involved in prison problems, in California and elsewhere. A series of television and personal appearances (and even more gratifying, a number of requests for pinto membership on several establishment committees concerned with the penal system) confirmed their sense that the data *were* being effectively used in destroying stereotypes and modifying what they saw as destructive institutional arrangements. Second, they felt that the project would not be a simple discrete operation, but would have long-range consequences. The Final Report (like the Advance Report) was the product of full collaboration between the pinto staff and the project director.

When the funding ended, the core pinto staff (and some of the administrative staff) became a nonprofit corporation to ensure that the long-range goals would be achieved. Proposals were submitted, fund-raising benefits were held, and the pinto staff continued to seek opportunities for further training. It would be nice to say that this faith in research as a neutral tool was confirmed by the rapid success of this most unique pinto organization. Unfortunately, Horatio Alger is dead. It is far more difficult for this minority within a minority—the Chicano pinto-tecato—to be accepted in the establishment on its own terms, even with professional collaborators. After two years of unrewarded organizational activity carried on almost entirely by the ex-convict staff and affiliated ex-convicts, the group received a second grant from NIDA.

Research Consequences of the Collaborative Model

Up to this point we have discussed the Pinto Project as a pilot project to overcome the major value and subcultural conflicts and tensions between the world views of academia and the world views of sensitive populations. The experiment was stressful—so much so that one major element, most of the graduate student assistants, became alienated and withdrew. (There are exceptions. One woman underwent a major shift in career as a result of her participation, and became director of a project to work with women ex-offenders. One man retained his affiliation with the project, even during the lean years.) But the subsequent incorporation and continued two years of unfunded activity show that, at least on the organizational level, the model was successful in generating collaboration.

More serious for the academic side is the question of the consequences of the collaboration for the research itself. Was there any benefit? What were the disadvantages in this collaboration?

Gangs, Barrios, and Drug Markets

Outside the question of advantages and disadvantages, the effect of the collaboration was substantial. There were major modifications in research design. The design as presented in the original research proposals was flexible, but collaboration meant some major changes in direction and emphasis. For example, the material given in Chapters 2 and 3 was not in the original proposal. The straightforward historical and conceptualizing approach was not present at all.

Originally we had developed a game-like instrument (pretested with pintos) that was to produce systematic data from gang members of different ages and generations. This would allow us to rate each gang-barrio on several levels of social prestige or rank, over time. It was mildly successful in some respects, but was abandoned because the pintos felt the instrument was artificial and violated the seriousness of the research. It neither took the gang seriously as a social group, nor treated gang identity and loyalty in a serious manner. The pintos did not like the gangs treated as a kind of large-scale game.

Instead, we decided on an oral history approach emphasizing just three barrios and the evolution of their gangs from their beginnings as local sociability clusters of young male Chicanos. In addition, we decided that we had to deal with the background of narcotics and drugs in East Los Angeles and with the history of the prison self-help movement.

It did not take the researchers long to discover that, like all other poverty populations, the history of the Mexican population in the United States is poorly documented. For the barrios, written information is virtually nonexistent. Not until 1950 did the U.S. Census provide reliable, but limited, data on the basis of small areas. Census materials on larger aggregations prior to 1950 are damaged by shifting definitions of the Mexican American population, as well as by serious underenumeration. Historical materials sometimes can be extracted from descriptive M.A. theses, especially those done under the supervision of Emory Bogardus of the Sociology Department of the University of Southern California. Bogardus was one of the few scholars who was interested in Mexicans in the 1920s and 1930s. Although these studies are generally mediocre at best, they were culled extensively.

Both our general histories of the barrios and the gangs rely almost exclusively on interviews. Gangs began to interest academic researchers in the 1940s, but many of these early studies were related exclusively to various treatment techniques in vogue at the time, limiting their interest only to historians of sociology and the rather shabby history of approaches to juvenile delinquency. A few ethnographic studies of gangs were performed, but they tend to be deeply biased by the moralistic perspectives of reform-oriented researchers and the informants themselves. Usually these were the "reformed" boys who had their own stories to sell the researchers. Thus one such study appears to be based on the Cherries clique of White Fence (Ranker, 1957). Disguised as the Black Swans, the clique is shown as a savage gang with an insatiable appetite for sex and sadism. It is an accurate reflection of the newspaper stories of the time. The White Fence staff member was profoundly shocked. He had never heard of any of these things.

Oral history has a growing tradition among researchers interested in Chicanos, although it has been pursued under other names.[2] At the turn of the century, H. H. Bancroft's massive history of the Pacific Coast from Alaska to Central America compiled transcripts of interviews his assistants conducted with older members of prominent families, like Teresa Sepulveda (cited in Chapter 3, note 2). Amateur historians formed the California Historical Society in 1886; they and others began compiling reminiscenses relevant to local history.

The most extensive publications based on interviews with Chicanos were those of Manuel Gamio (1930) and Paul Taylor (1928–32). More recently, historians publishing in the Chicano journal *Aztlán* have applied oral history approaches in detailing labor strife (Weber, 1972; Gómez-Quiñones, 1972; López, 1970) and the economic adjustment (Gonzales, 1971) of Mexicans in the period before World War II, as have contributors to Servín's (1974) collection.

Our interviews of barrio residents about their early history are aptly characterized by C. Vann Woodward's comments (1974) on the slave narratives collected by the Federal Writer's Project in the 1930s:

> Sharing the normal shortcomings of historical sources, the slave interviews have an unusual character. Confusing and contradictory as they are, they represent the voices of the normally voiceless, the inarticulate masses whose silence historians are forever lamenting.

However, the data from our interviews represent not "the inarticulate masses," but rather interviewers' parents, uncles, brothers, friends, and friends of friends. The "confusion and contradiction," as well as missing information, can be resolved with another visit or a phone call. These resources are in jeopardy, however. Several respondents were in their 80s. One younger man died of an overdose of heroin between the first and second interview.

The "unusual character" of these interviews, however, is striking. They convey not only information, but—because they are taken by interviewers who really want to know about their own pasts—they convey an ambience and a quality of life with extraordinary impact. In addition, they provide the raw material for derivation of concepts.

Though oral histories had been envisioned from the outset of the project, their potential was slow in catching on with the pinto staff. Only as each individual found that his own special experience with his barrio was not generalizable to earlier or later periods did historical research begin to capture the imagination of the staff. This happened first with the history of White Fence, and for this reason the White Fence history (especially of the gang cohorts) is the fullest. The White Fence interviewer contacted at least two respondents from each crowd, and cross-checked when contradictions or gaps in information occurred.

The history of barbiturates was the primary responsibility of a pinto staff member who had been directly involved in barbiturate marketing. He interviewed a number of individuals who organized a distribution network of drugs in the barrios of East Los Angeles. He also took major responsibility for the history of the heroin market, drawing on interviews with people in the drug business, former and present addicts, and his own experience. Preliminary versions of both papers were distributed among prisoners and ex-convict groups, and were the subject of two staff seminars which included members of prison culture groups. Knowledgeable pinto staff members also contributed substantially to these two papers. Longer versions of each of these papers may be found in *The Los Angeles Pinto* (1975).

The history of the self-help movement was derived from interviews with participants, from the experiences of staff members who have been active in it, from a small-scale survey of culture group leaders (see Appendix C for a report), and from interviews with correctional personnel.

Thus the collaborative effort accidentally produced a major body of historical materials on four types of social phenomena that go almost totally unrecorded in urban history. These are the barrios, the gangs, the drug market, and the prison self-help movement. Los Angeles is, to say again, the major settlement of the second-largest minority in the United States. It is on the basis of the pintos' dissatisfaction with their own understanding of their roots, and their relatively easy access to normally inaccessible sources of historical data, that this body of materials was assembled.

Prison Experiences and Adaptations

The most striking effect of our unique collaboration occurred in the changes made in the analysis of Chicano prison adaptations. We originally planned to administer a modified version of a survey developed by John Irwin (1970), based on his own prison experiences. We tried this during a seminar with staff people, pintos in a community agency, and three convict visitors. We discovered immediately that the categories did not communicate to either convicts or ex-convicts. We were astonished when the Chicano prisoners asked for a questionnaire that could be administered inside the prison by Chicano self-help groups. We had assumed that the prisoners would resist questionnaires as they have done successfully for many years.

The resulting questionnaire was developed after a great deal of discussion and dispute within the pinto staff. During this discussion some of the basic divergencies within the pinto viewpoint appeared. The development of the questionnaire and the seminars with pintos outside the staff was the first substantive task for staff collaboration. Later another seminar was held with yet another group of visitors from a different prison. Thus the involvement of pinto expertise from presently incarcerated and from non-staff ex-convicts of varying backgrounds was established very early and in a significant research context.

This process of interaction became most important when the staff began to visit prison self-help groups. Two seminars included pintos from outside the staff, but the direct visits to prison and some long discussions impressed on the non-pinto staff the extreme importance of prison adaptations on the post-prison capacities of the Chicano prisoner. Thus a minor portion of the original research design was substantially expanded.

We discovered during this process that the existing literature was very nearly useless. After a staff consultation with John Irwin (author of the book we had been using for research questionnaire design), we realized it would be necessary to start from the beginning. A series of sensational television shows focussing on Mexicans in prison in the fall of 1974 helped solidify this conviction. More important, a sensationalist academic publication (Davidson, 1974) appeared at this time. The book projects a certain surface plausibility along with a deeply destructive fantasy of Chicanos as total masters of themselves and the prison environment, a conclusion that contradicts the most superficial observation of any prison environment in California. It alleges the existence of a dominant, but benign and movement-oriented, Brown Mafia which, he charged, actually controlled San Quentin. At the same time the development of the Mexican prison super gangs (Mafia and La Familia) were being used by correctional authorities as the rationalization for a newly repressive policy toward Chicano convicts. Newly incarcerated Chicanos (especially older men with previous sentences) were heavily interrogated upon arrival about possible Mafia involvement. Davidson presented his work to our staff, and met such hostility from the pintos (some of them earlier subjects at San Quentin, whom he presents as his friends and secret informants) that a collective critique of his book formed the jumping-off point for further investigation of prison adaptations.

This correctional policy also entailed a revived hostility from correctional administrators toward the Chicano self-help groups. In some cases these groups were simply eliminated from the prison program. Chicano prisoners reported increased discrimination in their assignments to prison work, to programs dealing with education or trade experience, and in their transfer from maximum- or medium-security institutions. From the point of view of our research, we then knew that the convicts we would be interviewing on release would be experiencing especially repressive attention from the California correctional system.

A final word about the post-release interviews. The pintos helped design the interview schedule and locate the appropriate number of pintos from each barrio. They persuaded the respondents to be interviewed honestly by their barrio homeboys (who often knew some of the facts of their cases), and they helped to interpret the responses. All of this was planned from the beginning. This portion of the research design would be impossible for an academic person to accomplish without direct exposure to the antecedent social worlds of the prisons and the barrios.

It should be clear that this book could not have been researched and written without pinto help at every step, from the research design to the final revisions of the manuscript. Nor could this book have been written without the peculiar insights of the academic world. Yet even with the collaboration of these two worlds it must not be considered a definitive study.

More important, it should not be considered as important or as intensive a collaboration as the world of academic sociology might produce in the future.

LUCHA Survey of Parolees*

1. Sex: (1) male = 78.1%, (2) female = 15.8%, (3) no answer = 6.1%
2. Ethnicity: (1) Mexican American = 76%, (2) black = 7.5%, (3) Anglo-American = 13%, (4) other = 0.5%, (5) no answer = 3%
3. Age: (1) under 20 = 3.4%, (2) 20–25 = 21.2%, (3) 26–30 = 41.9%, (4) 31–40 = 20.5%, (5) 41–50 = 4.1%, (6) over 50 = .7%, (7) no answer = 8.2%
4. Education: (1) less than 4th grade = 6.8%, (2) 4–8 = 32.2%, (3) 9–11 = 43.1%, (4) 12 (high school) = 2.1%, (6) no answer = 21.9%
5. How long have you been out on parole? (1) less than 6 months = 26%, (2) 6 months–1 year = 38.4%, (3) 1–2 years = 21.2%, (4) 2–3 years = 7.5%, (5) more than 3 years = 1.4%, (6) no answer = 5.5%
6. Is this your: (1) first parole = 17.8%, (2) second parole = 54.8%, (3) third parole = 25.3%, (4) no answer = 2.1%

For each condition of parole, indicate how much of a problem it has been for you:

	Very serious problem %	Moderate problem %	Not very serious %	No problem %	No answer %
1. Reporting at release	25.3	11	12.3	51.4	0
2. Residence	43.8	17.8	23.3	15.1	0
3. Maintaining employment	58.9	14.4	21.2	4.8	0.7
4. Monthly reports	27.4	12.3	16.4	43.8	0
5. Alcoholic beverages	45.2	8.2	15.8	30.8	0

*SOURCE: *People's Resolution* (1970), pp. 1–5. Number of respondents: 146.

	Very serious problem %	Moderate problem %	Not very serious %	No problem %	No answer %
6. Narcotics and drugs	67.8	13	8.9	10.3	0
7. Weapons	35.6	7.5	11.6	44.5	0.7
8. Association	51.4	20.5	21.2	6.2	0.7
9. Motor vehicles	46.6	26.7	12.3	13.7	0.7
10. Cooperation and attitude	50.7	9.6	17.1	11	11.4
11. Law and conduct	61	9.6	17.1	11	1.4
12. Civil rights	72.6	13.7	7.5	4.1	2.1
13. Cash assistance	71.9	15.1	5.5	6.8	0.7
14. Special conditions: a. nalline testing	65.1	11	11.6	9.6	2.7
b. other	58.2	9.6	10.3	6.2	15.8
15. Certificate of rehabilitation	63	11.6	11	8.2	6.2

For each area of service, indicate how much help your *parole agent* has been:

	Great Help %	Con-cerned but not much help %	Not con-cerned; not much help %	Negative %	No answer %
1. Job development	1.4	9.6	13	74	2.1
2. Personal counseling	1.4	11.6	15.1	69.9	2.1
3. Awareness of referral services: Medical	2.7	12.3	19.2	63.7	2.1
Housing	2.1	11.6	15.8	67.8	2.7
4. Referrals: Clothing	0.7	13	11.6	72.6	2.1
Food stamps	0.7	10.3	20.5	66.4	2.1
Financial aid	0.7	11	19.9	66.4	2.1
Transportation	0.7	11.6	19.9	65.8	2.1
5. Attitude toward race	0.7	17.1	17.8	62.3	2.1

	Great Help %	Concerned but not much help %	Not concerned; not much help %	Negative %	No answer %
6. Willingness to respond to an after-hour emergency	0.7	3.4	15.8	78.1	2.1
7. Awareness of parolee's whole history	0.7	15.8	18.5	63	2.1
8. General overall attitude	0.7	19.2	13	65.1	2.1

Now, some questions about the prison experience itself:

1. Did you experience group therapy?
   Yes: 72.6%   No: 12.3%   No answer: 15.1%
2. If yes, did you find it:
   Helpful   4.8%
   Waste of time   39.0%
   Destructive   37.7%
   No answer   18.5%
3. What was your maximum pay in prison?
   3¢: 28.1%; 6¢: 17.8%; 9¢: 13.7% 12¢: 10.3%; 16¢: 2.7%; 18¢: 0.7%;
   24¢: 2.1%; No answer: 24.7%
4. What was your longest job in prison?
   1. Professional (dental technician, etc.)   6.8%
   2. Machine shop   10.3%
   3. Administration and school programs   7.5%
   4. Laundry, tier tendng   22.6%
   5. Yard sweeper   14.4%
   6. Other   24.7%
   7. Unclassified   9.6%
   8. No job: education program   0%
   9. No answer   4.1%
5. What kind of vocational training did you have?
   1. Semiprofessional, professional   13.7%
   2. Machine shop   8.9%
   3. Textile mill   11.0%
   4. Furniture factory   6.2%
   5. Other   52.1%
   6. No answer   8.2%

6. Do you feel that the prison classification system discriminates against Mexican Americans?
    Yes: 97.3%; No: 0.7%; No answer: 2.1%
7. Against blacks:
    Yes: 93.8%; No: 0; No answer: 6.2%
8. Do you feel that the psychological tests administered to you on your entry into prison were: (1) used by the officials to control you, or, (2) used by the officials to help you, or, (3) not used by the officials, or, (4) don't know.
    (1) 79.4%, (2) 1.4%, (3) 4.1%, (4) 11.6%, (5) No answer, 3.4%
9. Were you ever returned to prison for parole violation?
    Yes: 83.6%; No: 10.3%; No answer: 6.2%
10. If yes, do you think you would have been returned if you had been through a regular trial procedure, with a lawyer?
    Yes: 32.9%; No: 46.6%; Don't know: 13.0%; No answer: 7.5%
11. In sum, prison was: (1) helpful, (2) waste of time, (3) destructive to rehabilitation:
    (1) 2.1%, (2) 32.9%, (3) 61.0%, (4) No answer, 4.1%
12. In sum, is parole, (1) helpful, (2) waste of time, (3) destructive to your present rehabilitation?
    (1) 3.4%, (2) 37.0%, (3) 56.2%, (4) No answer, 3.4%

MASH Survey*

Results of survey on Chicanos incarcerated in McNeil Island Federal Penitentiary in 1971. This survey was conducted by members of the Mexican American Self-Help Group (MASH) and it was learned that Chicanos serve longer sentences than other ethnic groups for the same offense.

This survey was conducted in secret and the results were given to concerned Chicanos from the academic community so that they could be aware of the harsh penalties meted out to Chicanos.

Age (104 members)

The youngest was 23 years old (serving an 18-year sentence); the oldest was 57 years old. Mean average, 37 years old; median average, 40 years old.

I.Q. (84 members) (excludes those from Mexico and/or non-English speaking)

Low: 49 (this man serving life for murder, English spoken very broken so not true reading); high: 130 (this man serving 30 years). Mean: 106; median: 104.

G.P.A. (84 members; excludes those from Mexico)

Mean: 7.2; Median: 7.6.

*SOURCE: MASH Survey (1971), pp. 6–7.

Offenses (111 members)

Narcotic (paroleable sentence): 25
Narcotic (nonparoleable sentence): 56
Bank robbery: 18
Alien-related offense: 5
Assault: 1
Forgery: 1
Counterfeit: 1
Interstate Theft: 1
Homicide: 2
Fraud: 1

Tentative Release Dates (91 members)

1971: 2	1974: 10	1977: 10	1981: 3
1972: 12	1975: 19	1978: 1	1982: 1
1973: 12	1976: 15	1979: 2	1985: 1
		1980: 3	1986: 1

Residence (106 members)

Mexico: 18	Washington: 3	Colombia: 1
California: 72	Colorado: 4	Alaska: 1
Texas: 2	New Mexico: 2	Chile: 1
Arizona: 1	Venezuela: 1	

Trades/vocations (106 members)

50% have trades
50% do not have trades

Length of service (105 members)

2 years: 3	6 years: 5	10 years: 32	18 years: 2
3 years: 3	7 years: 13	12 years: 5	20 years: 1
4 years: 3	8 years: 16	14 years: 1	22 years: 1
5 years: 11	9 years: 1	15 years: 5	25 years: 3
			30 years: 1

Mean: 8.6 years; median: 16 years (not valid); mode: 10 years (excludes homocide).

Appendix C

Culture
Group Survey

FROM THE BEGINNING of the Pinto Project in 1974, relationships were set up with culture groups in prisons in the local area. Four culture groups encouraged the project to submit questionnaires to them (see Appendix A).

At the four institutions, respondents to our survey included:

35 members of the executive council of MAYO at the minimum-security California Rehabilitation Center (Norco);
22 members of COPA at the minimum-security California Institution for men (Chino);
35 members of MACHO and other self-help groups at the minimum-security California Correctional Institution (Tehachapi);[1] and
31 members of PUMA at the maximum-security Federal Correctional Institution (Lompoc).

We can get further insight into the extent to which these culture group members are representative of other Chicano pintos from the comments of officers of the three state prison groups to a series of questions sent by our staff. These men acknowledge a considerable variation in their ability to keep their fellow pintos participating in these groups. Only 10 percent of the Chicano convicts at Tehachapi, for example, attend the MACHO meetings. Forty percent of those incarcerated at CRC attend MAYO meetings. In this latter group, the 35 members of the executive council were the survey target; the remaining three hundred-odd members were too diffiicult to reach. The Chicano culture groups have had a strong history at CRC and CIM, but at the time of our survey, that group at Chino (CIM) was facing considerable harassment from the prison administration. Group officials tend also to disagree about the impact of prison participation on parole decisions, but they all agree that such activity is more controversial than, for example, participation in such groups as Alcoholics Anonymous. (AA attracted a total of 2,580 inmate members in March of 1975 in the California prison system, and was actually introduced to the correctional system by the administration. Many of the members join because attendance looks good to the parole board.)

The accompanying table shows respondent characteristics in each of the four prisons. Relationships were also established with the groups at CMC-

East and at the men's and women's federal prisons at Terminal Island, after overcoming many administrative obstacles. There relationships were established so late in the project's existence that questionnaires were not administered.

Background Characteristics of Culture Group Members, by Prison

	Prison			
Characteristics	CRC* %	CIM† %	CCI‡ %	FCI§ %
Age				
20–24	41	14	20	47
25–29	29	29	32	47
30–+	30	57	48	6
Median school years completed	10.2	11.2	12	10.8
Marital status				
single	25	54	32	43
married	64	32	41	37
other	11	14	27	20
Number of dependents				
none	22	57	34	23
1–2	31	14	47	29
3 or more	47	29	19	48
Ever in				
foster home	44	9	11	12
Juvenile Hall	25	36	54	53
Youth Authority institution	36	59	51	47
other adult prison	91	62	53	75
Ever addicted to				
heroin	79	57	56	72
amphetamines	33	14	18	15
barbiturates	22	14	21	31
Time served on this offense				
1 year or less	51	6	6	34
1–5 years	20	22	35	53
5 years or more	29	72	59	13
Occupational level				
skilled	34	41	30	38
semiskilled	11	5	7	12.5
unskilled	34	36	44	34
none	17	18	19	12.5
student	3	0	0	3
Total N (= 100%)	(35)	(22)	(35)	(31)

*California Rehabilitation Center, Corona, California.
†California Institution for Men, Chino, California.
‡California Correctional Institution, Tehachapi, California.
§Federal Correctional Institution, Lompoc, California.

Appendix D   Chicano Culture Groups

In California State Prisons

Prison	State	Name of culture group	Acronym
*San Quentin	California	El Mejicano Preparado Listo Educado y Organizado	EMPLEO
*Susanville	California	La Raza Unida	LIBRE
*Folsom	California	League of Inmates of Brotherhood Rehabilitation and Education Empleo Por Unidad	
Vacaville	California		GEMA
*Soledad (Central)	California	Grupo Ejemplar Movimiento de Aztlan	CAUSA
*Soledad (North)	California		
*Tracy	California		
San Luis Obispo	California	La Raza Unida	MACHO
Tehachapi (min.)	California	Movimiento Aztlan Chicano Organizado	
Tehachapi (med.)	California	La Raza Unida	COPA
Chino	California	Chicanos Organizados Pintos de Aztlan	MAYO
CRC (Women)	California	Mexican American Youth Organization	MAYO
CRC (Men)	California	Mexican American Youth Organization	MARA
CIW	California	Mexican American Research Association	

In Federal Prisons

Prison	State	Name of culture group	Acronym
McNeil Island	Washington	Mexican American Self Help	MASH
Lompoc Inst.	California	Pinto Unidos Mejicanos de Aztlan	PUMA
Lompoc Camp	California	Mexican American Rehabilitation Culture Organization	MARCO
*Terminal Island (Women)	California	Mujeres Unidas Juntas en Revolucion	MUJER

*Denotes those prisons that do not have sponsors and/or are non-functional due to other causes.

199

Prison	State	Name of culture group	Acronym
*Terminal Island (Men)	California	Teson Respeto Unidad Cultura Historia Amistad Sabaduria	TRUCHAS AZTLAN
*Leavenworth	Kansas		
La Tuna	New Mexico	Los Mejicanos	
*Sanford Camp	Arizona		
Springfield Medical Center	Missouri	La Causa Latina	
*Marion	Illinois	Chicano Culture Center	
Fort Worth	Texas	El Azteca Cultural Group	
El Reno Reformatory	Oklahoma		AIMA
Terre Haute	Indiana	Hermanidad Pan American	
Seagoville Camp	Texas		
In Other State Prisons			
Arizona State Penitentiary	Arizona		MACHO LADS
Canon City Penitentiary	Colorado		
Michigan Youth Reformatory	Michigan		
Walla Walla Penitentiary	Washington	United Chicanos	
Shelton Reformatory	Washington	Chicano Carnalismo y Cultura	
Monroe Reformatory	Washington	Los Mejicanos	
Salem Penitentiary	Oregon		
Youth Training School	California	Chicano Cultural Club	COPA

*Denotes those prisons that do not have sponsors and/or are non-functional due to other causes.

Appendix E

Pinto and Non-Pinto Interviewers in the Barrios

ACCORDING to the conventional wisdom of professional survey researchers, the best interviewer is a warm, preferably middle-aged, woman. Because we wanted all of the staff to visit all barrios, everyone (man, woman, pinto, and non-pinto) interviewed residents of the three gang barrios. Nonetheless, we expected that the more respectable, that is, the non-pinto, interviewers would do the best, especially the women.

These interviews were, of course, extremely difficult in these very poor, village-like barrios, and the questionnaire was long and controversial. (Classically, these are questions of respondent motivation; cf. Kahn and Cannell, 1957, 1968.) We realized that students were having more, rather than less, discomfort and difficulty, but we did not realize at the time that the pinto interviewers obtained nearly three times as many interviews as did non-pintos (pinto mean number = 15; non-pinto mean number = 5.2). Regardless of sex, the student interviewers were the least productive (obtaining a mean of 3.25 interviews).

Why the difference? The factors that must be sorted out are many. Pintos were generally older by ten to fifteen years; all were male. Four of the non-pintos were women. Perhaps most important, the pintos included a larger number of natives of the barrios (five of the six pintos were natives of one of the three barrios; four of the nine non-pintos were natives). The educational differences were great. Only one pinto had a college degree (MSW); four of the non-pintos were graduate students and one was an undergraduate. Age was clearly associated with productivity; the older interviewers averaged 15; the younger only 4.6. Nativity was associated: the natives obtained 11.9; the non-natives just 5. Yet although the pinto and non-pinto distinction is somewhat confounded with other factors, we asked a second question: what differences appear in those questions in which pintos may have a strong interest?

In traditional terms, this is a question of bias. But, first, did the respondents get cues in the pinto interviewer's behavior about the questions about prison and ex-convicts? Second, did the pinto expect, and therefore elicit, a different pattern of responses?

First, the cues. Whatever cues might be put forth by the interviewer are not immediately analyzable. Analogously, Mulford and Miller (1959, 1960, cited in Calahan, et al., 1969) found that teetotalling interviewers found lower rates of drinking than did drinking interviewers. In a classic study, Rice found that interviewers' own diagnosis of the causes of skid row destitution was reflected in respondents' response patterns (1929, cited in Kahn and Cannell, 1957). These are all invisible characteristics, unlike age, race, sex, social-class cues in clothing and language, and the like. Neither are they simple questions of ideology—or at least not in our group of interviewers (cf. Hyman, et al., 1975). Our interviewers seemed to share ideological commitments to the Chicano movement, to developing community-based alternatives to incarceration, and to other issues presented in the questionnaire. Whatever the cues presented to respondents, they must have been very subtle. And (speculatively) they must have had more to do with the ease and comfort with which problems of gangs, drugs, and prison were dealt with by pintos as compared with non-pinto interviewers.

Second, what were the possible expectations of pinto interviewers as compared with non-pinto interviewers of the neighborhood respondents? Hyman (1975) argues cogently that the interviewer's role expectations of the respondents tend to come out most strongly when there is questioning in a difficult area. Certainly, the questions we asked were difficult, calling for respondent opinions about a wide range of disturbing social problems. Here our data tend to be of some use: we did find differences in certain selected items between respondents interviewed by pintos and by non-pintos. And, oddly, we must conclude that it is the non-pintos who probably projected their own stereotypes onto respondents more than did the pintos. This set of findings (see accompanying table) suggests that non-pinto interviewers had an inhibiting effect on respondents' estimates of extensiveness of illegal activity in their neighborhoods.

If we argue that the non-pintos tended to inhibit the estimate of high rates of illegal activity, we must ask further how it works. The pintos were older and tended to be natives of the barrios. It is likely these factors cued rerespondents that it was all right to admit the existence of barrio problems, because the interviewer could accept such unpleasant knowledge. By contrast, the younger, more feminine, somewhat more middle-class non-pinto interviewers may have created an unwillingness to admit to something that the interviewers themselves may have felt was shameful.

We have some corroboration to this comfort hypothesis. It occurs in responses to the question about whether or not the respondent is comfortable in talking about drugs. Although it is not statistically significant, it is worth noting that 42 percent of the persons responding to non-pinto interviewers said they did not like to talk about drugs. Only 25 percent of the pintos' respondents felt such constraints.

To summarize to this point, we feel we have discovered another Mulford and Miller effect. Interviewers who are comfortable with, and participate in, a controversial act elicit from respondents more admission of such acts than do interviewers who are uncomfortable with, and do not participate in, such acts. We feel that non-pinto interviewers inhibit the willingness of barrio residents to admit the existence of what an outsider might consider to be illegal activities in the barrio.

Estimates of Illegal Activities in Neighborhood, by Pinto and Non-Pinto Interviewers, 1975

	Estimate		
Illegal activity	High or moderate (%)	Low or none (%)	D.K. (%)
Gang activity in neighborhood*			
pinto interviewers	78.5	21.4	n.a.
non-pinto interviewers	53.4	46.7	n.a.
Neighborhood families with drug problems†			
pinto interviewers	19.3	43.1	37.5
non-pinto interviewers	0	51.1	48.8
Neighborhood families with pill problem‡			
pinto interviewers	17.5	42.0	39.5
non-pinto interviewers	4.3	45.7	50.0
Neighborhood men who have served time§			
pinto interviewers	12.8	43.0	44.2
non-pinto interviewers	2.1	29.2	68.8
Neighborhood youth who have served time‖			
pinto interviewers	13.9	36.0	50.0
non-pinto interviewers	0	27.6	72.3

*$x^2 > .005$ †$x^2 > .01$ ‡$x^2 > .10$ §$x^2 > .02$
‖$x^2 > .01$

Then there is the traditional question of bias: did the pinto interviewers elicit more pro-convict, anti-prison responses than did the non-convicts? The simple answer is: they did not. In a set of five questions about the functions and effects (good or bad) of prison, and in a set of social distance items involving ex-convicts, pinto and non-pinto interviewers were indistinguishable.

Yet a set of seven questions on the role of the ex-convict in the local community showed statistically significant differences. More respondents to pinto interviewers felt that the community should help the convicts—and the convicts should help the community. They felt there should be halfway houses for newly released convicts, and that other barrio problems did not override the issues of convict reabsorption. This finding (that pintos elicit no bias in respondent attitudes toward ex-convicts and prison, but do elicit bias with regard to community-convict relationships) seems congruent with the earlier conclusion that barrio residents are more comfortable in discussing community problems with convicts than with non-convicts. We suggest that the earlier admission of the extensiveness of the problem may have put the respondents into a frame of mind in which they saw the problems of ex-convicts as something of concern to them as community members.

These findings about differences between the types of interviewers were unexpected. They clearly suggest that some of the traditions of survey research should be examined when sensitive populations are asked about sensitive local problems.

Appendix F

Statistical Analyses Relating to Barrio Surveys

Factor Analysis

THOUGH FACTOR ANALYSIS has been widely criticized in the analysis of survey data it has the great advantage of reducing large amounts of data to just a few indices. Factor analysis "uses the intercorrelations among a large number of variables and summarizes their common variations in to a relatively small number of 'hypothetical' variables or 'factors.' . . . [Each factor] represents a group of highly correlated variables and constitutes an index describing the characteristics displayed by those variables" (Burns and Harman, 1968, p. 87). Our project employed the factor analysis program available through the SPSS package.

At the outset we selected 62 attitudinal variables in 5 categories that appeared to relate to the primary issues in this chapter. After preliminary analysis these variables were pared down to 38 items. A three-factor solution summarizes 36 percent of the common variation in these items, and the factors appeared to make intuitive sense.

The accompanying table shows the loading for each variable. (Coefficients lower than .200 were omitted from the table.) The variables are ordered in the table by the strength of their association with each factor, irrespective of sign.

Factor 1 is termed "Perception of Neighborhood as Problem-Filled," or "Problems" for short. The factor summarizes 16.7% of the common variation among the items, and the loadings on neighborhood problem items is quite high.

Factor 2 we termed "Desire for Social Distance from Problems," or "Distance" for short. The highest loadings were on items derived from two "social distance" scales, having to do with relations with ex-convicts and ex-addicts, and other items with relatively high loadings are similarly oriented. It summarizes 11.5% of the common variation among the items.

Factor 3 is the weakest of the three factors, summarizing only 7.9% of the variance. It is also the most difficult to name. We call it "Reliance on Institutions for Solutions," or "Institutional" for short, because it is loaded on questionnaire items that relate to the respondent's belief in the political system (regardless of his understanding of politics), his willingness to turn to institutional officials for help with neighborhood problems, and positive attitudes toward the criminal justice system. It can be seen as describing the extent to which respondents trust—or are critical of—institutions, and rely— or don't—on institutional agencies for help with local problems.

The mean score for Factor 1 is −.006, with a standard deviation of .970. The mean score of Factor 2 is .060, with a standard deviation of 1.022. The mean score in Factor 3 is −.014, with a standard deviation of .939.

For additional information, the next section in this appendix shows the actual patterns of response on each of the items included in the factor analysis.

Factor Loadings, Los Angeles Barrios, 1975

Variable	Factor 1 Problem	Factor 2 Distance	Factor 3 Institutional
1. Crime in streets problem	.781	*	*
2. People worry about personal safety	.768	*	*
3. Gang activity in neighborhood	.704	*	*
4. Many thefts in neighborhood	.693	*	*
5. Youth present serious problem	.649	*	*
6. Occurrence of violent behavior	.627	*	*
7. Drug addiction problem	.623	*	*
8. Neighborhood not good influence on children	.616	*	−.235
9. Ex-cons have enough help	.389	*	*
10. Distasteful to party with ex-addicts	*	.804	*
11. Distasteful to work with ex-addicts	*	.723	*
12. Distasteful to dance with ex-convicts	*	.723	.217
13. Distasteful to work with ex-convicts	*	.660	.272
14. Distasteful to dance with ex-addicts	*	.624	*
15. Distasteful to party with ex-convicts	*	.614	.213
16. Distasteful to marry ex-cons	*	.517	*
17. Ex-convicts should have halfway house in this community	*	−.356	*
18. Community has (not) too many problems to care about ex-cons	*	−.288	*
19. Hire woman ex-convicts as baby-sitter—no	*	.296	.256
20. Need community help for drug abuse	*	.217	−.200
21. Need programs to help addicts	*	(.103)	*
22. People like you have say in government	*	*	.582
23. To help with narcotics: more police	*	.310	.576
24. To help with narcotics: social workers with family	*	*	.537
25. Prison punishes bad people	*	.379	.502
26. Prison creates criminals (no)	*	*	.496
27. Public officials care about people like you	−.259	*	.472

Variable	Factor 1 Problem	Factor 2 Distance	Factor 3 Institutional
28. Suggest probation department to kid on drugs	*	*	.460
29. Use of narcotics a sin	*	*	.452
30. Ex-convicts are a problem to the community	*	.296	.428
31. Prison teaches trades	*	*	.424
32. People like me can't understand politics (no)	*	*	−.409
33. Suggest juvenile police to kid on drugs	*	*	.399
34. Community halfway houses are bad (no)	*	*	−.397
35. Prison dehumanizes (no)	*	*	.388
36. Suggest school teacher to kid on drugs	*	*	.352
37. Ex-convicts' problems are related to crime and drugs	*	*	.287
38. Crime would rise if offenders served terms in community	*	*	(.191)
39. Poor schools are a problem (no)	*	*	(.168)
Percent of Variance by Factor (Total = 36.0%):	16.7%	11.5%	7.9%

*Indicates a coefficient of less than .200, except for three variables in parentheses.

Patterns of Response to Questionnaire Items in Factor Analysis

1. Crime in streets problem. Questionnaire: Here are some problems that other communities have talked about—do you feel these are problems that are serious in your community. Crime in the streets: (1) very serious 18.5%, (2) moderate 24.4%, (3) minor 17.8%, (4) not serious 34.1%, and (5) don't know 5.2% (100% = 135).

2. People worry about personal safety. Questionnaire: Do people in this neighborhood have to worry about their personal safety? If alot or some, why would they have to worry? (1) alot 15.2%, (2) some 20.5%, (3) a little 29.5%, (4) not at all 34.8% (100% = 132).

3. Gang activity in neighborhood? Questionnaire: What about gang activity, is there much in this neighborhood? (1) yes, alot 28.7%, (2) some 41.4%, (3) little or none 30.2% (100% = 129).

4. Many thefts in neighborhood? Questionnaire: There are many thefts in this neighborhood—would you say, (1) very true 14.3%, (2) somewhat true 42.1%, (3) not true 39.8% and (4) don't know 3.8% (100% = 133).

5. Youth present serious problem. Questionnaire: Would you say that youth present serious problems or not: (1) serious 31.8% (2) fairly serious 30.3%, (3) not serious 28.0%, and (4) not at all 9.8% (100% = 132).

6. Occurrence of violent behavior. Questionnaire: Is this neighborhood ever disturbed by people engaged in violent behavior such as gang fighting? (1) many times 8.3%, (2) sometimes 39.1%, (3) seldom 24.1% and (4) never 28.6% (100% = 133).

7. Drug addiction problem. Questionnaire: Here are some problems that communities have talked about—do you feel these are problems that are serious in your community. Drug addiction: (1) very serious 35.8%, (2) moderate 17.9%, (3) minor 6.7%, (4) not serious 17.9%, and (5) don't know 21.6% (100% = 134).

8. Neighborhood good influence on children. Questionnaire: This neighborhood is a good influence on children. (1) very true 32.8%, (2) somewhat true 36.6% (3) not true 27.6%, and (4) don't know 3.0% (100% = 134).

9. Ex-cons have enough help. Questionnaire: For a person coming out of prison back to the neighborhood, how true do you feel the following statements are: Ex-convicts have enough social agencies to help them deal with the problem they face: (1) very true 7.3%, (2) true 3.7%, (3) somewhat true 11.9%, (4) not so true 12.8%, and (5) not true 64.2% (100% = 109).

10. Distasteful to party with ex-addicts. Questionnaire: Now I'd like to ask you something about how you feel about people with different backgrounds. Some people have strong feelings about people who are different, while others don't mind. Do you think you would ever find it distasteful to: go to a party where most of the people are ex-heroin addicts: (1) distasteful 25.6%, (2) reservations 17.8%, and (3) not distasteful 55.8% (100% = 128).

11. Distasteful to work with ex-addicts. Questionnaire: for leading-in wording see item 10 above. To work with an ex-heroin addict: (1) distasteful 30%, (2) reservation 30%, and (3) not distasteful 38.5% (100% = 128).

12. Distasteful to dance with ex-convicts. Questionnaire: see item 10 above for correct wording. Dance with an ex-convict: (1) distasteful 17.1%, (2) reservations 24%, and (3) not distasteful 55% (100% = 124).

13. Distasteful to work with ex-convict. Questionnaire: see item 10 above. Work with an ex-convict: (1) distasteful 14.4%, (2) reservations 20.5%, and (3) not distasteful 63.6% (100% = 130).

14. Distasteful to dance with ex-addicts. Questionnaire: see item 10 above. To dance with an ex-heroin addict: (1) distasteful 34.1%, (2) reservations 28.7%, and (3) not distasteful 34.9% (100% = 126).

15. Distasteful to party with ex-convicts. Questionnaire: see item 10 above. Go to a party where most of the people are ex-convicts: (1) distasteful 29%, (2) reservations 32.8%, and (3) not distasteful 36.6% (100% = 129).

16. Distasteful to marry ex-convicts. Questionnaire: see item 10 above. To have someone in your family marry an ex-convict: (1) distasteful 11.7%, (2) reservations 14.8%, and (3) not distasteful 71.9% (100% = 126).

17. Ex-convicts should have halfway houses in this community. Questionnaire: Convicts coming back to the community should have places to stay right in their own community, such as halfway houses: (1) strongly agree 66.2%, (2) agree 5.3%, (3) neutral 9.0%, (4) disagree .8%, (5) strongly disagree 4.5%, and (6) don't know 14.3% (100% = 133).

18. Community has too many problems to care about ex-convicts. Questionnaire: There are too many other problems in the neighborhood for anyone to care about people coming out of prison: (1) strongly agree 23.7%, (2) agree 8.4%, (3) neutral 5.3%, (4) disagree 4.6%, (5) strongly disagree 48.9%, and (6) don't know 9.2% (100% = 131).

19. Hire a woman convict as babysitter. Questionnaire: What about a female ex-convict, would you hire her as a babysitter: (1) yes 8.0%, no 42.5%, (3) depends on person 4.4%, (4) depends on offense 45.1% (100% = 113).

20. Need community help for drug abuse. Questionnaire: There is a need in this community for programs to help solve problems of drug abuse. (1) strongly agree 63.4%, (2) agree 6.7%, (3) neutral 3.7%, (4) disagree 4.5%, (5) strongly disagree 3.7%, and (6) don't know 17.9% (100% = 134).

21. Need programs to help drug addicts. Questionnaire: In some neighborhoods they have opened offices to help drug addicts. The programs have been successful in some neighborhoods and not successful in others. If they opened a program for addicts here, how successful do you think it would be: (1) needed and would work 54.3%, (2) moderately needed 21.3%, (3) neutral 17.6%, (4) wouldn't work at all 2.9%, and (5) don't know 1.5% (100% = 129).

22. People like you have a say in government. Questionnaire: Do you feel that people like you have a say about what the government does: (1) yes 32.2%, (2) no 55.9%, and (3) don't know 11.8% (100% = 127).

23. To help with narcotics: more police. Questionnaire: Here are some policies some people talk about with regard to controlling drugs: More police: (1) good—should be done 45.5%, (2) bad—should avoid 24.4%, (3) no effect 29.3%, and (4) don't know .8% (100% = 123).

24. To help with narcotics: Social workers with the family. Questionnaire: See item 23 above. Social workers with the family: (1) good—should be done 75.7%, (2) bad—should avoid 5.2%, (3) no effect 18.3%, and (4) don't know 0.9% (100% = 115).

25. Prison punishes bad people. Questionnaire: Prison had a good effect because it punishes people who have done wrong: (1) strongly agree 26.5%,

(2) agree 8.1%, (3) neutral 11.0%, (4) disagree 2.9%, (5) strongly disagree 34.6%, and (6) don't know 15.4% (100% = 134).

26. Prison creates criminals. Questionnaire: Prison has a bad effect because people learn how to become better criminals: (1) strongly agree 53.4%, (2) agree 6.9%, (3) neutral 9.2%, (4) disagree 0.8%, (5) strongly disagree 11.5%, and (6) don't know 18.3% (100% = 131).

27. Public officials care about people like you. Questionnaire: Do you think that public officials really care much about what people like you think: (1) strongly agree 19.2%, (2) agree 5.8%, (3) neutral 8.3%, (4) disagree 2.5%, (5) strongly disagree 61.7%, and (6) don't know 2.5% (100% = 120).

28. Suggest probation department to kid on drugs. Questionnaire: Suppose somebody you knew had a kid who was involved with hard drugs; where do you think you would suggest that he go for a solution; how likely would you be to send him to . . . probation department: (1) very likely 21.0%, (2) maybe 21.0%, (3) never 42.7%, (4) don't know 14.5%, (5) don't know agency 0.8% (100% = 124).

29. Use of narcotics a sin. Questionnaire: There are alot of different ways of thinking about drugs and drug addicts. Some people, for instance, believe that drug addiction is a crime, some people believe that it is a sin, others believe that it is a psychological problem, etc. For each of the following statements, please tell me whether you feel this way very strongly, moderately, or disagree. Using narcotics is a sin: (1) strongly agree 40.0%, (2) moderately agree 14.1%, (3) disagree 40.7%, (4) don't know 5.2% (100% = 135).

30. Ex-convicts are a problem to community. Questionnaire: For a person coming out of prison, back to the neighborhood, how true do you feel the following statement is: Ex-convicts represent a problem to the community. They can't be reabsorbed: (1) very true 27.1%, (2) true 6.2%, (3) somewhat true 15.5%, (4) not so true 3.1%, and (5) not true 48.1% (100% = 129).

31. Prison teaches trades. Questionnaire: Prison has a good effect because people can learn a trade for when they are released: (1) strongly agree 53.4%, (2) agree 6.9%, (3) neutral 9.2%, (4) disagree 0.8%, (5) strongly disagree 11.5%, and (6) don't know 18.3% (100% = 131).

32. People like me can't understand politics. Questionnaire: Some people feel that politics and government are so complicated that people like themselves, don't realize and can't understand what is going on: (1) strongly agree 19.2%, (2) agree 5.8%, (3) neutral 8.3%, (4) disagree 2.5%, (5) strongly disagree 61.7%, and (6) don't know 2.5% (100% = 120).

33. Suggest juvenile police to kid on drugs. Questionnaire: Suppose somebody you knew had a kid who was involved with hard drugs; where do you think you would suggest that he go for a solution; how likely would you be

to send him to . . . police (juvenile): (1) very likely 10.7%, (2) maybe 19.1%, (3) never 58.8%, (4) don't know 10.7%, and (5) don't know agency 0.8% (100% = 131).

34. Community halfway houses are bad. Questionnaire: It would be bad to have a small halfway house for ex-convicts in this neighborhood: (1) strongly agree 26.1%, (2) agree 3.0%, (3) neutral 5.2%, (4) disagree 1.5%, (5) strongly disagree 45.5%, and (6) don't know 18.7% (100% = 134).

35. Prison dehumanizes. Questionnaire: Prison has a bad effect because it dehumanizes people: (1) strongly agree 58.1%, (2) agree 7.4%, (3) neutral 7.4%, (5) strongly disagree 6.6%, (6) don't know 18.4% (100% = 133).

36. Suggest school teacher to kid on drugs. Questionnaire: Suppose somebody you knew had a kid who was involved with hard drugs; where do you think you would suggest that he go for a solution; how likely would you be to send him to . . . school teacher: (1) very likely 21.5%, (2) maybe 26.9%, (3) never 40.0%, (4) don't know 10.8%, and (5) don't know agency 0.8% (100% = 130).

37. Ex-convicts' problems are related to crime and drugs. Questionnaire: For a person coming out of prison back to the neighborhood, how true do you feel the following statement is: Ex-convicts' main concerns are connected with their drug or crime patterns: (1) very true 50.4%, (2) true 8.5%, (3) somewhat true 20.5%, (4) not so true 4.3%, and (5) not true 16.2% (100% = 117).

38. Crime would rise if offenders served terms in community. Questionnaire: Some people are talking about doing away with prisons and having some offenders serving sentences in the community. Do you feel there will be a rise in crime if offenders were to serve out their sentences in the community: (1) strongly agree 29.9%, (2) agree 8.7%, (3) neutral 6.3%, (4) disagree 2.4%, (5) strongly disagree 33.9%, and (6) don't know 18.9% (100% = 127).

39. Poor schools are a problem. Questionnaire: Here are some problems that other communities have talked about—do you feel these are problems that are serious in your community . . . poor schools: (1) very serious 24.1%, (2) moderate 25.6%, (3) minor 7.5%, (4) not serious 27.8%, and (5) don't know 15.0% (100% = 133).

Analysis of Individual Factor Scores

Once individual respondents were allocated scores on each of the factors, a variety of hypotheses were tested using a variety of statistical techniques.

For linear background variables (age, number of years living in Los Angeles, and number of years living in the current residence), a multiple regression analysis was used. On partial correlations, the first two of these variables were significantly related to the scores on each of the three factors (see accompanying table); years in current residence was not significantly related to these sets of attitudes summarized in the factor scores. For sex, a chi-square test was used.

For measures of acculturation, chi-square and simple correlations were used, as they were in measures of neighborhood linkage.

The outcomes of these analysis are presented in the accompanying table. As indicated in the text of Chapter 7, the patterns are far from simple to interpret. Therefore, the interpretation developed into a "profile" analysis, which is based on the data presented here.

Variables Related to Factor Scores

Variables	Factor 1 Problems		Factor 2 Distance		Factor 3 Institutional		Statistic Used
	signi-ficance	sign	signi-ficance	sign	signi-ficance	sign	
Background							
Age*	$>.06$	$(+)$	$>.02$	$(-)$	$>.03$	$(-)$	partial r
Years in L.A.†	$>.05$	$(+)$	$>.02$	$(-)$			partial r
Years in current residence‡							partial r
Sex			$>.05$	§			x^2
Acculturation							
Nativity status‖			$>.001$	$(-)$	$>.01$	$(-)$	r#
(For those not born in L.A.) where living before L.A.							x^2
Fluency in English							x^2
Neighborhood Linkage							
Number of families known by name							r
Neighbor visits by man			$>.05$	$(-)$			r
Neighbor visits by woman	$>.09$	$(+)$			$>.10$	$(-)$	r
Like to move	$>.003$	$(-)$					x^2
Problems will improve	$>.01$	$(-)$					x^2

*Partial correlation, holding years in L.A. and years in current residence constant.

†Partial correlation, holding age and years in current resident constant.

‡Partial correlation, holding age and years in L.A. constant.

§Males high, females low.

‖The question read: born in L.A., moved here as a child, moved as an adult The negative association means that those that were born in L.A. were low, and those migrating as an adult were high.

#x^2 was also used here.

Notes

Introduction

1. A good illustration of this common situation is given by a study in which three hundred inmates, newly admitted to the Los Angeles County Jail, were asked for a urine test. Later they were interviewed in a long attitudinal survey; one question was about current heroin use. The respondents all answered the question, but a measure of the covert noncompliance is given by the finding that only 46 percent of the inmates whose urinalysis showed signs of heroin use admitted to being "current users." The study was replicated in five other cities: Los Angeles showed the lowest "candour" in admitting current narcotics use—a result almost certainly connected with the fact that many inmates are on their way to prison and that California narcotics laws are very severe (Eckerman, el al., 1971).

2. These prison groups included COPA from California Institute for Men, Chino (CIM) MACHO from Tehachapi, and MUJER from Terminal Island. The very name of the project was a pinto decision. The study had no name until January, 1975, when the MACHO self-help group presented the research staff with a carved plaque labeled "U.S.C. Pinto Project."

Chapter 1

1. The information in this section of Chapter 1 is not assembled elsewhere. Much of it is based on ephemera in the personal files of the principal author. For general reference, in addition to Grebler, et al. (1970), see Acuña (1972) and Moore (1975).

2. Using county relief statistics, in 1975 the Los Angeles County Director of Public Social Services developed a brief "profile" of a typical "illegal alien" who earned two dollars per hour and lived in the "inner city." This marginal individual would be expected to drive 7,000 miles each year (Memo to Each Supervisor from Harry L. Hufford, Chief Administrative Officer, County of Los Angeles, March 20, 1975).

3. "Drunk" and drunk driving arrests account for "more than half of East L.A. arrests, largely because the area is policed by 13.5 officers/sq. mile compared with 3.5 officers/sq. mile in the white community (both with equal alcoholism and major crime rates)" (Morales, 1972).

4. Ginzberg (1976) argues that only 36 percent of the labor force "had good jobs characterized by stability, security of employment and above-average earnings" in 1970. This statement is based on Freedman's analysis, which entailed partitioning all jobs in the economy into fourteen labor market "segments" which varied in earnings. Segments were also characterized by typical differences in five other factors associated with labor market forces, especially those having to do with stability and continuity of employment on the one hand and bargaining power of worker groups on the other hand. Freedman found that "the primary variable distinguishing above and below-average [earnings] segments was the percent of full-time, full-year employment. Eight of the ten segments with above-average earnings had at least 65 percent of [the jobs in] the full-time, full-year category. Taken together, these eight segments constituted the jobs held by 36 percent of the labor force, including all managerial positions, 53 percent of all semi-professional and technical jobs, and 46 percent of all professional positions" (p. 23). By contrast, the four "lowest" segments (i.e., segments with below-average earnings) were "nonprofessionals . . . in education and health; operatives in 14 industries; laborers in 16 industries; office clericals in 23 industries; non-managerial jobs in retailing and service jobs in 'other consumer services' " (p. 28).

5. From the point of view of the conventional labor economist, the availability and utilization of workers with these kinds of characteristics is a current condition for the operation of peripheral firms. If such workers became unavailable, this view argues, either mechanization would replace them, or new sources of labor would be tapped—e.g., undocumented Mexicans would be more in demand.

6. Approaching this from a different perspective, O'Connor (1973) views the economy as divided into three sectors: the oligopolistic, the public or state, and the competitive. The primary sectors in today's economy are the oligopolistic and the public or state, as well as those occupations that are sheltered by licensure, unions, etc. (cf. Freedman). Freedman's "peripheral" is O'Connor's "competitive."

7. Wiley (1977) follows O'Connor's distinction between oligopolistic, competitive, and government sectors but takes a complementary view to that given here. He argues that positions in the labor markets (Weber's "life chances") have become the coequal of positions in the consumption market in determining class identity (both are controlled by oligopolistic interests). This means that a new kind of labor-consumer identity is more salient than the late nineteenth-century labor-identification for the determination of classes. The discrepancies between these two class positions muddle the issue of class solidarity.

Chapter 2

1. Both law-enforcement officers (cf. *L.A.*, 1972) and black gang members (cf. Klein, 1971, p. 135) consider Chicano gang members to be exceptionally violent, a belief echoed by prison officials and the mass media.

2. "Fear" of gangs is not the only impact on Chicano teenagers. Police tend to stereotype all teenagers as gang members—as did a policeman interviewed by Malcolm Klein (1971) in nearby Lincoln Heights (p. 18).

3. A fairly extensive study of delinquency in San Antonio and Monterrey

in Mexico makes no mention of barrio gangs, even though they clearly exist in San Antonio (Rosenquist and Megargee, 1969).

4. Klein's knowledge was so limited that he actually includes two distinct barrios in his "Ladino Hills gang cluster"—Clover and Eastside Clover, assuming that the latter referred to "East Los Angeles," rather than to the special location near the Eastside Brewery.

5. Chicano *Movimiento* leaders noted that the number of American soldiers killed in Vietnam was disproportionately Chicano. The reasons for this seem obvious: not only is service in the Army a favored alternative for young Chicano men, but youthful first-time enlistees tend to appear in large numbers in combat ground troops.

6. The article in the *Bulletin* reported: "McBride said that Dr. Klein's indepth study into street gangs, which he believes to be the most complete done of gangs in Los Angeles County, showed that incidents of violence increased among East Los Angeles gangs when many programs were instituted to 'help' them." This resistance to programs is not new in Los Angeles history. In 1943 Police Captain V. Rasmussen claimed that gangs were "a vicious outgrowth of a recreational system established several years ago by the juvenile authorities, i.e., the city playgrounds" (UCLA Special Collections, Sleepy Lagoon Papers Box 4-file 8). By contrast, Bogardus (1946) complains that playgrounds in the Chicano areas close too early.

7. An exception is represented in the work of Stumphauzer, et al. (1977), who emphasize a peer "helping" relationship among adolescents, possibly related to the self help movement discussed in Chapter 6.

8. Bullock's Chicano respondents were scattered throughout the East Los Angeles area, with some concentration in the Pico-Union housing project community in which his principal assistant, Jacopo Rodriguez, worked with a local organization.

9. In the mid-1970s, the Pinto Program at the "open door" East Los Angeles College, a two-year college, successfully led a campaign to eliminate the consideration of arrest and conviction records in granting work-study funds to students. This was an important obstacle to utilization of the college.

10. It was in 1904 that G. Stanley Hall invented the term adolescence. Bakan (in Kagan, 1972) notes that in 1832, 40 percent of New England's factory workers were children, and that the labor force participation rate of children under 15 actually increased until 1900. Bakan identifies the source of adolescence as a new phase of life as the result of three major social movements which exempted teenagers from work: compulsory education, child labor legislation, and special legal procedures for juveniles—all products of the late nineteenth century.

11. Only 5 percent of the Chicago gangs were composed of "Americans," or boys whose parents were native-born white (as compared with 26 percent of the "boy population" of the city, aged 10 to 24). Eighty-seven percent of the gangs were composed of boys of foreign extraction (compared with 70 percent of the city population), while blacks were relatively insignificant both in gangs (7 percent) and in the city juvenile population (4 percent). (Thrasher, 1927, p. 193.)

12. Chicano parents can (and do) consider the presence or absence of a gang as one of the factors in their residential choice. Thus it is sometimes possible for families to protect their adolescent children from involvement by avoiding rough gang barrios.

Chapter 3

1. Clique is a translation of the Chicano term klika. It refers to the entire age cohort and not to any particular solidary group within it, as it does in the conventional gang literature (cf. Klein, 1971, pp. 66–69).

2. Some specific technical points on data-gathering for this table and for Table 2 are given in Appendix A. Given the common professional distinction between core and fringe members, it is worth repeating here that at least two members of each clique decided who was included as a clique member—and all who in their judgment participated were included. Some were not only fringe members but were despised fringe members, that is, ratas.

3. The origin of the name White Fence is controversial. Teresa Sepulveda, an upper-class Californian interviewed at the turn of the century, referred to the entire Boyle Heights area (which contains the barrio of White Fence) as "Paredon Blanco" (white walls), referring to large white bluffs over the Los Angeles River that look like walls. William Mason of the Los Angeles County Museum of Natural History believed this to be the origin of White Fence. Barrio residents jeer at this, because the river and its bluffs are a couple of miles west of the barrio (see Map 3). Others cite the building of Whittier Boulevard into East Los Angeles in 1913, when a number of barricades were erected to keep pedestrians and cars from falling over the steep embankments; these fences were painted white for night visibility. Gang youngsters point to a particular small fence in the heart of the barrio as their White Fence.

4. By 1975 this territory had expanded greatly, stretching twelve blocks north from Whittier (to Evergreen Cemetery) and ten blocks west from Lorena to Soto Street.

5. It may be worth noting that the gang can "take over" territory only through a process of conversion, or subversion, of residents to gang membership. In the 1940s White Fence was surrounded by other highly cohesive gangs. The expansion of territory by 1975 was due to the fact that boys in the new area were eager to affiliate themselves with White Fence.

Chapter 4

1. Narcotics are secret and illegal. Therefore the sources of information and understanding must come almost entirely from official, usually law enforcement, agencies. Yet nobody is likely to obtain much insight from the police or from jail-based research on the structural context of drug use and marketing. Very few people are allowed to enter this context in real life; outsiders are simply too dangerous for addicts. In our case the participant researchers were able to offer some unique insights.

There is no accurate information on even the number of heroin addicts in the U.S., nor about their geographic distribution. The best data sources come from New York—yet seven different estimates of the number of addicts in New York were made between 1968 and 1971, many using the same basic data sources (Blumstein, et al., 1973). Estimates range from 70,000 to 302,547 addicts. Blumstein also gives details on the estimation procedures. New York City has the best data available on narcotics, thanks to a narcotics register established in 1964 that is derived from "hospitals, addiction service agencies, police and correctional agencies, private practitioners and other health and social agencies" (Richards and Carroll, 1970, p. 1037). Other techniques include extrapolation from overdose deaths in the files of the local coroner, the "good old three-to-one ratio" (in which there are assumed to be three unknown addicts for every known addict), working backward from the amount of heroin illegally consumed, and the "fish pond count" procedure (tagging), which is based on a system used by conservationists to count the number of fish in a lake. The base is always institutional, with treatment and/or law enforcement the two major sources. Recent federal efforts have emphasized coordinated data from treatment sources in an attempt to improve this information. The two official sources of information on heroin addiction give widely different estimates. The Bureau of Narcotics and Dangerous Drugs estimates 559,224 heroin users in the United States and 302,547 in New York City; the Treasury Department reports 700,000 nationwide, but only 184,000 in New York (Mushkin, et al., 1973).

2. See also Preble and Casey (1969) and Ianni (1974) for the argument that heroin caused the New York gangs to die out.

3. Few snitches are, in fact, killed. They are ostracized—a fate almost as bad for many barrio addicts. Snitching is quite common and the rumor that a man "has a jacket" is enough, if verified, to cut off his sources of livelihood as well as of drugs.

Chapter 5

1. Park (1961), cited in Acuña (1972), reports 9,330 Mexicans counted by the U.S. Census in 1880 out of a total population of 30,440 (U.S. Dept. of Commerce, 1960).

2. In 1969 opiate offenses were the third most common crime for Chicanos received by the California correctional system. Such offenses were twelfth (out of twelve) for Anglos and fifth for blacks (California, 1969, 1973). These data exclude civil commitments of addicts to the California Rehabilitation Center, thus understating the magnitude of heroin as a source of incarceration. Chicanos were one-third of the men sent to prison in 1972 on narcotics offenses in California and about a third of the inmates of CRC in 1971.

3. An extensive survey of inmates of state institutions in the U.S. in 1974 showed that 30 percent of the inmates had used heroin (Barton, 1976). Twenty-six percent of the population of all federal institutions had "used narcotics" (ibid., source not given). Thirty-two percent of the jail inmates surveyed in six cities had used heroin (Eckerman, et al., 1971).

4. Between 1969 and 1973 the number of "incidents" rose from 303 to 778 and the rate per 100 inmates rose from 1.1 to 3.6 (California, 1974). No definition of incidents is provided. They appear to include fights that are reported to the captain and are followed by disciplinary action.

5. It should be recognized that even the routine activities of gang members reinforce the familistic quality of barrio relationships. When asked what they do, gang youngsters are likely to respond with something like "get loaded, party, sometimes fight, hang around." Each of these activities entails extensive interpersonal involvement. Just as members of a football team become intricately involved with one another by virtue of the activity of playing ball, so each of the typical activities of the barrio gang could be analyzed in terms of its function in rearranging the social world of the members.

6. These necessities may appear petty to the outsider, but they actually become critical to morale and survival. The strategy of the correctional system to reduce prisoners to essentials is an open invitation to enter the barter economy of the prison.

7. For the purposes of public relations, there appears to be a good deal of exaggeration by law enforcement officials. The article "Chicano Gangs of the Barrios" in the last issue of *L.A.* magazine estimated the gangs at about five times their actual numerical strength (*L.A.*, 1972). Cliques of the gangs were listed separately, exaggerating their importance.

8. An amazing total of three million people are processed every year through the county jails in Los Angeles. This gives some indication of the scale of operation at what is, in effect, a holding level of incarceration (information provided by the Los Angeles County Sheriff's Department, 1974).

9. Only 80 percent of the felony arrests in Los Angeles County resulted in a filing in Superior Court. Of those, only a tiny fraction (such as 4 percent of the narcotics sales arrests) received a jury trial (Greenwood, et al., 1973). Some indication of the depth of disillusion may be seen in the thriving operations of the writ writers in prison. These jailhouse lawyers are often quite adept. They measure in their numbers a delayed response by perfectly legal procedures to a mechanism seen as not only unjust but illegal (see Chapter 6).

10. Both machismo and the convict code have long been cited to explain Chicano convict behavior. Both are special ad hoc norms used to explain behavior. One is specific to Chicanos and the other to all prisoners. We feel neither idea is necessary for the sociological understanding of prison norms as they affect men from the barrio.

11. Throughout this chapter, our prime referent for prison is San Quentin. Not only is this particular prison historically significant in the development of the Chicano self-help movement in the mid-1960s, but it is singled out so often both by the mass media and academic research that it is very nearly a prototype of institutional experience. See, for example, Toch (1969) and Wright (1973). Much of Irwin's (1970) analysis is based on experiences at San Quentin.

12. Newer prisons are designed to minimize such large spaces in which inmates from the entire facility mingle. Prison architecture now tends to structure inmate relationships by residential units, rather than by outside linkages. New buildings appear to enhance and facilitate custodial control, further handicap the real-world orientation of the prison, and eliminate the constructive influences of real-world contacts. But this is speculation, and only research can answer this question definitively.

13. A study of prisoner stabbings before and after 1973, when the California prison system implemented stricter security measures, shows little success in reducing prison violence. Bowker (1977) argues that the study "shows the limitations on any attempt to solve prison problems by merely changing administrative and custody procedures."

14. For those who may remain skeptical about the capacity of a prison-based organization to have an impact on street narcotics traffic, the 1977 indictment of thirty men in a reputed "$50 million a year heroin operation . . . directed from a prison cell" should be of interest (*New York Times*, April 5, 1977, p. 1A).

15. Readers may be puzzled by the extent to which inmates turn to "exchanging goods" to help with personal problems. As shown in Table 4, the

overwhelming majority reported "family" and "money" to be their greatest worries when they entered prison. Although we are not sure they are referring to "personal problems," the worry about money may explain some of the rare reliance on "exchanging goods" for help with problems.

16. The availability of hard drugs in prison and its relationship to race relations is detailed in Carroll (1974).

17. Increasing pro-staff orientations were found among inmates in the last six months of their sentence. The "U-shaped curve of prisonization" in the studies cited by Bowker are interpreted as anticipatory resocialization. Our data do not permit this kind of analysis, but men at CRC were mostly short-termers and men at CIM were mostly in the last few months of their sentences. Neither group appeared to show a pro-staff attitude in comparison with other prisons. This seems to confirm our argument that resocialization to the outside world does not involve rejection of one's prison peers nor acceptance of the prison staff as surrogates for Chicano squares to be encountered upon release.

18. Both men were outsiders sponsored by authority who believed their informants were interested in improving the quality of scholarly literature, rather than in utilizing these researchers as resources (see the remarks on methodology in the Introduction and Appendix A).

Chapter 6

1. A self-survey of Folsom inmates from Los Angeles County done in the late 1960s included 54 men from Los Angeles county serving 10 and 15 years to life sentences for narcotics violations. Of these, 36 were Chicano and 11 were black. The quality of their legal service is shown by the fact that only nine were tried by a jury, 39 opted for a court trial, and six pleaded guilty. Thirty-six were represented by private attorneys and 18 by public defenders (see *People's Resolution*, 1970).

2. There are three main routes open to the prisoner: direct appeal from the judgement; petition for a writ of *habeas corpus* (which can appeal not only convictions but also "improper or unlawful prison and parole practices and treatment"); and writ of *erron coram nobis*, directed specifically at plea bargaining abuses (van Geldern, 1975).

3. *Miranda* v. *Arizona* 384 U.S. 436 (1966). These include the right to remain silent, the right to counsel, the warning that what the subject says may be used against him in a court, the information that the court can appoint a lawyer before the subject is questioned, and the request for feedback on the subject's understanding of these rights and the securing of a waiver of rights if the subject so chooses (Wicks, 1974, pp. 134–35).

4. Requirements for enrollment in many programs have been at least an eighth-grade education, a level reached by few Chicanos, especially in the 1960s, a maximum age (under thirty is insisted on by many unions), plus a low custody rating.

5. These insights are derived from interviews with prison staff people, former staff members, and only occasionally from convicts. They do not represent the views of disgruntled inmates, but rather are predominantly the perceptions of treatment staff inside the prison.

6. In the California Rehabilitation Center, the Chicano culture group had to resist an administrative notion that all Chicanos be *required* to join MAYO.

7. None of the charges of fiscal mismanagement of these agencies appear to have been substantiated—at least to the extent of embezzlement. The idea of embezzlement is so strongly fixed in the official mind that it reappears constantly, an unpleasant reminder of the correctional system and its firm conviction that convicts and money are never to be trusted together, even if the money is their own.

8. We are distinguishing here between agencies that hire ex-convict counsellors as paraprofessionals (cf. Bullington, et al., 1969, and Munns, et al., 1972), and those rare ones that are formed and directed on the self-help principle.

Chapter 7

1. The first factor we call Perception of Neighborhood as Problem-Filled. It deals with worries about personal safety, gang violence and related matters. Each respondent received an overall score on this cluster, summarizing a general position in responses to ten questions scattered throughout the interview.

The second factor is Desire for Social Distance from Problems and summarizes attitudes in fourteen items. These ask how people feel about their own personal relationships with addicts, convicts, and other people who represent neighborhood problems.

The third factor, Reliance on Institutions for Solutions, summarizes attitudes about what can be done about gangs, narcotics, and ex-convicts in the neighborhoods. A high score on this cluster means that the person generally trusts and would turn to the police, prisons, politicians, teachers and the like. A low score means that the person generally rejects these sources of possible help.

2. Survey data gathered in 1964 and 1965 (cf. Grebler, et al., 1970), and several years of participant observation. Autobiographical material (Acosta, 1972; Galarza, 1972) also provided insights. On the barrio types, there were extensive discussions among the ex-gang and ex-convict researchers.

3. Only the first three types of professionals (police, probation officers, and teachers) were involved in the factor analysis discussed earlier in this chapter, as they are related to the third factor of reliance upon institutions.

4. The proportion of respondents refusing to choose (don't know and no response) is higher here than on previous issues (and will remain so for the subsequent analyses). Nonetheless, they are not high enough to cast doubt on the findings, and relate to areas of controversy and of great ignorance, e.g., methadone programs.

Chapter 8

1. Whyte comments, "Cornerville's problem is not lack of organization [or disorganization] but failure of its own social organization to mesh with the structure of the society around it. This accounts for the development of the local political and racket organizations and also for the loyalty people bear toward their race and toward Italy" (p. 273).

2. Recently Alba (1976) has cast doubt on the validity of the notion that white ethnic groups are still segregated in primary-group relationships. Ex-

cept for Hispanics and French Canadians, "social assimilation [among Catholic ethnics] has proceeded much further than many acknowledge. While reports of the death of ethnic communities were premature, contrary reports of their continued vitality are greatly exaggerated" (p. 1,045).

Appendix A

1. One of the main problems is that "action," "policy," or "applied" research suffers from a lack of clear definition among academics. We were doing collaborative research in which one element had a major stake in social change. If that group had been part of the establishment (e.g., the schools), what we did might well have been called policy research. We were working as outsiders to the institutional establishment. "Action" or "applied" research with outsider groups is frequently done, not with the groups themselves, but with institutional advocates—social workers, and the like—for such groups. It is such a situation that is addressed by Klein (1971), who warns against "action seduction" in the study of juvenile gangs. What he refers to is the risk of contamination of "research purity" in research that involves "practitioners." Clearly this is very different from the approach developed in the Pinto Project.

2. We are indebted to Kaye Briegel for assembling the materials on oral history.

Appendix C

1. At Tehachapi the members of MACHO viewed the survey as an opportunity to strengthen already fairly strong relationships with members of other culture groups. Thus nine of the thirty-five respondents were Anglo, five American Indian, and three were black, while eighteen identified themselves as Chicano.

References

Acosta, Oscar Z.
    1972 *The autobiography of a brown buffalo.* San Francisco: Straight Arrow Books.
Acuña, Rodolfo
    1972 *Occupied America: the Chicano's struggle toward liberation.* San Francisco: Canfield Press.
Aiken, Thomas W., Jerome S. Stumphauzer and Esteban V. Veloz
    1977 Behavioral analysis of non-delinquent brothers in a high juvenile crime community. *Behavioral disorders* 2:212–222.
Alba, Richard D.
    1976 Social assimilation among American Catholic national origin groups. *American sociological review* 41:1030–1046.
Bakan, David
    1972 Adolescence in America: from idea to social fact. In *Twelve to sixteen: early adolescence,* ed. Jerome Kagan and Robert Coles. New York: W. W. Norton.
Bancroft, Hubert H.
    1884–
    1890 *History of California.* 7 vols. San Francisco: The History Company.
Banfield, Edward C.
    1974 *The unheavenly city revisited.* Boston: Little, Brown.
Baridon, Philip C.
    1976 *Addiction, crime, and social policy.* Lexington, Mass.: Lexington Books.
Barker, George C.
    1947 Social functions of language in a Mexican-American community. *Acta americana* 4:189–92.
Bartlett, Dana W.
    1907 *The better city: a sociological study of a modern city.* Los Angeles: Neuner.
Barton, William I.
    1976 Drug histories of prisoners: survey of inmates of state correctional facilities, January 1974.
    1976 Heroin use and criminality: survey of inmates of state correctional facilities. Drug Enforcement Administration.

223

Bernard, Jessie
  1973 *The sociology of community.* Glenview, Ill: Scott, Foresman.
Berry, Brian and John Kasarda
  1977 *Contemporary urban ecology.* New York: Macmillan.
Berry, Brian J. and Donald C. Dahmann
  1977 Population redistribution in the United States in the 1970's. *Population and development review* 4:443–471.
Blackwell, James
  1975 *The black community: diversity and unity.* New York: Dodd, Mead.
Blackwell, James and Morris Janowitz, eds.
  1975 *Black Sociologists.* Chicago: University of Chicago Press.
Blumstein, Alfred, Philip Sagi, and Marvin Wolfgang
  1973 Problems of estimating the number of heroin addicts. In *Drug use in America: problem in perspective*, National Commission on Marijuana and Drug Abuse, vol. 2. Washington, D.C.: U.S. Government Printing Office.
Bogardus, Emory
  1926 *The city boy and his problems: a survey of boy life in Los Angeles.* Los Angeles: Rotary Club.
  1943 Gangs of Mexican-American youth. *Sociology and social research* 28:55–56.
Bowker, Lee H.
  1977 *Prisoner subcultures.* Lexington, Mass.: Lexington Books. D. C. Heath.
Bowles, Samuel
  1972 Unequal education and the reproduction of the social division of labor. In *The capitalist system*, ed. Michael Reich and Thomas Weisskopf. Englewood Cliffs, N.J.: Prentice Hall.
Bullington, Bruce
  1969 Purchase of conformity: ex-narcotic addicts among the bourgeoisie. *Social problems* 16:456–463.
  1977 *Heroin use in the barrio.* Lexington, Mass.: D. C. Heath.
Bullock, Paul
  1973 *Aspiration vs. opportunity: "careers" in the inner city.* Ann Arbor, Michigan: Institute of Labor and Industrial Relations, University of Michigan-Wayne State.
Burgess, Ernest W.
  1925 The growth of the city. In *The city*, ed. Robert E. Park, Ernest W. Burgess and Roderick D. McKenzie. Chicago: University of Chicago Press.
Burns, Leland S. and Alvin J. Harman
  1968 *The complex metropolis.* Los Angeles: University of California Graduate School of Business Administration, Research Report no. 9.
Cain, Glen G.
  1976 The challenge of segmented labor market theories to orthodox theory: a survey. *Journal of economic literature* 65:16–22.
Calahan, Don, Ira H. Cisin and Helen M. Crossley
  1969 *American drinking practices.* New Brunswick, N.J.: Rutgers Center of Alcohol Studies.
California Department of Corrections
  1959 *California prisoners.* Sacramento, Calif.
  1964 *California prisoners.* Sacramento, Calif.

1969 *California prisoners.* Sacramento, Calif.
1973 *Characteristics of felon population in California state prisons by institution.* Sacramento, Calif.
California State Department of Industrial Relations
1930 *Mexicans in California: report of Governor C. C. Young's committee.* Sacramento, Calif.
Cannell, Charles F. and Robert L. Kahn
1968 Interviewing. In *The handbook of social psychology,* ed. Gardner Lindzey and Elliot Aronson, vol. 2. Reading, Mass.: Addison-Wesley.
Carroll, Leo
1974 *Hacks, blacks and cons: race relations in a maximum security prison.* Lexington, Mass.: Lexington Books.
Casavantes, Edward J.
1976 *El tecato: cultural and sociologic factors affecting drug use among Chicanos.* Washington, D.C.: National Coalition of Spanish Speaking Mental Health Organizations.
Cavan, Ruth Shonle and Ferdinard Theodore
1975 *Juvenile delinquency.* Philadelphia: J. B. Lippincott.
Chambers, Carl D., Walter Cuskey and Arthur D. Moffett
1970 Mexican American opiate addicts. In *The epidemiology of opiate addiction in the United States,* ed. John C. Ball and Carl D. Chambers. Springfield, Ill.: Charles C. Thomas.
Chavez, A.
1973 A demographic analysis of narcotic addiction among Mexican Americans. *Proceedings* of the Institute on Narcotic Addiction among Mexican Americans in the Southwest. National Institute of Mental Health.
Chein, Isidor, et al.
1964 *The road to H.* New York: Basic Books.
Chicano Pinto Research Project
1975a *The L.A. pinto: background papers and advance report.* Los Angeles: Chicano Pinto Research Project, Inc.
1975b *Final report.* Los Angeles: Chicano Pinto Research Project, Inc.
Clark, Janet and Helen MacGill Hughes
1961 *Fantastic lodge.* Boston: Houghton Mifflin.
Clark, Kenneth B.
1965 *Dark ghetto: dilemmas of social power.* New York: Harper & Row.
Clark, Margaret
1959 *Health in the Mexican-American culture.* Berkeley, Calif.: University of California Press.
Cleaver, Eldridge
1968 *Soul on ice.* New York: McGraw-Hill.
Clemmer, Donald
1958 *The prison community.* New York: Holt, Rinehart & Winston.
Cloward, Richard A. and Lloyd Ohlin
1960 *Delinquency and opportunity.* New York: Free Press.
Cohen, A.
1955 *Delinquent boys.* New York: Free Press.
Coleman, James
1961 *The adolescent society.* New York: Free Press.

Conwell, Chic and Edwin H. Sutherland
1937 *The professional thief.* Chicago: University of Chicago Press.
Coombs, Orde
1974 "Three faces of Harlem." *The New York Times Magazine,* Nov. 3.
Cressey, Donald
1955 Changing criminals: the application of the theory of differential association. *American Journal of Sociology* 61:116–120.
Davidson, Theodore
1974 *Chicano prisoners: the key to San Quentin.* New York: Random House.
Davis, Allison, Burleigh B. Gardner and Mary R. Gardner
1941 *Deep south.* Chicago: University of Chicago Press.
del Castillo, Richard Allan Griswold
1974 La raza hispano-americana: the emergence of an urban culture among the Spanish Speaking of Los Angeles, 1850–1880. Unpublished Ph.D. diss.: UCLA.
del Pinal, Jorge H.
1973 The penal population of California. In *Voices.* Berkeley: El Grito.
Doeringer, Peter B. and Michael J. Piore
1971 *Internal labor markets and manpower analysis.* Lexington, Mass.: Heath Lexington.
Drake, St. Clair and Horace R. Cayton
1962 *Black metropolis: a study of Negro life in a northern city.* 2 Vols. New York: Harper & Row.
Dunbar, Ellen R.
1975 Politics and policy change. Unpublished Ph.D. diss.: University of Southern California.
Duster, Troy
1970 *Legislation of morality.* New York: Free Press.
Eckerman, William C., James D. Bates, J. Valley Rachel and W. Kenneth Pool
1971 *Drug usage and arrest charges: a study of drug usage and arrest charges among arrestees in six metropolitan areas of the United States.* U.S. Department of Justice, Bureau of Narcotics and Dangerous Drugs, Office of Scientific Support, Drug Control Division.
Farrell, Barry
1977 The power politician behind the badge. *New West,* Dec. 19, pp. 28–36.
Feigenbaum, Roy A.
1976 The economics of heroin. In *An economic analysis of crime,* ed. Lawrence J. Kaplan and Dennis Kessler. Springfield, Ill.: Charles C. Thomas.
Finney, Graham S.
1975 *Drugs: administering catastrophe.* Washington, D.C.: Drug Abuse Council.
Freedman, Marcia K.
1976 *Labor markets: segments and shelters.* Montclair, N.J.: Allanheld, Osmun, and Co.
Friedlander, Stanley L.
1972 *Unemployment in the urban core.* New York: Praeger.
Galarza, Ernesto
1972 *Barrio boy.* New York: Ballantine.

Gamio, Manuel
  1930 *Mexican immigration to the United States: a study of human migra-
       tion and adjustment.* Chicago: University of Chicago Press.
Gans, Herbert
  1962 *The urban villagers.* New York: Free Press.
Garcia, F. Chris
  1973 *Political socialization of Chicano children: a comparative study
       with Anglos in California schools.* New York: Praeger.
Gintis, Herbert
  1971 Education, technology, and the characteristics of worker produc-
       tivity. *American Economic Review/Proceedings* 61:266–279.
Ginzberg, Eli
  1976 Labor market: segments and shelters. Abstracted in *Research and
       development projects.* U.S. Department of Labor, Employment and
       Training Administration. Washington, D.C.
Goffman, Erving
  1961 *Asylums.* Garden City, N.Y.: Doubleday.
Goldfarb, Ronald L. and Linda R. Singer
  1973 *After conviction.* New York: Simon and Schuster.
Goldschmidt, Walter
  1947 *As you sow.* New York: Harcourt, Brace.
Gómez-Quiñones, Juan
  1972 The first steps: Chicano labor conflict and organizing, 1900–1920.
       Aztlán.
Gonzales, Gilbert
  1971 Factors relating to property ownership of Chicanos in Lincoln
       Heights, Los Angeles. *Aztlán.*
Gordon, David
  1972 *Theories of poverty and underemployment.* Lexington, Mass.: D. C.
       Heath.
Grebler, Leo et al.
  1966 *Mexican immigration: the record and its implications.* Los Angeles:
       Mexican American Study Project.
Grebler, Leo, Joan Moore, Ralph Guzmán et al.
  1970 *The Mexican American people.* New York: Free Press.
Greeley, Andrew M.
  1972 The new ethnicity and blue collars. *Dissent* 19:270–77.
Greenwood, Peter W., Sorrel Wildhorn, Eugene Poggio, Michael Strumwas-
ser and Peter de Leon
  1973 *Prosecution of adult felony defendants in Los Angeles County: a
       policy perspective.* Santa Monica: Rand.
Griffith, Beatrice
  1948 *American me.* Boston: Houghton Mifflin.
Gustafson, Floyd V.
  1940 An ecological analysis of the Hollenbeck area of Los Angeles. Mas-
       ter's thesis: University of Southern California.
Handlin, Oscar
  1962 *The newcomers.* Garden City, N.J.: Anchor.
Hannerz, Ulf
  1969 *Soulside.* New York: Columbia University Press.

Harrison, Bennett
    1973 Education, training and the urban ghetto. In *Baker's dozen: abstracts of 13 doctoral dissertations completed under Manpower Administration research grants.* Manpower Research Monograph no. 27. U.S. Department of Labor, Manpower Administration.
Haskell, Martin R. and Lewis Yablonsky
    1974 *Juvenile delinquency.* Chicago: Rand McNally.
Healy, William and Bronner, Augusta R.
    1936 *New light on delinquency and its treatment.* New Haven, Conn.: Yale University Press.
Heller, Celia S.
    1966 *Mexican American youth: forgotten youth at the crossroads.* New York: Random House.
Hirschi, Travis
    1969 *Causes of delinquency.* Berkeley: University of California Press.
Hoffman, Abraham
    1974 *Unwanted Mexican Americans in the great depression: repatriation pressures, 1929–1939.* Tucson: University of Arizona Press.
Hughes, Patrick H. and Gail Crawford
    1974 Epidemiology of heroin addiction in the 1970s: new opportunities and responsibilities. In *Drug use: epidemiological and social approaches,* ed. Eric Josephson and Eleanor Carroll. Washington, D.C.: Hemisphere.
Hyman, Herbert H., William J. Cobb and others
    1975 *Interviewing in social research.* Chicago: University of Chicago Press.
Ianni, Francis A. J.
    1974 *Black Mafia: ethnic succession in organized crime.* New York: Simon and Schuster.
Irwin, John
    1970 *The felon.* Englewood Cliffs, N.J.: Prentice Hall.
Irwin, John and Donald R. Cressey
    1962 Thieves, convicts and the inmate culture. *Social Problems* 10: 145–47.
Jackson, George
    1970 *Soledad brothers.* New York: Bantam.
Jeffrey, John Mason
    1969 *Adobe and iron.* La Jolla, Calif.: Prospect Avenue Press.
Kahn, Robert L. and Charles F. Cannell
    1957 *The dynamics of interviewing.* New York: John Wiley & Sons.
Kaplan, Lawrence J. and Dennis Kessler eds.
    1976 *An economic analysis of crime.* Springfield, Ill.: Charles C. Thomas.
Keiser, R. Lincoln
    1969 *The Vice Lords: warriors of the street.* New York: Holt, Rinehart and Winston.
Kennedy, Will Charles
    1970 Prisonization and self concept. Unpublished Ph.D. diss.: UCLA.
Klein, Malcolm W.
    1971 *Street gangs and street workers.* Englewood Cliffs, N.J.: Prentice Hall.
Kornblum, William
    1974 *Blue collar community.* Chicago: University of Chicago Press.

Krisberg, Barry
  1975 *Crime and privilege: toward a new criminology.* Englewood Cliffs, N.J.: Prentice Hall.
L.A.
  1972 Chicano gangs of the barrio.
Lanigan, Mary
  1932 Second generation Mexicans in Belvedere. Master's thesis: University of Southern California.
Lemert, E. and J. Rosberg
  1946 Crime and punishment among minority groups in Los Angeles County. *Proceedings* of the Pacific Coast Sociological Society, pp. 133–145.
Lewin, David, Raymond Horton, Robert Shick, and Charles Brecher
  1974 *The urban labor market: institutions, information and linkages.* New York: Praeger.
Lewis, Hylan
  1955 *Blackways of Kent.* Chapel Hill: University of North Carolina Press.
Lieberson, Stanley
  1963 *Ethnic patterns in American cities.* New York: Free Press.
Liebow, Elliot
  1967 *Tally's corner.* Boston: Little, Brown.
López, Ronald
  1970 The El Monte berry strike of 1933. *Aztlan* 1:101–112.
Los Angeles County Probation Department and Youth Studies Center
  1963 Study of delinquent gangs, second annual progress report. July 1, 1962–June 30, 1963. University of Southern California.
Maddux, James F.
  1973 Characteristics of Mexican American addicts. National Institute of Mental Health, *Proceedings* of the Institute on Narcotic Addiction among Mexican Americans in the Southwest.
Madsen, William
  1964 *The Mexican-Americans of south Texas.* San Francisco: Holt, Rinehart & Winston.
Malcolm X
  1964 *Autobiography of Malcolm X.* New York: Grove Press.
Matza, David
  1969 *Becoming deviant.* Englewood Cliffs, N.J.: Prentice Hall, Inc.
McWilliams, Carey
  1949,
  1968 *North from Mexico.* New York: Greenwood Press.
Merton, Robert K.
  1972 Insiders and outsiders: a chapter in the sociology of knowledge. *American Journal of Sociology* 67:9–48.
Miller, Walter B.
  1958 Lower class culture as a generating milieu of gang delinquency. *The Journal of Social Issues* 14:5–19.
Mitford, Jessica
  1974 *Kind and usual punishment.* New York: Vintage Books.
Moore, Joan W.
  1970 Colonialism: the case of the Mexican Americans. *Social Problems* 17:463–472.

1972 LUCHA in agencyland: a Chicano self-help organization meets the establishment. *Growth and Change* 3:43–50.

1973 Social constraints on sociological knowledge: academics and research concerning minorities. *Social Problems* 21:65–76.

1975 *Mexican Americans.* Englewood Cliffs, N.J.: Prentice Hall.

1976 American minorities and "new nation" perspectives. *Pacific Sociological Review* 19:447–467.

Moore, Joan W. and Frank G. Mittelbach
1966 *Residential segregation in the urban southwest.* Mexican American Study Project, Advance Report 4, U.C.L.A.

Moore, Mark
1970 *Economics of heroin distribution.* Croton on Hudson, N.Y.: Hudson Institute.

Morales, Armando
1972 *Ando sangrando (I am bleeding): a study of Mexican American-police conflict.* La Puente, California: Perspective Publications.

Morse, Richard
1971 Trends and issues in urban research. *Latin American Research Rev.* 6:3–52.

Mulford, H. A. and D. E. Miller
1959 Drinking in Iowa. I. Sociocultural evaluation and interpretation of findings. *Quarterly Journal of Studies of Alcohol* 20:704–726.

1960 Drinking in Iowa. II. The extent of drinking and selected sociocultural categories. *Quarterly Journal of Studies of Alcohol* 20:704–726.

Munns, J. G., Gilbert Geis and B. H. Bullington
1972 The Boyle Heights project: former narcotics addicts as street workers. In *Major modalities in the treatment of drug abuse,* ed. L. Brill and L. Lieberman. New York: Behavioral Publications.

Murphy, Suzanne
1978 "A year with the gangs of East Los Angeles." *Ms.* July, pp. 56–60.

Mushkin, A., B. Surmeier, C. Karre and D. Detling
1973 Federal funding and intergovernmental coordination for drug addiction programs. In *Drug use in America.* Washington, D.C.: U.S. Government Printing Office.

National Commission on Marihuana and Drug Abuse
1972 *Appendix: technical papers.* Washington, D.C.: U.S. Government Printing Office.

1973 *Drug use in America: problem in perspective.* Washington, D.C.: U.S. Government Printing Office.

Novak, Michael
1972 *The rise of the unmeltable ethnics.* New York: Macmillan.

O'Connor, James
1973 *The fiscal crisis of the state.* New York: St. Martin's Press.

Orleans, P.
1967 Differential cognition of urban residents: effects of social scale on mapping. *Science, Engineering and the City.* Washington, D.C.: National Academy of Engineering.

Oxnam, G. Bromley
1920 *The Mexican in Los Angeles: Los Angeles city survey.* Interchurch World Movement of North America.

Pachon, Harry
1976 Michigan Pinto Prison Survey.
Park, Joseph F.
1961 *The history of Mexican labor in Arizona during the territorial period.* Tucson: University of Arizona Press.
Park, Robert E. and Herbert A. Miller
1921 *Old world traits transplanted.* New York: Harper and Row.
Patoski, Joe Nick
1977 Tex-Mex: the music that's becoming America's reggae. *Mother Jones* 2:33–38.
Paz, Octavio
1961 *The labyrinth of solitude: life and thought in Mexico.* New York: Grove Press.
People's Resolution
1970 Los Angeles: League of United Citizens to Help Addicts.
Pitt, Leonard
1966 *The decline of the Californios.* Berkeley: University of California Press.
Preble, Edward and John J. Casey Jr.
1969 Taking care of business: the heroin user's life on the street. *The International Journal of the Addictions* 4:1–24.
President's Commission on Law Enforcement and Administration of Justice
1967 *The challenge of crime in a free society.* Washington, D.C.: U.S. Government Printing Office.
"Profile: California"
1974 *Corrections Magazine* 1:3–49.
Quicker, John C.
1974 The Chicana gang: a preliminary description. Presented at the Pacific Sociological Association meetings.
Quinney, Richard
1977 Class, state and crime. New York: David McKay.
Rainwater, Lee
1966 Fear and the house-as-haven in the lower class. *Journal of the American Institute of Planners* 32:23–30.
Rainwater, Lee and William L. Yancey
1967 *The Moynihan Report and the politics of controversy.* Cambridge, Mass.: MIT Press.
Ranker, Jess
1957 A study of juvenile gangs in the Hollenbeck area of Los Angeles. Master's thesis: University of Southern California.
Reckless, Walter C.
1960 *The crime problem.* New York: Appleton Century Crofts.
Redlinger, Lawrence J.
1969 Dealing in dope. Unpublished Ph.D. diss.: Northwestern University.
Rice, Stuart
1929 Contagious bias in the interview: a methodological note. *American Journal of Sociology* 35:420–423.
Richards, Louise G. and Eleanor Carroll
1970 Illicit drug use and addiction in the United States. *Public Health Reports* 85:1035–1041.

Rist, Ray C.
   1973 *The urban school: a factory for failure.* Cambridge, Mass.: MIT Press, 1973.
Rosenquist, Carl M. and Edwin S. Megargee
   1969 *Delinquency in three cultures.* Austin: University of Texas Press.
Rubel, Arthur J.
   1966 *Across the tracks: Mexican Americans in a Texas city.* Austin: University of Texas Press.
Rudoff, Alvin
   1964 Prison inmates, an involuntary association. Ph.D. diss.: University of California-Berkeley.
Rufener, B. L., J. V. Rachel and A. M. Cruze
   1976 Final report: management effectiveness measures for NIDA drug abuse treatment programs. Vol. 2. Costs to Society of Drug Abuse. Research Triangle Institute. Washington, D.C.: Office of Program Development and Analysis, NIDA.
Ryan, William
   1971 *Blaming the victim.* New York: Vintage Books.
Sale, Kirkpatrick
   1975 *Power shift.* New York: Vintage Books.
Sandberg, Neil C.
   1974 *Ethnic identity and assimilation: the Polish-American community. Case study of metropolitan Los Angeles.* New York: Praeger.
Schwendinger, Herman and Julia R. Schwendinger
   1974 *The sociologists of the chair.* New York: Basic Books.
Scott, Robin F.
   1971 The Mexican-American in the Los Angeles area, 1920–1950: from acquiescence to activity. Doctoral thesis: University of Southern California.
Sells, S. B., ed.
   1974 *Research on patients, treatment and outcome.* Cambridge, Mass.: Ballinger Publishing.
Servín, Manuel
   1974 *An awakening minority: the Mexican Americans.* Los Angeles: Glencoe.
Shaw, Clifford R.
   1930 *The jack-roller: a delinquent boy's own story.* Chicago: University of Chicago Press.
Sheehan, Susan
   1976 *A welfare mother.* Boston: Houghton Mifflin.
Simirenko, Alex
   1964 *Pilgrims, colonists and frontiersmen: an ethnic community in transition.* New York: The Free Press of Glencoe.
Solzhenitsyn, Aleksandr
   1974– *The gulag archipelago, 1918–1956: an experiment in literary investigation.* Vol. 2. New York: Harper and Row.
   75
Soref, Michael
   1975 The structure of illegal drug markets: an organizational approach. Presented at American Sociological Association.
Spergel, Irving
   1964 *Racketville, slumtown and haulburg: an exploratory study of delinquent subcultures.* Chicago: University of Chicago Press.

Stumphauzer, Jerome S., Thomas W. Aiken and Esteban V. Veloz
  1977 East side story: behavioral analysis of a high juvenile crime community. *Behavioral Disorders* 2:76–84.
Suttles, Gerald
  1971 *The social order of the slum*. Chicago: University of Chicago Press.
Tappan, Paul
  1949 *Juvenile delinquency*. New York: McGraw-Hill.
Taylor, Paul
  1928 *Mexican labor in the United States: Imperial Valley, California*. Berkeley: University of California Publications in Economics.
Taylor, Paul
  1931 The Mexican immigrant and the problem of crime and criminal justice. National Commission on Law Observance and Enforcement, *Report on Crime and the Foreign Born*. Washington, D.C.
Thomas, W. I. and Florian Znaniecki
  1918 *The Polish peasant in Europe and America* (5 vols.). Boston: Badger.
Thrasher, Frederick L.
  1927 *The gang*. Chicago: University of Chicago Press.
Toch, Hans
  1969 *Violent men*. Chicago: Aldine Publishing.
Tuck, Ruth
  1946 *Not with the fist*. New York: Harcourt, Brace.
U.S. Bureau of the Census
  1966 Characteristics of the south and east Los Angeles areas, November 1965. Washington, D.C.: U.S. Government Printing Office.
U.S. Bureau of Prisons
  1936 *Federal offenders 1934–35*. Fort Leavenworth: Federal Prison Industries.
U.S. Bureau of Prisons, Education Branch
  1973 Population breakdown of Spanish-speaking residents.
U.S. Department of Commerce, Bureau of the Census
  1918 *Prisoners and juvenile delinquents in the United States: 1910*. Washington, D.C.
  1960 *Historical statistics of the United States: colonial times to 1959*. Washington, D.C.
U.S. Department of Labor
  1976 *Manpower report of the President*. Washington, D.C.
van Geldern, John
  1975 A prisoners guide to legal research in California prisons. *On the Line* 3:5–7.
Wald, P. M.
  1972 *Dealing with drug abuse*. New York: Praeger.
Ward, David
  1971 *Cities and immigrants*. New York: Oxford University Press.
Warner, W. Lloyd
  1937 *A black civilization*. New York: Harper.
Warner, W. Lloyd and Leo Srole
  1945 *The social systems of American ethnic groups*. New Haven: Yale University Press.
Weber, Devra Ann
  1972 The organization of Mexican agricultural workers, the Imperial

Valley and Los Angeles, 1928–34: an oral history approach. *Aztlán* 3:307–312.

Wheeler, Stanton
 1961 Socialization in correctional communities. *American Sociological Review* 26:697–712.

Whyte, William Foote
 1942 *Street corner society*. Chicago: University of Chicago Press.

Wicker, Tom
 1975 *A time to die*. New York: Quadrangle Press.

Wicks, Robert J.
 1974 *Applied psychology for law enforcement and correction officers*. New York: McGraw-Hill.

Wiley, Norbert
 1977 A Weberian interpretation of monopoly capitalism. Paper presented at Max Weber Colloquium, University of Wisconsin, Milwaukee.

Williams, Virginia L. and Mary Fish
 1974 *Convicts, codes and contraband*. Cambridge, Mass.: Ballinger.

Wirth, Louis
 1928 *The ghetto*. Chicago: University of Chicago Press.

Wood, Arthur Evans
 1955 *Hamtramck: then and now*. New York: Bookman Associates.

World Opium Survey
 See National Commission on Marihuana and Drug Abuse.

Wright, Erik Olin
 1973 *The politics of punishment: a critical analysis of prisons in America*. New York: Harper and Row.

Yancey, William L., Eugene P. Ericksen and Richard N. Juliani
 1976 Emergent Ethnicity: A Review and Reformulation. *American Sociological Review*, 41:391–402.

Index